Empowering Ourselves
and Transforming Schools

SUNY Series, Teacher Preparation and Development
Edited by Alan R. Tom

Empowering Ourselves and Transforming Schools

Educators Making a Difference

Judith W. Irwin

STATE UNIVERSITY OF NEW YORK PRESS

Published by
State University of New York Press, Albany

© 1996 Judith W. Irwin

For information, address State University of New York Press,
State University Plaza, Albany, N.Y., 12246

Production by Cathleen Collins
Marketing by Theresa Abad Swierzowski

Table 5.1 on pages 132–33 is reprinted from *Affirming Diversity: The Sociopolitical Context of Multi-Cultural Education* by Sonia Nieto. Copyright 1993 by Longman Publishers. Reprinted with permission.

Library of Congress Cataloging in Publication Data

Irwin, Judith Westphal.
  Empowering ourselves and transforming schools : educators making a
difference / Judith W. Irwin.
     p.   cm. — (SUNY series, teacher preparation and development)
  Includes bibliographical references and index.
  ISBN 0-7914-3103-7 (hardcover : alk. paper). — ISBN 0-7914-3104-5
(pbk. : alk. paper)
    1. Educational change—United States. 2. School management and
organization—United States. 3. Educational change—United States—
Case studies. I. Title. II. Series: SUNY series in teacher
preparation and development.
  LB2805.I7 1996
  371.2'00973—dc20   95-51392
                                                            CIP

10 9 8 7 6 5 4 3 2 1

This book is dedicated to
Christina
and all the brave children
who go to school.

Contents

Activities

x / ACTIVITIES

Tables

Acknowledgments

First, I would like to gratefully acknowledge the kind assistance of Judy Hofer, Robin Roberts, and Nancy Mangano Rowe who gave me many useful suggestions for the manuscript while it was in progress. I would also like to thank the reviewers at SUNY Press for their revision suggestions and my editor at SUNY Press, Lois Patton, for her kind encouragement. I would like to thank my students at the University of Connecticut who have helped me to develop and refine my ideas. Specifically I would like to thank Patricia Tierney, Sandy Philipson, and Debby Young for providing me with feedback and support. Of course, I also owe much to the five teachers who graciously consented to be interviewed and visited and discussed in this text. I am also grateful to my colleagues at the Synthesis Center in Amherst, Massachusetts for their numerous insights and for their sincere friendship during this period of my life. I would particularly like to thank the director, Didi Firman, for sharing her wisdom and advice. Finally, I would like to thank Judi Goodman for things too numerous to mention.

Introduction

I really care about this book. I hope you will care about it too, for this book is about putting caring and empowerment back into the center of our educational endeavors. It is about finding the personal and collective power to transform schools as they presently exist into places where a truly empowering education can take place.

When I first began to write this manuscript, my audience was limited to teachers. I firmly believed, as I do now, that teachers are the ones who most directly affect what happens to kids, and that they are the best group to lead any reform movement. While writing, however, I realized that this emphasis on teachers as a distinct group was really divisive. I know many administrators, parents and lawmakers who are just as concerned about the future of education as are teachers.

Nothing is to be served by dividing all these good people from one another. Thus, I have changed my title and audience to include all citizens concerned about education, and I have called them educators. I count myself among this group. We parents, administrators, college professors, lawmakers and concerned community members can work together to empower ourselves to transform schools.

The purpose of this book is to inform and to inspire. It seems to me that reflection, no matter how profound, is of little use unless it is tied to action. Thus, this book is about changing ourselves and taking action in the world. It is both practical and scholarly, personal and political, objective and subjective. (Yes, I really think these divisions are unreal in any case.)

When we look toward transformations in society, we must look at both the transformation of individuals and the transformation of external structures. In this text, I struggle throughout with the tension between individual and collective efforts, between personal and institutional change. I try to show that these are not necessarily opposite but that, in a conscious community in which autonomy and difference are valued, they are mutually constitutive forms of empowerment. The individual cannot become actualized without a supportive community and an empowering community can only become such if it is composed of authentic individuals.

You may have noticed that I have not even attempted to define empowerment here. I hope that I have piqued your curiosity in this matter, for empowerment is the subject of my first chapter. In that chapter I also attempt to explain why empowering the self inevitably leads to empowering others (unless you are a hermit). Moreover, this relationship between empowering self and other is the reason that a book on educators empowering themselves must also deal with empowering students.

In the second and third chapters, I take a close look at the aspects of our current system that disempower educators and students. Please note that I am not saying that everything that we are doing is disempowering. I am just focusing on those practices which are problematic.

In chapters 4 through 6 I try to make some suggestions about how we can empower our students through transforming our notions about the educational process and the content of that process. I use literacy as an example of these ideas because it is the area with which I am the most familiar.

In chapters 7 and 8 I present what I have found about empowering ourselves and creating empowering communities. My assumption is that the reader of the earlier chapters will have made some decisions about what needs to be changed and will be looking for ways to implement those changes. I encourage the reader to look within him- or herself first and then to connect with others. Indeed, that is the way that I hope this book will be used. Individuals can read and write response to the suggested activities by themselves, and they can get together with a friend or a support group to share their responses.

Chapter 9 presents the results of case studies of teachers who reflect the definition of empowered educators suggested in chapter 1. Because I am committed to developing knowledge about education that is grounded in real experience, I could not write a book on this topic without looking at the lives of real teachers in real classrooms. The results echo much of what was said earlier in the book.

In chapter 10 I try to tie everything together. I also share my own story in the attempt to be present to the reader as a person with her own struggles and successes. For none of us is ever completely where he or she wants to be. Empowering ourselves and transforming schools is a lifelong process, one that I have found to be worth the effort.

But it is not easy. It requires that we invest our whole selves. To this end, I have provided activities to get the reader involved with the text using his or her intellect, imagination, intuition and senses. For it is only by integrating these that we can truly change. I hope that you will find these activities to be a bridge from reflection to action and from theory to practice. I encourage you to spend time doing them in your own way. This is not a book designed to tell the reader what to think. It is a book designed to encourage the reader to develop his or her own beliefs and strategies for change. Enjoy!

PART ONE

Understanding the
System of Domination

CHAPTER ONE

Understanding Empowerment

Everywhere I look these days, it seems, I see the word "empowerment." I see it in newspapers and magazines; I see it in the subtitles of the new textbooks on teaching; I see it in my own writing. Having been in the field of education for over twenty years, I have learned that such enthusiasm warrants great caution. Fads worry me, and I am only beginning to discover why this one is so troublesome.

In the first place, why is it always a noun? "The empowerment of teachers" is the phrase I hear and read again and again. The problem with this phrase is that the agent is missing. Making it a noun allows us to avoid focussing on who is doing the empowering. It seems to me that if someone else is empowering you, then you still don't have the power. Empowering you to do what? Who decides? I believe that educators must be the ones to appropriate power and then define empowerment for themselves. We must decide what empowerment is. We must decide what we are being empowered to do. We must decide what our students are being empowered to do.

The answers to these questions are not nearly as easy as all the books referring to empowerment would have us believe. When I asked my colleagues for information on teacher empowerment, I got a bewildering array of articles on changing the organization of schools so that teachers had more responsibility and more of a chance to move into semi-administrative positions. Neither of these opportunities really captured my feelings about empowerment. The idea of giving teachers increased responsibility for a failing system made me shudder. This would make already overburdened lives more stressful. Increased ability to make decisions for others in traditional administrative positions did not make me feel any better. It went against all my beliefs about empowering others.

So I began to think about empowerment. If these organizational changes are empowerment, then maybe I am not so interested. And yet I am very interested in something else, both for myself and for my students. What is it? I began to search for new ideas that could ease my misgivings.

Possible Definitions of Empowerment

My first attempt was to read Gene Maeroff's book *The Empowerment of Teachers*. In it, he speaks of teacher empowerment in terms of "their individual deportment, not their ability to boss others." He speaks of the power involved as "the power to exercise one's craft with confidence and to help shape the way that the job is to be done" (p. 4). Similarly, I read in Ashcroft (1987) that "[a]n empowered person . . . would be someone who believed in his or her ability/capability to act, and this belief would be accompanied by able/capable action" (p. 143). This emphasis on the psychological state of the person contrasted with the external emphasis of organizational change and offered me a different way of looking at empowerment. Empowerment means believing in yourself and your own ability to act. Power, within this psychological definition, is thought to be an internal state of self-confidence that is accompanied by action.

On its face, this was very satisfying focus. It felt more like what I meant when I thought of myself as feeling empowered. When I feel empowered I make decisions and take action based on those decisions. I have self-confidence and feel good about what I am doing. I feel energized and full of enthusiasm. Perhaps this is why so many of us are drawn to the idea of becoming empowered. This is the definition of empowerment that is appealing to most people.

But my questioning self soon realized that this definition, though perhaps containing some necessary components, is not sufficient. If empowerment is becoming confident about one's decisions and ability to act, then we would characterize great tyrants as, perhaps, the most empowered individuals of them all. Yet this was surely not the result I was seeking. I soon realized that defining empowerment as feeling capable and taking action actually eschews another critical question: Capable of what? Acting in what way?

Those who would use their power to control others are clearly empowered in a different sense than the one about which I wish to speak. If people use their power to oppress others, then they have internalized a tyrant/rebel duality that keeps them from becoming truly empowered. They remain stuck in one side of a relationship in which neither person is truly free (Gawain, 1986). Certainly, this is not the kind of empowerment we want for teachers or students. Confidence, a sense of capability, yes, but within a context that enables persons to move beyond oppressive roles.

I thus began to expand what I am calling psychological definitions with political ones which address issues of power in society. For instance, Bookman and Morgan, in the introduction to their book entitled *Women and the Politics of Empowerment*, have supplied such a definition: "We use the term empowerment to connote a spectrum of political activity ranging from acts of individual resistance to mass political mobilizations that challenge the basic power relations in our society" (p. 4). They suggest that psychological definitions which stress "individual self-assertion" and "feeling powerful" can only be achieved for many people when they become aware of the causes of their powerlessness and act to change the conditions of their lives. Power, in this definition, is assumed to be "a social relationship between groups that determines access to, use of, and control over the basic material and ideological resources in society" (p. 4).

In a similar vein, Peter McLaren, when speaking of the empowerment of students, says

> I am using the term empowerment to refer to the process through which students learn to critically appropriate knowledge existing outside their immediate experience in order to broaden their understanding of themselves, the world, and the possibilities for transforming the taken-for-granted assumptions about the way we live. . . . It also refers to the process by which students learn to question and selectively appropriate those aspects of the dominant culture that will provide them with the basis for defining and transforming, rather I than merely serving, the wider social order. (p. 186)

From this politically aware point of view, empowerment is about changing society. It is about getting the knowledge and understanding of how things work that will allow one to transform the conditions of one's life. The assumption is that this transformation would be toward conditions of increased social justice.

Again, in my own life, becoming aware of the possibility of working to end social inequality has been empowering for me. As I have begun to question the very assumptions under which I work as a professor of education, I have begun to feel energized by my work for the first time. There is no question in my mind that, for me, the commitment to social change has empowered me to act.

Moreover, these political definitions of empowerment take into account the purpose of the power being accrued; they speak of feeling powerful as coming from knowledge and action that works against the unequal distribution of resources, and they answer the question of "empowerment for what?" Empowerment is to improve the conditions of one's own life *and* the conditions of other lives, especially those lives limited by discrimination and social injustice.

Activity 1.1[1]
DEFINING EMPOWERMENT FOR YOURSELF

For this activity, find a quiet space. You may wish to get yourself a journal for the activities in this book, or you may wish to write in the space left here. Just make sure you have a pencil and somewhere to write or draw.

Now, close your eyes and think of a time when you felt "empowered" as a teacher or educator (whatever that means to you). Let yourself feel those feelings again. How does it feel? How does your body feel? How do your emotions feel? What are you doing? Stop and list some words to describe the feeling of empowerment.

---

1. In order for this book to be useful to you, the reader, in your own process of empowerment, it seems essential that it be more than a monologue from me to you. To help you get involved and to develop your own opinions regarding the topics discussed, I have included what I am intending to be empowering activities. These are not meant to be dry academic writing experiences, but, rather, opportunities for you to go deeply within yourself in order to really change in ways you determine are best for you. Thus, though it is tempting to read on, figuring that you might do the exercises later (and later seldom comes), it would probably be best to take time when you come to these activities to become actively involved in responding to the ideas I have presented.

Next, think about the circumstances that led to this feeling. Were there students, teachers, administrator or parents involved? Was it a realization of some sort? A commitment or sense of purpose? Describe these circumstances.

Finally, did you take action as a result of feeling so empowered? What kind of action? Or did you change as a result of this feeling? In what way?

Now, look back over what you have written. Describe what teacher empowerment means to you at this time.

Defining Power and Domination

For me, all this thinking about empowerment seems to come down to definitions of power and domination. It seems to me that one's definition of empowerment depends fundamentally on one's definition of power . . . and since empowerment is in some way opposed to domination, this should also somehow figure in. I want a definition of empowerment that works against all forms of domination.

So what is domination? I would define it as "power over." (When someone asserts power over us, we experience it as oppression. Thus, domination and oppression are two sides of the same experience.) Though domination is sometimes limited to systematic asymmetrical relations of power at an institutional level, I think that it is important to expand this to include any individual power relations in which one person has "power over" another. (Of course, this may involve more than persons; the attempt to dominate nature is the most important example of this.) (See Merchant, 1980; Griffin, 1978). This seems to be the most predominant definition of power in our society (Kreisberg, 1992). Indeed, one colleague of mine says that she has a visceral negative reaction to the word "power." I suspect that this is because she associates it exclusively with "power over." (How do you feel when you hear the word "power"? Why?)

In the competitive world in which we live, there is an assumption that either you have power over me or I have power over you. We are constantly urged to a mentality of "one upmanship" (Schaef, 1981). Unfortunately, this power-over mentality depends on the objectification of others, that is, we must see them as objects to be manipulated in order to have power over them. Thus, it results in a fundamental estrangement from our connection with other living beings. Feminists, and others, have argued convincingly that this mentality is responsible for much of the suffering that we see today, because it isolates us from community and from nature (Kreisberg, 1992; Merchant, 1980).

To overcome this, we can look to the concept of "power to" or "power from within" (Starhawk, 1982). We can replace the myth that says that some people have worth and some do not with a belief that each person has inherent value; each has his/her own truth and this truth must be respected. With this belief system, the need to have power over others as objects can be abandoned for an emphasis on self-expression and fulfillment and a commitment to this for each person. This "postinstrumental" value system would result in collaborative rather than dominating relationships and a respect for diversity within a sense of unity (Balbus, 1982).

Moreover, radical belief in the dignity and humanness of every person is inherently empowering because it applies to the self as well as to others. Pat Collins (1990) makes this connection when she says

> Empowerment involves rejecting the dimensions of knowledge, whether personal, cultural or institutional, that perpetuate objectification and dehumanization. African-American women and other individuals in subordinate groups become empowered when we understand and use those dimensions of our individual, group, and disciplinary ways of knowing that foster our humanity as fully human subjects. (p. 230)

Empowerment comes from finding the power-from-within or power-to within us and rejecting models of power that imply power-over. To do this we must respect all people as fully human and self-actualizing and reject the temptation to objectify or to think of some humans as more fully human than others.

In *The Empowerment Book*, David Gerson and Gail Straub express it this way: "You will learn how to harness to passion of your mind and create your fullest expression of being human. We call this empowerment" (p. 5). Empowerment is finding your deepest human self and manifesting it in the world. It is respecting and promoting this for each person, for it is only through valuing this for all persons that we can truly expect it for ourselves.

Activity 1.2
EXPERIENCING POWER AND CONTROL
IN YOUR CLASSROOM OR SCHOOL

Find a quiet place and decide whether you wish to write or draw for this activity. Make sure you have the material you need.

Now, close your eyes and picture a time when you felt that you had to control your students (or teachers). It may have been a time when you were giving an assignment, monitoring their completion of an assignment, or just trying to keep order and quiet while you transmitted information. How are they reacting? How do you feel? How does your body feel? Stay in the situation for a minute and then jot down a few words describing how you feel in this situation, or draw a picture representing your feelings or the situation itself.

Now, think of a time in which you were allowing students (or teachers) to make choices of their own. They may be deciding what they want to learn or do, how they want to do something or when. How are they reacting? How do you feel? How does your body feel? Jot down a few words about what you want to remember about these feelings or draw a quick picture of yourself in this situation.

What does all this tell you about power and domination and how you and your students feel about it? Which situation made you more comfortable? Why?

Power-With

Another way to look at the power-from-within that respects the humanness of others has been suggested by Seth Kreisberg in his book *Transforming Power*. He suggests that "power with" is "characterized by collaboration, sharing, and mutuality" (p. 61). This is the form of power that is embedded in relationships. Each person in the relationship is empowered through relations of mutual respect. The power is "jointly developed" (Follett, 1924) because people are "developing their capacities by working together" (p. 71). Kreisberg's (1992) study of six teachers working together in the Boston Area Educators for Social Responsibility from 1984 to 1986 supports the possibility of developing these empowering communities in which power is experienced as co-agency through consensus, mutuality and respect for each individual voice. In that group, each member felt included, each was listened to fully even when he or she dissented, and decisions were made by consensus. Members reported feeling empowered in various ways by their participation in this group.

It seems that when we experience this power individually, it is experienced as power-to or power-from-within. When we participate in empowering communities, (which may indeed be necessary in order for us to empower ourselves—see chapters 8 and 9), then it is experienced as power-with. Power-to and power-with are just different expressions for the kind of power that respects the independent subjectivity of self and others. Neither of these can really exist without the other; we cannot sustain power-to without some sort of empowering community and we cannot participate in a truly empowering community unless we are able to hold onto our power rather than giving it away to a leader. To stress this interdependency I use the term power-to/power-with, Power-to/power-with reminds us that work in our classroom and community must involve sharing, mutual respect and collaboration if it is to be empowering for any of us as individuals.

Empowerment and Will

Finally, it is important to remember that respect for the dignity of all includes respecting our own self-assertion as well. Asserting our human will, or power to, is an essential part of being empowered and need not result in the domination of others. In *The Act of Will* (1973), Roberto Assagioli has developed a psychological theory of will that describes the kind of person that expresses his or her own humanity while also respecting that of others. He suggests that the truly effective will involves a balanced working of at least three components:

1) *Good will:* an awareness of "ethical considerations," a consideration of the needs of others, a "sense of love and compassion." (p. 15)

2) *Skillful will:* "the ability to obtain the desired results with the least expenditure of energy" (p. 15); practical knowledge and the ability to use it.

3) *Strong will:* the strength to use the will when necessary. This is only one aspect and, "when dissociated from the others, it can be, and often is, ineffectual or harmful to oneself or other people." (p. 15)

If these are out of balance or weak, there is a problem with will.

Tyrants exemplify overages of skillful and strong will combined with a very weak good will. They can get things done but they have little concern or respect for the rights of others. (Actually, this combination is encouraged for men in our society, who are expected to be "tough.") Overages of good and skillful will, with a weakness in strong will, will result in a person who is concerned about people and able to get things done but unable to assert him or herself in difficult situations. The third possibility, a weakness in the practical will, would probably manifest as a strong and compassionate person who has little common sense and thus accomplishes very little.

The empowered person must have a balance among these three types of will. He or she has compassion for others, seeing them as fully human and as having worth. He or she has the strength and practical knowledge to actualize him/herself and to encourage this in others. Do you have a sense of your own development in relation to these three aspects of will? Do you feel strong enough to stand up for what you believe? Can you be practical and get things done? Do you tend to act in the best interests of others? This may give you insight into where you wish to concentrate your energies in empowering yourself. Take a minute and jot down ideas about how you might strengthen any weakened aspect of will you find in yourself.

Empowered Educators[2]

All of the notions I have discussed in this chapter seem, to me, to supply a piece of the puzzle called empowerment. All must be included in any definition of empowerment. All are involved in my purpose for writing this book . . . so let me attempt here to put all this together into a working definition of empowered educators:

> Empowered educators are persons who believe in themselves and their capacity to act. They understand systems of domination and work to transform oppressive practices in society. They respect the dignity and humanness of others and manifest their power as the power to actualize their own unique humanity. They are strong, practical and compassionate as they work individually and with others to support the self-realization of all persons in their classrooms, schools and communities.[3]

There is something very satisfying to me about this definition. Of course, no one can meet this ideal all of the time, but it seems to me that it can serve as a goal or inspiration to help us achieve the real personal growth that has drawn us to the word "empowerment" in the first place. We must avoid being sidetracked by partial definitions that leave us feeling disillusioned yet again. Most importantly, this description includes the opposition to domination or power-over mentality, the power-to actualize one's highest self, and the power-with that comes from working with others. It also reminds us of the empowering of others that automatically results when we are empowered ourselves.

---

2. I have used the word "educator" rather than "teacher" to avoid contributing to the division between teachers, parents and administrators, all of whom can empower themselves to work for change and all of whom are educators.
3. It is also interesting to see how this definition can be translated to apply to students:

> Empowered students are persons who believe in themselves and their capacity to act. They understand systems of domination and work to transform oppressive practices in society. They respect the dignity and humanness of others and manifest their power as the power to actualize their own unique humanity. They are strong, practical and compassionate as they work individually and with others to support the self realization of all persons in their classrooms, schools, and communities.

What kind of curriculum would result in this kind of student empowerment? (See chapters 4–6.)

My experience leads me to suspect that empowering ourselves as teachers or educators is the first step toward empowering our students. Moreover, it probably requires at least three recursive stages: First, we must come to understand the systems of domination that operate in the lives of teachers and students in our schools. I have attempted to describe some of these systems part 1 of this book. Such things as bureaucracy, scientific rationality, internalized domination, isolation and sexism all work to disempower educators in their daily lives. Tracking, labelling, cultural privilege, and the overemphasis on schedules, rules, cognitive tasks and competition are examples of power-over practices that disempower students.

Secondly, we must decide what we really value, our deepest beliefs about the dignity and worth of each person and how these can be reflected in our educational practices. In part 2 of this book, I have provided some suggestions for empowering alternatives to our present educational practices. These include such things as emphasizing process, sharing authority, encouraging voice, redefining multiculturalism and integrating forms of knowledge.

Finally, we must find ways to manifest our vision and support ourselves in these efforts by creating empowering communities. The third part of this book contains suggestions for self and community empowerment. Teachers who have read this book have told me that reading or at least skimming these chapters (7 and 8) before reading chapters 1–6 helps clarify one's direction as one reads the earlier chapters.

Part Three concludes with descriptions of five teachers who exemplify the definition of an empowered educator given in this chapter. Each of these teachers is in a unique situation and yet, taken together, these descriptions provide a compelling picture of the possibilities inherent in teacher and student empowerment. To ground theory in reality, I have used examples from these teachers' lives throughout the text.

The process of empowerment requires us to be willing to change, and we cannot change by thinking and analyzing alone. We must enlist the help of our feelings, senses and imagination as well. Indeed, a basic premise of this text is that neither we nor our students can or should devalue or isolate these natural psychological functions. To do so would be to deny our wholeness as persons. (See chapter 5.) Thus, the empowering activities provided in this book will encourage you to think, sense, feel and imagine and to draw and/or write to connect with those thoughts, sensations, feelings and images as you go through what I hope will be the liberating process of empowering yourself to make positive differences in your own life and the lives of others. These activities will also encourage you to connect with others in dialogue and community, for we cannot empower ourselves without the support of other empowered persons. Power-with is the community experience of power-to and provides us with the ground on which we can stand.

CHAPTER TWO

How Educators
Experience Domination

In the activities in chapter 1, you may have gotten a sense of how you feel when you are empowered. You may have also realized that you wish to feel that way more often. Yet you may be wondering why you don't. You may be finding youself attempting to control and manipulate your students (or others) in ways that make you uncomfortable. You may also feel alienated from many of the professional decisions that you implement each day. For me, it was this sense of alienation from my own teaching that led me to explore how I might come to feel more empowered. The truth is that even though teachers and other educators seem to have a large amount of autonomy, domination operates in our professional lives on a daily basis. What are the unstated and often unseen ways in which we are controlled? This is the subject of this chapter.

Scientific Rationality

One of the most pervasive controlling forces in education today is the belief in scientific rationality. Most of the programs we implement boast that they have been "scientifically tested" or that they have the theoretical support of "scientific" research. Reading instruction, the area with which I am most familiar, is a classic example. Most teachers have believed that there has been scientific evidence for the subskill lists that have driven the basal curriculum. The fact is that these subskill lists vary tremendously from series to series and no one set of skills has been sub-stantiated by research at all (Rosenshine, 1980).

Of course, there are some programs that have been "proven" to be "effective." What we forget to ask is "effective in what way? for whom? under what circumstances?" The criteria on which these programs are judged are determined by the biases of their creators. Most programs are tested against standardized test scores, results that are limited in many ways and do not reflect natural life tasks. Many programs are tested in small, specialized settings with specially trained personnel. These results do not necessarily apply to you and your classroom. Almost no program is tested for social and attitudinal outcomes that are long-range, probably because these are not highly valued by those doing the testing and be-cause they are difficult and expensive to measure.

"Scientific rationality" is the term often used to refer to the myth that educational programs are scientifically justified rather than based on value systems and controlling interests. For me, the major flaw in this myth is that there can be no such thing as pure objectivity. Lorraine Code, in a wonderful discussion of how knowledge is constructed, states that we must see knowledge as a synthesis of the objective and the sub-jective. Objectivity and subjectivity form a continuum rather than a di-chotomy. We can be more or less "objective" depending on the situation. *We can never be completely objective* because we are always operating on the basis of our basic beliefs about the ways things work and the way things should be. "Emotions and intellect are mutually constituative and sus-taining rather than oppositional forces in the constuction of knowledge" (Code, 1991, 27). (The ironic thing is that the ideal of objectivity is ac-tually the result of emotional needs: Its appeal is security, safety and con-trol of the world around us [Code, 1991].)

Moreover, what does is mean for something to be "scientific" any-way? Usually we mean that it was determined using "scientific method." This method was originally developed to study questions in physics where the subject matter is much less complex than children learning in classrooms. One can question whether such a method is the best for studying social situations which involve numerous uncontrol-lable variables (see Code, 1991). Moreover, this method is based on taking numerous observations and then generalizing to groups. Indi-vidual differences are "variability" to be "controlled." Yet, in working in schools, we may find that it is just those individual differences that most affect our work.

The point here is that educators can question the scientific legitimacy claims that are used to justify programs. What works "in general" may not work for the individuals in my home, class or school. The values (as reflected in methods and goals) of the program creators may not match mine or those of my students or those of my school and community. There is no curriculum that is not value-laden, and claims for scientific legitimacy do not change this fact. (Note: Yes, there is a place for scientific investigations. The critical step is acknowledging biases and limitations rather than overgeneralizing and mystifying values.)

Activity 2.1
QUESTIONING SCIENTIFIC LEGITIMACY

Think of something that you do or is done in your classroom or school that has scientific legitimacy and still makes you uncomfortable. What is it? _____

What about it makes you uncomfortable? _____
_____

Why does this make you uncomfortable? (Does it represent a value that you do not share?) _____
_____

How would you change it? Why? _____
_____
_____

Finally, let's dethrone the program altogether. (If it makes you uncomfortable, there is a good chance that the research support is based on a value that you do not support or was conducted in a different kind of setting than the one about which you are concerned.)

How was its legitimacy determined? Better performance on what tests or in what situations? _____

Is this what you value the most? Is this relevant to your situation? _____

What else have the program "scientists" failed to consider? _____

What biases did they have when they created this program? _____

Share your realizations with your colleagues!!

Technical Control

Of course, educators, like other workers, are under certain pressures, just because they work for someone else. Simple, observable control in the workplace comes from direct contact with one's employer or manager and control through merit raises, hiring and firing, and so on. Administrators are accountable to other administrators and to school boards, for instance. Once tenured, many teachers escape the most insidious features of this kind of control, though we must never forget that structural changes like ending tenure and breaking teacher's unions could reinstate it.

However, in his book, *Contested Terrain: The Transformation of the Workplace in the Twentieth Century*, Edwards speaks of the recent growth of two new forms of control as the size of the workplace and the complexity of work has increased. These are technical control and bureaucratic control (Edwards, 1979). I believe that these forms of control are much more insidious and pervasive in the lives of educators than the simple hierarchical control mentioned above.

Put simply, technical control is control embedded in the technology of the work activities themselves. The managers are simply enforcers of the dictates of the technical structure of the work. In my work as a teacher educator, technical control is asserted by the state requirements related to testing teachers for certification and by the state teaching competencies by which beginning teachers are judged. Whether these are my beliefs about good teaching or not, they must be taught if these young people are to succeed. (Luckily, I also have time to expose my students to other philosophies of teaching and critical reflection about the alternatives.)

In the case of teaching, such control is embedded in prepackaged programs like basal series and other textbooks in which the teacher is supposed to implement the program as designed. Here the text is controlling the educator rather than the educator controlling the instruction. Other curriculum guidelines can also control what the teacher is allowed to do. Here, again, we are not controlled by a person but by a program (Apple, 1982). Several of the teachers I interviewed for chapter 9 mentioned having experienced being compelled to implement a specific curriculum with which they did not agree.

The common result of technical control is "deskilling" and "reskilling": Teachers (and administrators) are not expected to know much about reading or math (or teaching) or whatever in order to implement a prepackaged program (deskilling). Instead, they are taught to be managers and implementers of programs prepared by others (reskilling). Preparers of these programs used to talk about them as "teacher proof," meaning that they would be effective in spite of the supposed ignorance of the teacher. Though this terminology is no longer acceptable, it is quite possible that many of the designers of such programs still work with this basic mindset.

I believe that the popularity of current programs like writing workshop and teaching reading through literature rests in the fact that technical control is greatly relaxed in these approaches. Of course, many teachers, parents, administrators and schools boards fear just this, and, in many places, some are attempting to reestablish technical control over these programs by writing literacy curricula with clearly specified procedures and outcomes and by adopting traditional textbooks and basal series that are "whole language" based.

Several years ago I was involved in a training program related to reading instruction in the Archdiocese of Chicago elementary schools. Funded by the state of Illinois, we had the opportunity to monitor on site the changes made by the teachers involved. I was also interested in monitoring the changes in attitude that accompanied the changes the teachers were making in their classrooms. I was particularly interested in whether the type of substantive "reskilling" we were providing gave them the support they needed to resist the technical control exerted by the basal readers.

After a year of training on teaching the reading process (Irwin, 1991), I found that the two most noticeable attitudinal changes were the renewed sense that they, as teachers, had the knowledge they needed to make decisions about literacy instruction and the new awareness that the basal series did not have the scientific legitimacy they had previously assumed. These two attitudinal changes were accompanied by a noticeable weakening in the technical control of the basal.

To some extent we can resist technical control by resisting the de-skilling it requires. By remaining knowledgeable about the curriculum, we can continue to make our own decisions and to refuse to be imple-menters of someone else's program when that program does not fit the needs of our students. (See chapter 7 for a further discussion of substan-tively reskilling ourselves.) One of the teachers interviewed for chapter 9 told a story about how she designed a whole literature-based program years ago as soon as she could tell how bored she and her students were with the basal. Another teacher told about how she and her colleagues got together and designed a whole new content-area reading curriculum on their own. (See chapter 9.)

There is one problem with this, however, that must be confronted directly, and you have already probably thought of it . . . having the time. Social theorists have found that work load increases tend to accompany deskilling and the separation of conception and execution (Apple, 1988). They have referred to this as intensification. In recent times, intensifica-tion has increased, especially for jobs involving mental labor (Larson, 1980). Apple (1988) found that, in a school in which control by pre-specified objective and constant measurement was implemented, intensi-fication increased. He noted that intensification of the work load has several unfortunate side-effects: destruction of sociability leading to pro-fessional isolation, destruction of time necessary for self-direction, and the loss of the time necessary to keep up with developments in one's field. All of one's time is taken up with meeting the immediate demands of the job which are, by themselves, increasingly difficult to handle. Thus, intensification and deskilling go hand in hand. The high school teacher I interviewed put it this way:

> Do you address anywhere the idea of time as empowering or the lack of time as disempowering? This year, as I rush from lunch duty to two classes then to our new writing conference center, without even time to go the the bathroom, I wonder a lot about time. As I read drafts late into the night or get up early to plan what to do that day, I wonder about time.

The number of responsibilities being handled by the typical educa-tor in the nineties has increased geometrically. Paperwork and bureau-cratic demands on time are often reported as taking all the extra time teachers might spend on planning and professional growth. The intensification of the teaching profession must be addressed at the same time that we address deskilling and technical control. If Apple's observations are correct, then there may be a way to resist technical control, deskilling and intensification simultaneously by searching for curriculum models and teaching routines that return to us the control of our classrooms while also allowing us the time we need to make needed decisions and to educate ourselves so that we can make the best decisions possible. We can question technical and bureaucratic demands that take us away from the business of teaching. We can question prepackaged materials in terms of the time and control they leave to the teacher. Filling out forms, grading tests, organizing worksheets, writing reports, going to ritualized meetings and filing folders are not the tasks that should be taking teachers' time. Planning and improving instruction, reflecting, having meaningful interactions with colleagues, doing collaborative research and keeping up with professional knowledge are much more appropriate activities for educators.

Activity 2.2
RESISTING TECHNICAL CONTROL

Is there a program in your classroom (or school) that is controlling you (or other teachers) or taking up too much time? What is it? _____

How could you adapt this program or create another that more appropriately reflects your values and meets the needs of students or that takes up less time with needless busywork? (Don't let yourself be stopped by internal voices that say you must follow the prescribed curriculum. Just pretend that you have unlimited freedom.)

Write three ways you would change it below . . .

1. _____

2. _____

3. _____

Now, how comfortable do you feel with implementing these changes? If you feel comfortable with them, then go ahead with it! If you do not feel comfortable with trying this program, describe why. What or whom is in your way? Are you sure? _____

_____

These blocks probably represent bureaucratic controls which also need to be addressed. Don't worry! This is the subject of the next discussion and activity.

Bureaucratic Control

As you may have noticed while doing the last activity, technical control and intensification are not the only factors controlling educators. We are also affected by bureaucratic control. Like technical control, bureaucratic control seems outside of the immediate relationship between the employee and manager. In this case, rather than arising from the structure of the activities as in technical control, bureaucratic control is built into the structure of the organization. In our case, this would include the organizational structure of school districts. Job categories and descriptions, assignments of responsibilities, promotion procedures, work rules and the like control what can be and is accomplished. A hierarchy of persons is established. Changes must go through mounds of red tape and through persons assigned decision-making responsibilities.

At its worst, bureaucracy can divide teachers from those who are making decisions. The junior high teacher I interviewed said:

> [The bureaucracy] totally disempowers teachers. . . . The current administration has as attitude of us against them. . . . It's like the administrators are the only people who care about the students. . . . What kind of garbage is that? . . . [N]ow there's this snide, undermining, demoralizing attitude, that is, this "us against them" attitude, and it's damaging.

Teachers, parents, and administrators who are compliant and follow the bureaucratic procedures set up for them are usually the most rewarded. Edwards (1979) says that the following types of behaviors are the most rewarded in a bureaucratic system: "rules-orientation," "predicatability and dependability," and "internalization of the enterprise's goals and values." Wise (1979) points out that in a bureaucratic system rules and procedures are thought to be superior to the exercise of judgement. Thus, it is no wonder that we feel insecure when we do not wish to go along with the current curriculum or when we want to make changes in spite of the supervisor whose job is defined as "the one who makes decisions."

An excellent example of how bureaucracy can inhibit change and quality performance is in the area of special education. Once children are identified as having special needs, they go into a system that sometimes chugs along impressively but accomplishes very little. Teachers are forced to spend endless hours in testing, writing reports, and preparing seemingly endless lists of "objectives" as required by law. Unfortunately, this often leaves very time for giving attention to how that child is to be taught or what might represent quality instruction. Moreover, in some systems, there is pressure to make decisions prematurely and apart from the instructional setting and then to lock those decisions in place. (Note: I am not suggesting that the laws protecting the rights of students with special needs are the problem. I am suggesting that we must resist the tendency to believe that the bureaucracy is the solution.)

Moreover, school bureaucracies often add to the intensification of our work, thus increasing our deskilling and our vulnerability to technical control. On almost every occasion on which I have gone into a district to work with teachers who have been asked by someone above them in the hierarchy to work on revising curriculum, someone has mentioned that the last time they did such work at the request of someone higher in the bureaucracy, "It got buried in someone's desk" or "No one ever did anything about it. No one could see any reason to change. They just filed the plan away." Teachers are understandably frustrated by the amount of time they often put in on projects that are never implemented or are implemented badly because they have little support from the actual teaching staff in the first place.

One of the biggest problems with bureaucracies is that the person who is actually blocking the change is often obscured. We get answers like "it can't be done," "it will never go through central office." My favorite, which I hear from teachers all the time, is "They won't let us do it." Usually, when I pursue this with "Who won't let you do it?" the answers are vague. No one is quite sure. And when we begin looking for a person, we often don't find one. The internalization of bureaucracy has made things look more hopeless than they really are.

Of course, bureaucracy doesn't stop at the district level. Governmental agencies are increasingly making decisions previously reserved for educators. State and federal governmental policies are increasing the bureaucratic push to rationalize schooling even as local districts are seeing the limitations of bureaucratic control and scientific management. For that reason, I would strongly recommend that lawmakers educate themselves by reading this and other books on educational reform. (See Wise, 1979.)

Fortunately, current trends in business and education reflect a desire to ameliorate some of the worst aspects of bureaucratic control. Shared decision-making is being tried in a variety of settings, from the shop floor to the artist's studio (Montouri and Conti, 1993). This is largely a result of the fact that the business community has found that when workers are too far removed from decisions, productivity and commitment to work begin to wane. (See Depree, 1989; Senge, 1990; and others.) As mentioned above, teachers forced to work on someone else's ideas about curriculum change rarely cooperate in their implementation. Moving decisions down the hierarchy or "localness" results in people taking more reponsibility for their actions (Senge, 1990). Administrators are finding that when teachers are involved in the decision-making, the results are much more positive. (See Lieberman, 1988; Meier, 1995; and others.) The teachers I interviewed for chapter 9 are wonderful examples of teachers who have been involved in both the planning and the implementation of curriculum changes that have been successful.

Activity 2.3
WORKING IN A BUREAUCRACY

Now, refer back to the changes you wanted to make in activity 2.2. Did you feel limited by bureaucracy? If so, then it is time to revisit those limitations. If not, then you may need to think of a time when you wanted to change something but the bureaucracy effectively prevented it.

Now, try to get specific about the block.
First, list specific persons who would *not* have supported this change:

Which of these actually have the power to block your change? Put stars by their names.

Now, think of persons who would support the proposed change. List them below.

Which of these have the most power to help you? Put stars by those names.

Now, for the persons who were not starred as able to help, how could they be gathered together to form a more unified power block?

Now, it is time to plan a strategy. Here are some ideas to choose from. You may have others of your own. Feel free to add to this list:

- Visit one or more of the persons expected to block the change and work out a compromise you both can live with. Ask for their support in the compromise plan.
- Meet with persons supportive of the change and ask how they can help you.
- Form a committee of persons interested in the change and work through the bureaucracy together.
- Find out why those opposed are so opposed. Is is a lack of information? Collect information and share it with those who need it in order to support you.
- Others:

Select your strategies and write them on the plan below. You may wish to keep track of the results. Good luck!

WORKING FOR CHANGE: Preliminary Plan
STRATEGY	DATE COMPLETED	RESULTS

Hegemony

Many of the factors I have been discussing seem to be external; that is, they exist in the environment around us. However, it is important to realize that these are also things in which we participate; they are inside us as well. For instance, the myth of scientific rationality is so pervasive that it is difficult to remember to question it. Moreover, we have internalized the demands of technical and bureaucratic control to such an extent that we usually blame ourselves when we can't meet them.

One of my students recently broke down into tears in my class saying that she was a "bad teacher." When I pursued this perception with her, I found that she was teaching a large class of students who for various reasons were alienated from schooling. She had tried to motivate them by team teaching with another teacher and by bringing in journals and cooperative learning. Lately, however, she had begun to think about what others thought of her. She was sure that her classroom was perceived as too "noisy" and not sufficiently curriculum-based. The part of her that had internalized these values was at war with the part of her that believed in something else.

This tendency for domination to perpetuate itself through social consensus is often called hegemony. (See Apple, 1979; Gramsci, 1972; Kreisberg, 1992; McLaren, 1989; and others.) We accept certain social beliefs and practices because it is "just the way it is." (I hear this phrase a lot in class.) Thus, my student believed that quiet classrooms are good classrooms, regardless of how this conflicted with her other values. Even more insidious is the internalization of socially accepted notions of unequal worth:

Women often struggle with internalized notions of female inferiority; gay people struggle with internalized homophobia, and so on.

Moreover, it is extremely difficult to step outside this system of socially accepted assumptions legitimizing domination. For instance, when everyone around us thinks of teachers as not particularly bright or prepared to make decisions, it is difficult for us to think of ourselves differently. This "common sense" view of teachers is supported by practices that take away our autonomy, as well as by comments that are thought of as acceptable like "Well, we can't just have teachers deciding what is acceptable on their own." When everyone around us views these comments as sensible, it takes great courage to hear and question the belief system the statement is supporting. (The teachers I interviewed were quite vocal in their questioning of the "common sense" notion that elementary school teachers are less competent than high school teachers; see pages 268–69.)

Taken for granted beliefs about the world (which are sustaining our current system of power-over) are perpetuated in at least four ways (Thompson, 1987). Defined simply, they are:

1. Legitimization: domination is presented as "just" or "fair."
2. Dissimulation: domination is concealed.
3. Fragmentation: subordinate groups are divided and turned against each other.
4. Reification: practices of domination are presented as if they have "always been this way" rather than being rooted in a particular historical period.

Each of these is easy to see when we examine the educational system around us. Understanding them can help us to notice and question blocks to our own empowerment.

A classic case of legitimization is the myth of scientific rationality discussed earlier in this chapter. Programs that have scientific legitimacy are presented as if they are not laden with the values of their creators. Labelling students disabled or disadvantaged has also always struck me as an attempt to legitimate the school's failures by blaming them on the students.

Dissimulation is best represented by what has been called the "hidden curriculum." This would include all those things children learn from the everyday practices of schooling; things like it is best to do what you are told, there are few situations in which it is acceptable to question authority and so on. Few schools admit that this is what they teach, and yet they all do.

Fragmentation, for me, is best represented by the divisions I see every day between teachers and parents and students. Parents and students see teachers as dominant. Teachers do not feel dominant; they feel dominated by administrators from whom they are thereby alienated as well. Administrators doe not feel dominant either; they have to report to the school boards and the parents. Each of these groups fears the other. Whenever I hear references to "them," I see fragmentation slowing things down.

Finally, reification exists whenever we think that the way we are doing something is the only way it can or has ever been done. Teachers used to reify the basal as the way of teaching reading (Shannon, 1983, 1987, 1989), though this has been changing now that other philosophies like whole language have challenged them. (See chapter 6.) Whenever you hear someone say "because we have always done it this way", you will know that it is not a reason not to change; it is as expression of reified thinking.

One of my students gave me a great example of reified thinking. A friend of hers always cut pot roast into two parts before putting it in the oven. When she asked her friend why, she said she had always done it that way. Her friend became curious and called her mother to find out why. Her mother had always cut it into parts because she didn't have a pan big enough! This is a great example of how practices continue even when the original need is gone.

Resisting hegemony is a lifelong project; it is not something we can ever finish. We can start by questioning everything we do. We can question scientific legitimacy and other myths that perpetuate programs that we suspect are not in the best interests of our students. We can look for the hidden curriculum in the everyday workings of the classroom. What are the children really learning? How could we change the hidden curriculum? We can resist fragmentation by emphasizing the common bond among parents, students, teachers and administrators (educators). We can realize that every practice can be changed. Nothing is written in granite, as they say. There are many activities I could suggest at this point, but I do not want to give the impression that resisting hegemony is reducible to one writing activity or visualization. I will suggest one on resisting the hidden messages about the role of teachers, but it is important to remember that this whole book is about resisting hegemony or the perpetuation of practices of power-over through social consensus.

Activity 2.4
RESISTING HEGEMONIC CONCEPTS OF TEACHERS

What is the "hidden curriculum" in your school (or community) concerning the role of teachers?

	Never	Sometimes	Usually	Always
1. Look at memos sent to teachers . . . Are they respectful of them as professionals?				
2. Listen at meetings . . . Are teachers' views taken seriously?				
3. Is the teacher supported when a parent challenges a teacher?				
4. How many times do teachers have opportunities for meaningful conversations with colleagues?				
5. Are teachers able to challenge and change curriculum?				
6. Do teachers feel free to make situation-specific decisions about instruction in their classroom?				
7. Are teachers given adequate time for professional development and/or serious scholarly study?				
8. Do teachers have input into in-service topics and procedures?				

TO THINK ABOUT: What are some ways that teachers can have meaningful input into the decisions made in your school and district? How can these avenues be explored and expanded?

Internalized Domination

Thus, practices which limit our autonomy are perpetuated through a whole set of social beliefs and practices which most people accept as common sense. They are also perpetuated by our own internalization of the psychology of domination. Many psychologists have written about the internalized "self-hater" (Starhawk, 1982) or "tyrant" (Gawain, 1986) or the "inner critic" (Stone and Stone, 1993). For instance, Starhawk (1982) says:

> The self-hater is the inner representation of power-over. We have internalized it, not just from our parents but from every institution in society with which we have contact. It is the structure in the psyche that perpetuates domination. It reminds us of our helplessness, our powerlessness. It blames the victim; it tells us we are bad when bad things happen to us, that we do not have the right to be, to feel, to do what we do. It is the inner gun that keeps us in an inner prison. (p. 63)

Gawain (1986) identifies this "tyrant" as "the inner voice that tells us what we should and shouldn't do" (p. 86). Gestalt psychologists call this the "topdog." "It represents the 'shoulds' that are introjected by the individual, usually mainly from the parents. It is righteous, perfectionistic, authoritarian, bullying, and punishing" (Patterson, 1986). Other psychologists call it a "subpersonality" (Brown, 1983; Ferruci, 1982; Sliker, 1992; and others) which may have various unique characteristics depending on the individual and his/her life-experiences.

The important thing to remember here is that this inner voice, this subpersonality, developed when we were very young, when doing what authority prescribed actually did help us to survive. It was, and is, our friend. The best way to overcome the effects of this internal authority figure is not to repress it or banish it from existence. Then it will just go underground and bother us more. It is more effective to respect and know the needs of this subpersonality, to understand its fears, to accept this part of ourselves and to begin to meet its needs in more productive ways. (See Brown, 1983; Ferrucci, 1982; Sliker, 1992; and others.) Often we find that it is the voice of a critical parent who loves us but is afraid for our welfare.

When we hear this voice inside ourselves, we can recognize it for what it is, a part of us that is trying to protect us within a system of domination. Then we can engage other parts of our personality to help us to meet its need for security without sacrificing our autonomy. (For example, the tactician within us can reassure the tyrant that communication will be handled carefully.) Often, when we befriend the inner critic, we find that it helps us to be discriminating and wise (Stone and Stone, 1993).

Activity 2.5
OVERCOMING INTERNALIZED DOMINATION

Now, think of a time you wanted to change things but you didn't try because you *expected* the bureaucracy to prevent it. You may have just *assumed* that your "superiors" wouldn't approve. This internalized bureaucracy is just as powerful as the real one. It can be as if you have a bureaucratic voice inside your head telling you that you must conform.

Get a picture in your mind of the tyrant inside you. This may be a person like you or someone very different, that is, a different gender, age or personality. It may be a parent or authority figure. Let your imagination create a specific chaacter to represent this voice. You may even want to give him/her a name. Sketch you inner critic here:

Now let him/her talk for a while. Ask this personality what s/he needs and how he or she is useful to you. Ask what you can do to assuage his/her fears. What does s/he say?

Now, try to get an image of the empowered educator within you. What does he or she look like? Again, this personality may have a different gender or age than you. This is fine. Sketch this figure if it would be helpful. What does he or she have to say about the changes you want to make? Write with the voice of this empowered educator.

If possible, let these two internal voices have a dialogue. Can they get to a point of mutual acceptance?

Becoming aware of this internal tyrant can be the first step to accepting and understanding it. It developed at a time in your life when it was useful to you. It is still useful to you sometimes. Take a minute to think about what you have learned about yourself from doing this activity. Make notes below.

Make a promise to yourself to be aware of this internalized critical voice, to treat it with compassion, and to recognize its needs by making empowered decisions that take your whole self into account.

Note: As with many of the exercises in this book, you may find that it is useful to you to share what you have written with others who have completed the activity themselves. Also, such an inner dialogue may take more than one sitting. Finally, if feelings come up that are difficult to handle or if you want to pursue this in more depth, you may wish to seek professional assistance. Gestalt, transactional and psychosynthesis therapists all work with "subpersonalities" as a way to achieve personal growth.

Surplus Powerlessness

Current forms of domination also perpetuate themselves through what has been called "surplus powerlessness" (Lerner, 1986). This can be defined as the way in which we see ourselves as being more powerless than we really are. Psychologist Michael Lerner (1986) describes this as "the set of feelings and beliefs that make people think of themselves as even more powerless than the actual power situation requires, and then leads them to act in ways that actually confirm them in their powerlessness" (p. ii). How many of us feel that we are helpless to change things? I think this is the primary reason that some teachers become burned-out workers rather than aggressive change agents and some parents avoid school meetings rather than requesting them.

Surplus powerlessness is perpetuated through a process of "self-blaming." This is thinking that all our problems, such as stresses and frustrations at work and at home, are the result of our own inadequacies and failures and that it is our responsibility to fix them by ourselves. As a result, we do not feel that we have a right to demand real systemic changes, and we do not feel comfortable sharing our stress with others (Lerner, 1986). Even as I write this, I can think of the stresses I know my colleagues are enduring in isolation. Why aren't we coming together to discuss how things can be changed? We each think that we have to handle things on our own.

This leads to a very real isolation which only increases our self-blaming. Indeed, my conversations with teachers have suggested to me that isolation is a big source of disempowerment for educators (see chapter 9). When asked about external obstacles to her development as a change agent, one of the teachers I interviewed for my case studies said, "The educational structure . . . it's predicated on isolation and individualism which can be pluses but . . . not collaborative or empowering." John Gatto (1995) has spoken of the "quasi-monastic commitment" of teachers in which each is virtually locked in a cell with no other adults for the majority of the day. (One teacher recently told me that she will know she has grown up when she can go to the restroom whenever she wants.) Even at the university, we rarely have the time to talk with each other in open-ended ways.

Of course, the myth of meritocracy is what provides the rationale for self-blaming and encourages isolation. This is the belief that individuals can make whatever they wish of their lives depending on the amount of effort they put into it and the amount of talent they bring to it. Thus, if you have less money than someone else or if you are unhappy at work, you have no one to blame but yourself. I think this is the biggest reason we don't look for support from our colleagues in schools and universities. We are all afraid of being judged inferior if we admit to feeling frustrated or inadequate to the challenges we face.

The truth is that individual advancement and rank in a hierarchy often has little to do with individual merit. Elementary teachers are not inferior to secondary teachers. Teachers are not inferior to administrators. Professors who primarily teach are not inferior to those who primarily publish.

Moreover, we are often given limited alternatives, and frustrations at work are often built into the way work is organized. For instance, in bureaucratic systems, following rules is rewarded more often than excellence. In our current system of technical control, the teacher whose students do well on the test is often rewarded more than the teacher whose students love learning. At the university level, the professor who publishes is often rewarded more than the professor who effectively teaches all the high enrollment courses. Collectively, we can do something to change these things but only if we stop blaming ourselves as individuals and see clearly that what needs to change may be in the system itself.

A second myth that contributes to surplus powerlessness is the belief that our personal life should make up for all the frustrations and sacrifices that go on in the world of work (Lerner, 1986). Most people think it is their own fault when this doesn't happen and self-blaming increases. The fact is that the way we come to feel about ourselves at work has a profound influence on the way we feel about ourselves in other areas. Most people cannot spend the day suppressing feelings of frustration and helplessness and self-blame and then return home ready for loving intimacy. Moreover, in order to hide feelings of failure, families (and singles) often isolate themselves from friendships and community involvement with other families, putting further pressures on family relationships that are already strained to the breaking point.

I know that in my life I have been unable to completely separate my work and home lives: If one area is difficult the other usually suffers as well. Perhaps if we are more realistic about this, we can begin to support each other at home and at work in ways that more realistically allow us to be whole persons.

A final major contributor to our feelings of powerlessness is the self-blaming that begins in childhood. When we are young, we often see the frustrations and unhappiness in our parents' lives caused by real and surplus powerlessness. As egocentric child selves, we interpret their resultant inability to take joy in our authentic being as a personal failure and blame ourselves whenever they are caught in this cycle. We interpret their looks of stress and frustration as resulting from something that is wrong with us . . . thus beginning a cycle of self-blaming through shame (Bradshaw, 1988). If you feel that this is a problem for you, you may wish to seek help in ridding yourself of these early feelings of failure.

For beginning to see that things can change involves ending self-blame and isolation. We need to see that our problems are shared. Technical control, bureaucracy and internalized domination are common experiences. We can stop blaming ourselves for our feelings of frustration. We can move beyond isolation and self-blame to a place where we can begin to share our feelings of frustration and powerlessness when we see that these problems are common. Then we can collectively begin to change things or, at least, to make things better by supporting each other. We can move from an "I" to a "We." *I* can't make things better, but *we* can.

This leads to a concern that I have about writing this book. To the extent that it is viewed as a way for an individually flawed educator to "empower him or herself," I will have failed. Too many self-help books actually contribute to feelings of powerlessness by making the individual feel that if only he or she could "get it together," his or her problems would go away. I do not believe this for one second. What I am trying to communicate is that it is the systemic organization of forms of domination that has led to our individual feelings of powerlessness; it is only when collective recognition of social realities and collective action are combined with individual self–understanding and empowerment that the situation can be significantly improved.

Activity 2.6
OVERCOMING SURPLUS POWERLESSNESS

Lerner (1986) has described two journal questions that he uses in his "Occupational Stress Groups" that seem to be a good place to start on overcoming the isolation and self-blaming he discusses:

"Ask your co-workers at the workplace [teachers, parents and administrators] to describe to you what things are most stressful for them at work. List what they say. Then ask them to suggest two or three changes that they would like to see, and how they envision them being implemented." (p. 312)

Stresses Identified by My Colleagues	Changes They Would Like to See

"Describe three incidents that happened this week at work [at school] that helped reinforce the divisions between workers, rather than encouraging their solidarity." (pp. 312–13) (In our case, let's look at students, teachers, parents and administrators.)

1.

2.

3.

What could be done to avoid or mediate these divisive factors? _____

Now, here's one of my own:

Think about something you have tried in your classroom or school (or district) recently that did not go well. Picture the situation. How did you feel? _____ Did you blame yourself for the problems? _____

What were the factors under your control that you can change the next time you do the activity? _____

Now, what were the factors *not* under your control that led to the problems? _____

How can you stop blaming yourself unnecessarily every time your plans go awry? _____

A final note: Do you think the others in your district experience these same problems? Have you shared your experience with them? How can you create an environment in your school community in which it is OK to take risks and fail?

Sexism

No discussion of the oppression of educators in the twentieth century would be complete without including sexism. The fact is that approximately 87% of elementary school teachers and 67% of all public school teachers are women (Apple, 1986, 9). By far the majority of administrators have been men, though this is changing (Apple, 1988; Strober and Tyack, 1980). For the purposes of this discussion, I think it would again be useful to look at sexism in the lives of educators in terms of both external and internal oppressors, though, of course, these work together in complex ways.

Apple (1988) has suggested that part of the explanation for why there is such a clear attempt to control teachers is the politics of gender. He points out that this is part of a larger social trend to deskill and technically control a profession as soon as it becomes "women's work." The secretarial profession went through similar changes when it changed from a male profession to a female one. Moreover, the history of the development of technical and bureaucratic control in the teaching profession "is the history of the state, in concert with capital and a largely male academic body of consultants and developers, intervening at the level of practice into the work of a largely female workforce" (Apple, 1988, 36–37). Go to any professional convention in education and look at the percentage of women that are in the audience listening, and the percentage of women in the group of "experts" telling them how to teach, to convince yourself that this is still an issue.

I suspect that a similar devaluation may happen for parents participating in schools because they are usually the mothers (women). I have attended many meetings as a parent in which I am allowed to speak only after everyone else has spoken. I am not expected to have much to say (though I usually do). I have often felt that, as parent representative, I am there to rubber-stamp the opinions of others. I wonder if this would be the same if it were fathers who were participating in these meetings.

Similarly, when I was in graduate school, all my professors (except one visiting professor) were male. All the professors on my doctoral committee, therefore, were also male. When I was in my first academic job and visiting a school district in which I was preparing to gather data for a research study, I was asked when Dr. Irwin was going to arrive. (Similarly, Sarah Weddinton, a former Texas state legislator, once received a plaque from the state bar association because she had been selected as one of the state's ten outstanding legislators. It read, "With grateful appreciation to the honorable Sarah Weddinton for his dedication and service to the state of Texas" [cited in Cantor and Bernay, 1992, 79].)

Studies support the notion that there is a general tendency to devalue women and their work. In one study, for instance, evaluations of articles, paintings and other products were higher when they were attributed to men rather than women (see Nieva and Gutek, 1980). Men are generally thought to succeed because of skill, whereas women are encouraged to seek external explanations for their successes (Safilios-Rothschild, 1979).

These everyday experiences have a way of affecting those of us who are women. They begin to limit our expectations of ourselves. The lack of role models leaves us with little on which to base our expectation that we can lead. The assumption that women are not usually leaders creeps into our consciousness. In spite of the above examples, I have found that

I have had to struggle against my own internalized sexism much more than I have had to struggle against any concrete external barriers existing because I am a woman. For instance, when I am to give a presentation, I usuallly worry more about what I will wear than what I will say. Though I have the appropriate credentials, I worry about whether I will be taken seriously. Most of the female teachers with whom I have worked have expressed similar doubts when they are put in the position of leading groups. I have not heard similar doubts from male colleagues.

In her essay "On Psychological Oppression," Sandra Bartky has spoken about this internal factor:

> To be psychologically oppressed is to be weighed down in your mind; it is to have a harsh dominion exercised over your self-esteem. . . . Differently put, psychological oppression can be regarded as the "internalization of intimations of inferiority." (Bartky, 1990, 22; citation to Cook, 1970)

Women come to believe in their own inferiority through stereotypes of women as childlike, incompetent and less capable of autonomous decision-making. This is enhanced by their exclusion from high-level jobs and the reduction of women to sexual objects who are valued more for how they appear than for how they act (see Bartky, 1992). (Though I am speaking about sexism here, it seems obvious and important to mention that racism operates in similar ways for teachers of color. The "experts" that come in to tell us how to teach are usually white. Stereotypes work against educators of color in terms of external advancement as well as internal feelings of competence. Moreover, classism also clearly has external and internal effects. One of the teachers I interviewed mentioned keeping track of teachers' expectations for graduate education and finding that these were related to socioeconomic background more than ability.)

Gilligan and co-workers (1990), in a series of studies of early adolescent white girls, found that these young women give up their assertive power in order to be socially acceptable. They seemed to move from being sure of themselves to "I don't know." (In one of the most interesting studies I have come across recently, the reported gender gap on a test in science was overcome by removing the "I don't know" option from the exam [Linn et al., 1987].) A recent report of the American Association of University Women has cited data that showed that while 67% of the nine-year-old girls surveyed reported being "happy with the way I am," only 29% of the high school girls surveyed reported feeling this way. For boys, the results fell only from 60% to 46%. Interestingly, the results of such research seem to change for girls of color. In the high school data, only 22% of the white girls were "happy as I am," but 30% of the Hispanic girls and 58% of the black[1] girls agreed with this statement (American Association of University Women, 1992a,b; Orenstein, 1994).

I believe that an internalized sense of inferiority for many women is related to the problematical relationship between these women and power. (Again, this may differ for different cultural groups.) Many women seem to fear power because they believe that if they are powerful it will ruin their relationships (Miller, 1987). Kestenbaum (1986) has even written an article entitled "The Professional Woman's Dilemma: Love and/or Power," reflecting many women's beliefs that they have to choose. Many women have been taught that their role is the enhancement of the power of others. Moreover, the mythology and fairy tales on which many of us were raised imply that when women get power, it is an evil power of which we should be afraid. Look at the powerful women in Cinderella and Snow White. Need I say more!

In a study of women who have succeeded in the difficult world of politics, Cantor and Bernay (1992) have suggested that leadership. for these women, was the result of redefining stereotypes about women and power. These women achieved effective leadership roles through a combination of a "Competent Self" plus "Creative Aggression" plus "Womanpower." They define "Competent Self" as knowing who you are, taking risks, and believing that you can achieve. "Creative Aggression" is being willing to take the initiative and to speak out when necessary. "Womanpower" is a redefinition of power as the ability to make people's lives better. They suggest that a redefinition of power as the "ability to make a difference in society for the greater good" (p. 39) no longer conflicts with women's values or self-definition. Moreover, "womanpower also encompasses the notion of empowering others" (Cantor and Bernay, 1992, 57). The definiton of power they heard from the successful women leaders they interviewed sounds very much like the power-to/power-with discussed in chapter 1!

---

1. There is little scientific evidence to justify the belief in separate races. I have used the terms black and white to refer only to socially constructed categories that permeate the American consciousness.

Anything we can do to help ourselves develop a competent self, creative agression, and a sense of power-to/power-with may help us to feel more comfortable and be more effective as leaders. Cantor and Bernay (1992) suggest five empowering messages that we can start giving ourselves:

1. You are loved and special.
2. You can do anything you want to do.
3. You are entitled to dream of greatness.
4. You can use and enjoy your Creative Aggession.
5. You can be courageaous and take risks. (p. 256)

Though they designed these messages specifically for women and girls, they seem appropriate for men and boys as well. Obviously, they can be helpful for persons from all cultural groups.

I would also hasten to add that we cannot overcome internalized sexism (or racism or classism) by ourselves. We need the support of others to overcome both internalized messages of inferiority and the real institutional barriers.

As we begin to take risks and flex our aggressive muscles, we may find this is not as dangerous as we had expected. Indeed, I have found that when I speak out authentically I am actually acknowledged much more than when I was inhibited and only spoke when I felt safe. As we begin to be more comfortable with taking the initiative to speak our minds, our sense of who we are and what we stand for will probably develop. As we come to understand that power does not have to be used to dominate others, but, rather, can be an expression of our concern for others or for ourselves (power-to) and can be used in concert with other empowered persons in a relationship of mutual collaboration (power-with), then we can cease to fear that power will damage our connections with others.

For the central problem in the system of domination (power-over) is the separation of love and power (see Griffin, 1981). In domination, strong will (power) is separated from compassionate will (love) resulting in a kind of tyranny of one person's needs over those of others. (See chapter 1.) Persons with compassionate will but little strong will tend to give themselves up for others. People with strong will but little compassionate will tend to dominate others. But persons who are both strong (powerful) and compassionate (loving) assert themselves and respect the right of others to do the same. Thus, the belief that will transform the power-over system into an empowering one (power-to/power-with) is the realization that true love is powerful and true power is loving. I call this caring power.

Activity 2.7
DEVELOPING CARING POWER

POWER:
What does this word make you think of? Without analysis, jot down every word that comes to your mind when you hear the word "power."

These pretty much describe what society has taught us about power. Notice also that they tend to be words associated with masculinity.

Now, do the same thing for the word **CARING**. What words pop into your mind when someone says "caring"?

This is our internalized notion of caring. Notice how many of these words seem to be associated with femininity.

Now, here's the trick. Let's change our concept of these terms by putting them together. Find words on your first list that you can put together with words in your second list to make a new concept. Be creative!

EXAMPLE: strong sweetness

Let's go about it one more way. Think of a person you know who is powerful but also caring. How can you describe his or her quality of caring power?

Finally, all this is pretty abstract unless we look at ourselves. Most of the words you have listed on all these lists probably can be applied to you at one time or another. But are you more comfortable with CARING or POWER? Which would others say is more true of you? _____

Whichever you choose is probably a good resource for your own empowerment . . . but look at the term not chosen. How could more of this be incoporated into your life as an educator?

Summary

As mentioned in chapter 1, domination, or power-over, is the predominant definition of power in our society. This psychology of domination is so pervasive that we are not even aware of the myriad ways in which it operates in our daily lives. The first step to becoming more empowered and operating from a power-to/power-with standpoint as we transform our educational institutions is recognizing the specific forms that this psychology of domination takes in schools.

We must also recognize that these forms of control exist not only in our environment but within us as well. We have internalized domination of various kinds. Beliefs about things like hierarchy, sexism, and meritocracy are perpetuated by social consensus, and that social consensus can only be changed by challenging our own beliefs as well as the beliefs of others.

Scientific rationality is one of the most obvious dominators in education. The pretense that prepackaged programs are designed "scientifically" and, therefore, are free from bias, keeps us from questioning practices that are oppressive. This domination is often enforced through technical control, the expectation that we are to be implementors of programs rather than decision-makers in our own right. The expectation that we will follow prescribed programs is a part of a bureaucratic system that has set up a hierarchy of power-over positions and procedures designed to insure our cooperation. Our work is intensified by the demands of these programs in such a way that there is very little time to connect with our peers or to keep ourselves informed so that we can make decisions on our own.

All of this is sustained not by a group of power-hungry oppressors, but by people just like us (including us!) who have been taught that hierarchy is the best way to get things done. I think it is important to stress that I do not think that there is a conspiracy of bad guys out there trying to oppress us. Instead, as I see it, these practices are perpetuated by a belief system that goes back thousands of years that we can, as a society, choose to bring to an end.

More specifically, most of the power-over practices in our schools are perpetuated by our acceptance of legitimization (usually through scientific rationality), dissimulation (the real curriculum is unstated), fragmentation (isolation), and reification (it has always been this way). Change will require that we question scientific rationality, uncover the hidden curriculum of domination, connect students, teachers, parents, administrators and lawmakers, and realize that current practice is historically determined and can be changed. When we end internalized oppression and self-blaming and unite with others to alter power-over practices, we will experience empowerment in terms of power-to/ power-with.

As women, we will have to battle stereotypes about femininity and power, but the experience of women in power tells us that our commitment to the well-being of others can sustain us. As men, we will have to battle stereotypes about caring men, but I suspect that this battle is not new to the men who are reading this book.

How Students
Experience Domination

In chapter 1, I discussed the relationship between our own empowerment and the empowerment of others. We cannot be truly empowered ourselves if we are caught in a tyrant/rebel duality or a power-over mindset. Indeed, many of the teachers with whom I have discussed empowerment have told me that they have felt the most empowered when they were empowering their students. In activity 1.2, you probably noticed something like this about your own experience. When you are trying to control your students or others in alienating ways, you feel disempowered. When you are sharing power and decision-making with your students and with other teachers, you feel empowered.

Thus, it is critical now to turn our attention to the workings of power-over in the way teaching is conducted in our schools. Whereas in chapter 2, I focussed on what structural and ideological factors disempower us as educators, I would like to focus here on what disempowers our students. It is often in the carrying out of these power-over procedures that our own disempowerment is embodied, and we feel unexplainably alienated from our work.

Reproducing Social Inequality

Much has been written aboaut how schools actually reproduce the class structure that they are supposed to be overcoming (see Bowles and Gintis, 1976; and others). Such reproduction of the existing social order in which

49

some racial, class, gender or ethnic groups have power over others is, put simply, the reproduction of domination. Many of our current discriminatory schooling practices were actually designed to prepare kids for different kinds of futures. When they were originated, the purpose of schooling was thought to be the Americanization of large numbers of immigrants and poor who were actually believed to be inferior in an evolutionary sense (see Oakes, 1985). (This "Social Darwinism" is a great example of scientific rationality covering up the biases of its proponents.)

The most obvious of these practices are ability grouping and tracking by ability. We know that poor kids and kids from ethnic minorities are more likely to be in the lower tracks than are white middle-class kids, due to various biases in the sorting procedures (see especially Oakes, 1985; and others). Unfortunately, the kids in the lowest tracks seem to get the worst education.

In a study of the effects of tracking in junior and senior high schools across the country, Jeannie Oakes (1985) found that there is a clear difference between upper and lower tracks in terms of the content of the instruction, the quality of the instruction, and the quality of the classroom climate. Upper-track students got more culturally valued content (e.g., Shakespeare, *New York Times* editorials) and were encouraged to think critically, whereas students in the lower tracks were exposed to content less culturally valued (e.g., adolescent novels, motorcycle magazines) and were encouraged to learn by rote. Upper-track students had more effective learning time in class, more homework time, and a better understanding of what they were to do and why when compared to lower-track students. Finally, the upper-track classrooms were characterized by warmth, concern and affiliation, whereas the lower-track classrooms were characterized by dominance, coercion and alienation, qualities that we know diminish rather than enhance the learning environment. Thus, the kids who seem to need the best opportunities for learning are given the worst, and the students are effectively sorted for an unequal class structure. Even more insidious, perhaps, is that fact that the failure of the students in the lower tracks is blamed on the students. (This is a good example of dissimulation in which the problem with a structure is obscured by blaming the victim.)

Similar results have been found for ability grouping in the elementary school. The most common ability-groups are for reading, and research again indicates that those who need it the most get the worst instruction. Poor readers are interrupted two to five times more, and often in the middle of sentences, whereas good readers are usually only corrected at the end of the sentence (Allington, 1980; Hoffman et al., 1984). Poor readers are given less time to correct themselves (Pflaum et al., 1980), read fewer words each day (Allington, 1977), do more oral reading (as opposed to silent reading practiced by good readers) (Allington, 1983), and are given a decoding rather than a meaningful focus (Allington, 1978). Taking children out of the classroom for remedial instruction does not ameliorate these problems (Allington, 1994; McGill-Franzen and Allington, 1991). Again, children of color and working class children are most likely to be in these "poor reader" groups, often simply because they do not exhibit middle-class social conditioning or because they are not competitive test-takers.

How are such practices legitimated? Jeannie Oakes has suggested that there are at least four assumptions that support our belief in ability grouping; that students learn better when grouped homogeneously, that students have a better self-concept when grouped with those of similar ability, that the placement process is "fair," and that homogeneous groups are easier to teach.

In fact, none of these assumptions is supported by the data. We have research to show that the lower-ability students learn less in ability groups and little to show that the upper-ability students learn better. Oakes' data indicate that self-esteem suffers in ability-grouping situations and that a disproportionate number of minority students end up in the lower groups due to the cultural bias of tests that are used and the cultural biases of the other subjective measures that supposedly temper them. Finally, one could make a case that cooperative learning and other nonlecture teaching techniques work equally well with heterogeneous groups. The only really effective (though hidden) argument for our current grouping practices is that they effectively sort the kids into the "have's" and the "have-not's" at an early age, though this effect is dissimulated by the unquestioned assumptions mentioned above. (I think this is an important point: Most—if not all—of the people advocating tracking procedures believe that they are in the best interests of the children.)

Of course, in some cases, the discriminatory nature of tracking is not adequately dissimulated. While writing this chapter, I came across an article in the *New York Times* (2 November 1993) entitled "School System Found to be Biased Against Bright Minority Students." According to the article, a federal magistrate found that Rockford, Illinois Public Schools had discriminated against minority students in a policy that "barred minority students from enrollling in accelerated classes, even though some of them had received higher test scores than white students who were permitted to enter the classes" (p. A24). The judge said that the system had "committed such open acts of discrimination as to be cruel and committed others with such subtlety as to raise discrimination to an art form." (Most districts dissimulate better by using test scores to sort students.)

In my own life, I see the results of such discrimination in the inability of colleges to fill their minority quotas with students who have been given the preparation they need to succeed. Why are college and universities not more vocally questioning the differential education given to so many minority students?

Moreover, in my opinion, a much more subtle part of this whole discriminatory sorting procedure is our current system of grading and evaluation. Clearly, here is an example in which, if we measure everyone against the same middle-class white cultural biases, some students are going to be penalized for their background. In addition, students whose abilities are not academic will be made to feel inferior.

Indeed, in the kind of competitive system we currently use, all but the top student is made to feel inferior. Competitive grades feed into the growing self-blame and surplus powerlessness of our students (see chapter 2). They discourage intrinsic motivation by encouraging the students to compare their performance with others (see Spaulding, 1992a), and they lower self-esteem (see Kohn, 1986). Even though I was always an A student, I remember feeling tremendous stress in school in terms of getting good grades. I hardly remember ever enjoying learning, and I never thought I was all that capable because there was always someone just a little higher on the grading scale.

Activity 3.1
GRADING RECONSIDERED

Close your eyes and picture how you feel when you are giving the students grades for the marking period. Bring yourself entirely into that space. What are you thinking? How is your body feeling? Take a moment to jot down the feelings that come to mind. . . . What are the pros and cons of the way you grade students?

PROS	CONS

How could you revise your grading procedure so that it is more empowering both for you and your students? _____

Note: Parents and administrators may wish to pretend that they are teachers to do this activity.

Looking at how these sorting and evaluation procedures really operate in schools has made me realize that equal opportunity is only a myth. A recent study of dropouts in an urban public school has supported this conclusion. Michelle Fine (1991) spent a year studying one urban public high school which had dropout rates between 40 and 60 percent. She found that this school was one of the worst-funded and most overcrowded. This was, in part, due to the fact that in this system students received fewer credits for remedial classes, and, therefore, schools with large numbers of remedial classes received less money per pupil, monies being based on numbers of credits being taken. Students who wanted to drop out were allowed to do so with relatively little real imformation about their choices, which consisted mostly of chronic unemployment, the military, and trade schools with even worse retention records than the high school. (Was this lack of effective counseling due to the fact that retention of these students with high absenteeism and high numbers of remedial classes was not seen as economically advantageous?) The teachers in this school seemed to feel particularly disempowered and unsupported by the administration.

Perhaps most importantly, Fine found that the students' voices were silenced by the curriculum and by the "systemic commitment to not name those aspects of social life or of schooling that activate social anxieties" (p. 33). For students to speak of the real problems in their lives, they had to go to the counselor's office. The students generally believed that to be a good student, you had to be silent, very much like the lower-track students in Oakes' (1985) study. Material was often taught in a right/wrong fashion that left little room for the students' opinions, again very much like the rote learning encouraged for the lower tracks found by Oakes.

Indeed, it seems that we may have different expectations of students from different social classes and that these are played out in the ways that teaching/learning is conducted in schools. These differences very much echo the track differences discovered by Oakes. Anyon (1981) observed and interviewed children in second- and fifth-grade classrooms in communities characterized by different social classes. She found that in the working-class school, knowledge was defined in terms of knowing basic facts and following rote procedures. In the middle-class school, content was to be learned, some students believed that knowledge could be constructed, and there was some discussion of general concepts. In the affluent professional-class school, the emphasis was on creative and critical thinking, and the majority of students said that they could make knowledge. Finally, in the "executive elite" school, the emphasis was on reasoning and problem solving as well as rigorous academics. I do not believe that these teachers felt that they were being classist in their teaching; they were simply acting out the dominant assumptions operating in their schools.

This sort of contrast was driven home for me one semester when I was doing inservice presentations on teaching reading comprehension to both a group of inner city teachers in Chicago and another group of teachers at an elite private school. My work at that time centered on getting students to organize, synthesize, and think critically about information. The teachers in the inner city, whose students were mostly working class, tried many of the techniques I suggested and were amazed at what their students could do. They said that they had not expected this level of thinking from their students before. The teachers in the elite private school, whose students were mostly from the affluent professional class, yawned a lot and asked what else was new. They were already doing lots of creative and critical activities, and their students were already excellent organizers and synthesizers. They had always expected these things from their students. (They wanted help working with the students with learning disabilities. This never came up in the inner city population, as few of their students had been identified in this way.)

For the knowledge that some kids bring to school from home is valued more highly than the knowledge brought by others. Kids that come from homes that value what the school values (punctuality, conformity, following directions, neatness) are likely to be thought of as having more potential. Bourdieu (1977) has called this "cultural capital," defined as sets of linguistic and cultural competencies which are inherited by each member of a cultural class or group. Some cultural capital is more valued than other cultural capital, and it puts its possessors in a privileged position as soon as they walk into the school building.

A good example of this is can be found in language practices. James Gee (1990) defines the "discourses" of communities as integral combinations of "saying the right sorts of things in the right way, while engaging in the right sorts of actions and interactions, and appearing to think and feel the right way and have the right sort of values" (p. xv). Picture the way people speak and act in a biker bar and compare it to the "discourse" you would imagine in a yuppie bar and you begin to have the point.

Gee gives an example of a young black girl in first grade "sharing" time who tells a wonderful story about her family baking a series of cakes and buying more cakes and eating them until they get sick. The class thoroughly enjoyed the story which reflected the child's discourse community and the value it puts on entertainment and performance. The teacher, however, did not respond positively because the story was not "true" and did not "inform." She judged the black child to be of lesser ability than the white child who gave only facts. She failed to reinforce the values and talents that this child brought from her particular home culture, and we can assume that by the time someone is ready to appreciate them, this little girl will have shut them down. (See also Houston, 1973.)

Bernstein (1971) has looked at what he calls the language "codes" of different social classes. The working-class students he studied used what he called a "restricted" code in which the context carries the meaning and there is an emphasis on connection to the listener and the present. "[T]he restricted code emerges where the culture or subculture raises the 'we' above the 'I'" (p. 146). In the "elaborated" code used by middle-class speakers, the meanings are made more explicit, possibly based on "an expectation of separateness and difference from others" (p. 133) in which shared meanings cannot be assumed. The point may be that as we ask children to shift to an elaborated code in school, we are actually asking them to shift social identities away from the communal one they share at home.

Thus it seems clear that our schools, as presently organized, do not adequately provide equal opportunity for all students. Students come to school with cultural capital including discourse styles that are differentially valued by the school. Often, on the basis of many of these differences, the children are grouped into tracks that result in unequal education, with those that seem to need it the most receiving the worst instruction.

Activity 3.2
WORKING WITHIN ABILITY GROUPING SYSTEMS

(Note: This is only useful to those working within these programs!)

Let's try a drawing activity. Don't worry about the drawing or its quality . . . just scribble to get your ideas down. (If you have trouble drawing to explore ideas, feel free to write verbal descriptions.) First, draw a picture of yourself as you are when you are teaching the "top" group or the "upper track." Include any details or symbols that seem relevant.

Now, draw a picture of yourself teaching the "bottom" group or the "bottom" track. Include any details or symbols that seem relevant.

What could you do to feel like you do in the first picture while you are teaching the lower groups?

Finally, as though racial, ethnic and class biases are not enough, we are only just learning how school practices have also legitimated the unequal education of girls. Research suggests that girls receive considerably less attention and reinforcement from their teachers than boys, starting at a very early age. Girls' successes are often attributed to outside forces rather than ability. The curriculum materials still do little to represent the real contributions of women and girls to our culture. The predominant teaching style tends to encourage competition even though there is research to indicate that girls may learn better in cooperative atmospheres (Belenky et al., 1985). For a summary of these and other issues related to gender, see the recent report *How Schools Shortchange Girls*, published by the American Association of University Women. (See also Kleinfeld and Yerian, 1995.)

I find that when I discuss gender issues in my education classes at the university, most pre-service and in-service teachers see gender problems as less insidious than those associated with race and class. The fact is that we can have no hierarchy of oppressions. Orenstein (1994) has provided us with graphic evidence of the seriousness of gender issues in schools in her ethnographic study of junior high school girls in California. After noting the denigration of the girls' classroom competence and the pervasive nature of sexual harassment as well as the invisibility of their mothers' achievements at home, she finds problems of bulimia, anorexia and suicidal depression even among the very small group of girls she selected. If we do not value the intellectual contributions of girls, if we do not attribute their success to ability, if we do not allow them to work cooperatively, and if we do not absolutely refuse to tolerate sexual harrassment, then we are leaving these girls with a legacy of low self-esteem that goes well beyond a few trivial moments of embarrassment or discomfort (as these things as often characterized to me). (See also Pipher, 1994.)

Activity 3.3
MONITORING CLASSROOM GENDER BIAS

Most teachers are not aware of the unconscious gender bias that operates in their classes. Thus, if you wish to check this for yourself, you will need to find a colleague you trust to observe you. Have the colleague tally the following things:

	GIRLS	BOYS
No. of times called on		
No. of times answers are called out and accepted by teacher		
No. of times interrupted		
No. of times speak for more than one sentence		
No. of times praised		
No. of times have eye contact with teacher		
No. of times supported by fellow students		

Resistance to Domination and Discrimination

It is, however, important that we do not portray schools as places where all this discrimination goes on uncontested and unnamed. Students and teachers often resist the pressure to value some students more than others.

"Resistance" theories, as they are called, look at schools in ways that show how individuals do not always carry out or participate in programs or policies that they see as unfair. This can result in an only incomplete reproduction of unjust social conditions. (See Giroux, 1983.)

One strength of resistance theory, in my opinion, is that it helps us to understand the unruly behaviors of kids in new ways:

> Resistance in this case redefines the causes and meaning of oppositional behavior by arguing that it has little to do with the logic of deviance, individual pathology, learned helplessness (and, of course, genetic explanations), and a great deal to do, though not exhaustively, with the logic of moral and political indignation. (Giroux, 1983, 107)

Kids may have some real moral and political reasons to resist the school culture. Girls may resist becoming docile; anyone might resist becoming alienated from his/her personal needs and feelings or from his/her home culture. (See also Kohl, 1994.)

Student resistance works itself out differently for different race, class and gender groups, but, in most cases without much ultimate success. In the struggle to survive, most groups are forced to trade one source of oppression for another. For instance, in his now classic study of a group of working-class boys in Great Britain, Willis (1977) found that in their rebellion against the insults of an alien school culture, the "lads" rejected mental labor as destructive and glorified manual labor as productive. Thus, in attempting to achieve self-respect, they actually participated in reproducing the class structure and destined themselves to remain in the working class. Moreover, they used racist and sexist attitudes to preserve a sense of superiority, thus perpetuating the psychology of domination. (See also Brake, 1980.)

Thomas (1980) studied two groups of antiacademic girls, one in a middle-class and one in a working-class school. She found that both groups of girls tended to express their resistance to schooling in the form of asserting their own sexuality in ways that the school culture deemed inappropriate. The working-class girls used their sexuality aggressively and as a form of power, especially in situations in which it was likely to offend. The middle-class girls were similar but much more steeped in the ideology of romance than were the working-class girls, and both groups were careful about their actual sexual relationships. Again, we see these girls attempting to resist school culture by glorifying an image that may ultimately destine them to subordination; in this case, they assert their own objectified role as sexual objects against the oppression of school culture, thus possibly limiting themselves to unpaid labor in the home.

Finally, in a study of black girls, Fuller (1983) found yet a different kind of resistance. Faced with the triple oppression of race, class and gender, these girls seemed to decide that succeeding within the school system provided them with the greatest chance to challenge stereotypes and gain control over their lives. There is some question abut whether this can be called resistance, however. Weiler (1988) suggests that this may help them to resist oppression in their own lives but should be seen more as "individual accommodation" rather than "collective resistance." It is interesting, however, to see that they chose to accept the classist nature of society and challenge its racist and sexist assumptions.

The point of all this, to me, is the gaining of a new perspective on some of the seemingly antisocial behaviors exhibited by our students. Though not all defiance is resistance to real oppression, a large part of it can be seen this way, and then it can take on a whole new meaning for us. For me, one of the most moving expressions of the source of student resistance has come from Peter McLaren (1989):

> I have argued that the major drama of resistance in schools is an effort on the part of students to bring their street-corner culture into the classroom. Students reject the culture of classroom learning because, for the most part, it is delibidinalized (eros-denying) and is infused with a cultural capital to which subordinate groups have little legitimate access. . . . To resist means to fight against the monitoring of passion and desire . . . students resist turning themselves into worker commodities in which their potential is evaluated only as future members of the labor force. . . . Students resist the "dead time" of school, where interpersonal relationships are reduced to the imperatives of market ideology. Resistance, in other words, is a rejection of their reformulation as docile objects where spontaneity is replaced by efficiency and productivity, in compliance with the needs of the corporate marketplace. Accordingly, students' very bodies become sites of struggle, and resistance a way of gaining power, celebrating pleasure, and fighting oppression in the lived historicity of the moment. (p. 188)

Unfortunately, such resistance leads to a reproduction of the class and gender structure in the students' lives unless the students' impulse to self-assertion is harnessed by an educational system that empowers them to be authentic and to develop strategies necessary for economic success at the same time. Also, their resistance to loss of spontaneity and meaningful human relationship is a resistance not related to class, race or gender but to our whole definition of schooling. (See chapter 4.)

My students at the university have told me that they sometimes feel more disempowered by their students than by bureaucratic and technical control. I believe that this sense of disempowerment is a result of participating in a power-over relationship in which one party is refusing to cooperate. (Of course, in schools as presently structured, we can only partially mediate the effects of this power-over relationship.) It also results from not understanding the source of the students' refusal to cooperate. Usually this refusal is not focussed on us personally, but is a result of years of alienating school experiences. Working with resistant students requires courage, patience and honest communication over a long period of time.

Activity 3.4
UNDERSTANDING STUDENT RESISTANCE

Close you eyes and picture a student (or a class) who (that) has really driven you crazy with his or her (or their) resistance. Picture the clothes the student(s) is (are) wearing, the makeup, the jewelry, the hairstyle(s). Watch his or her (or their) behavior for a while. Draw a quick sketch of these students.

What are they trying to express with their resistant behavior? _____

_____

_____

Now, imagine yourself having a conversation with these students about their resistant behavior. Do they know why they act this way? As you help them to understand this, encourage them to think about how they could resist in a manner that truly helps them to overcome some of the alienation they feel. Take a few minutes to carry on this conversation in your head and then jot down what you have learned. (If they refuse to communicate, what else can you do to facilitate this?)

How can this level of communication be incorporated into your classroom or school?

Finally, we can also take a lot of inspiration from the studies which have documented the successful resistance by teachers. Both Weiler (1988) and Fine (1991) have provided numerous examples of individual teachers who create liberatory moments in their individual classrooms. Kreisberg (1992) has provided a rich study of teachers involved in the steering committee of the Boston Area Educators for Social Responsibility. These teachers each found unique ways to empower their students within traditional schools. Similarly, my study, in chapter 9 of this book, gives inspiring examples of teachers who are finding ways to empower their students in spite of traditional power-over practices in their districts.

Lather (1984) has suggested that we distinguish between resistance and counterhegemonic action. She characterizes resistance as usually informal, individual and unsystematic whereas "counterhegemonic" action is grounded in a critical understanding, organized and often collective. Whereas resistance can be seen in small individual decisions, counterhegemonic action is geared toward changing whole institutions or creating permanent liberatory spaces within institutions. I suspect that we can each find instances of each of these in our work, as well as instances that seem to combine them. The point is not to devalue our acts of individual assertion but rather to see that our resistance is likely to be more effective if it is grounded in an understanding of the system of domination, planned, and, ideally, supported by a like-minded group of change-oriented individuals.

An example of work that began as individual resistance and then became truly counterhegemonic can be found in the detracking program in Montclair, New Jersey (Karp, 1993). Because she believed that tracking perpetuated inequalities and because she believed in the social importance of a multicultural curriculum, Dr. Bernadette Anand, the chair of the English Department there, developed, with the Social Studies Department, an untracked World Cultures and Literature course that was very successful. However, when she proposed that this course replace the current three-level tracked freshman English program for all students, she heard objections from administrators and parents alike. (Her department voted unanimously in favor of the program.) The major concern seemed to be that the "upper" track could not earn "honors" points in an untracked class. But supporters of the plan reached out to the community in meetings and the local media and, in the end, the board voted 4-3 in favor of the proposal (Karp, 1993).

Successful detracking experiments are going on around the country. (For example, see Christensen, 1992.) Wheelock (1994) has written an entire manual entitled "Alternatives to Tracking and Ability Grouping" which has been published by the American Association of School Administrators. This manual contains many of the empowering teaching strategies that I will be dicussing in chapters 4 and 5.

Indeed, much of the rest of this book is about both personally resisting the pressures to dominate and discriminate against students, and, perhaps more importantly, working with others to establish a system that does not perpetuate the power of one group over another. Before I turn to these issues, however, I would like to look more closely at the premises that support and define the power-over educational system we have now.

The Ideology of Inequality

As I said earlier, I do not believe for one second that educators today are sitting around planning unequal education for different students. As a group, we are one of the most caring and fair-minded I know. Instead, it is our belief in the ideology of meritocracy that legitimates the system that perpetuates inequality. Basically, this is the belief that we get what we deserve: Students who work hard and follow the rules will succeed. If you are in the bottom track, it is because you did not try hard enough or you did not have enough ability, and so on.

As we have seen, the idea that our schools are true meritocracies is a myth. Students come to school with different cultural capital that is differentially valued by the school. They are treated with differing expectations depending on their gender, ethnic background and class. The students with the greatest needs are often given the worst education.

But it is important that we challenge this whole idea of meritocracy at a deeper level. Even if it could be implemented effectively, is it really what we want? Do we really want people sorted into piles that determine their future access to resources according to some socially prescribed definition of merit or ability?

Actually, the ideology of meritocracy is based on two even more powerful and devastating myths that support it and all forms of power-over. These are the myths of scarcity and of the variability of human worth. Challenges to the inequalities we see in the ways that students are treated must begin by challenging these basic myths in all of their subtle manifestations.

The myth of scarcity says that we have limited resources and there is not enough to go around. Thus, we must fight over what is available (Katz, 1983/1984). This mentality pervades our society whether we are talking about food and housing, love, or self-esteem. Yet, in the United States, we clearly have the resources to feed, house and clothe everyone. Some believe that with current technology we have enough food to feed the world and enough resources to house and clothe everyone on the planet, if we use our resources wisely and avoid overconsumption. (Yes, we must only use that technology that does not destroy the planet.) When we love, more love is created, so certainly there is enough of this to go around. And there is just no logical reason to suggest that everyone can't feel good about him or herself at the same time. Everyone can be creative. Everyone can learn. How can these things be scarce?

The myth of the variability of human worth is even more pervasive and hidden. Though we talk about "all persons being equal" in our democratic documents, we have not yet internalized this concept as a society. Starhawk talks about the stories about either "Making It" or "The Fall" as stories that perpetuate this notion:

> This is a story about success and failure. The older religious version has given way to the secular American version. At first Making It and The Fall seem like two very different stories. In the first—a person of lowly birth is discovered (for some virtue or talent) and welcomed into the circles of the elect. In the second, a person who is a member of the elect, an inhabitant of the garden, owing to some weakness, some inherent evil or personal flaw, falls, and is cast down into the ranks of the ordinary.
>
> But looking closer, we see the two are the same story in reverse. A person who lacks value gains it; a person who has value loses it. Both reinforce a consciousness and a power structure in which some people have value and others don't. (pp. 22–23)

Both of these stories perpetuate individual self-blaming. If I have not made it, it must be my fault. (And, indeed, this was what the students in the lower tracks studied by Oakes seemed to believe.) But more importantly, they perpetuate the notion that some people are worth more than others.

Most of us would say that we do not believe this. Yet, if we do not believe this, then why do so many people fight to maintain a sense of self-esteem (Steinem, 1992; and others)? I know that I deal with self-esteem issues when I am not successful personally or professionally. Yet I ask myself how this could be so. Don't I believe in the absolute worth of every individual regardless of performance or achievement?

As long as we believe in the myths of scarcity and the variability of human worth, then meritocracy will make sense to us. If there are limited resources, then how else can we mete them out but through merit . . . especially if some persons are more worthy than others and merit can be gained or lost. As soon as we see those myths for what they are, we see that meritocracy is just an excuse for treating persons unequally, as less than fully human, and for giving some people power over others.

A Paradigmatic Shift

What we are really looking for is a paradigmatic shift in the educational enterprise, from one based on meritocracy and variable human worth to one based on valuing every person equally and absolutely, from one based on discrimination to one based on acceptance, from one based on power-over and separation to one based on power-to and connection (power-with).

Many recent writers have written about how these traditional and emerging paradigms seem to be competing in our current world. For instance, Steinem (1992) defines this paradigm shift as being from one centered on duality, linearity and hierarchy and to one centered on unity, cyclical time and cooperation. Montouri and Conti (1993) simlarly speak of a paradigm shift from one of dualism and separation to one based on systems theory and an awareness of connection. Kreisberg (1992) speaks of ending the old paradigm of linear causality and replacing it with a holistic one based on reciprocal influence and "interdependent relationships among parts of the whole" (p. 79). Similar ideas can be found in Oliver and Gershman (1989) who describe the "modernist" paradigm as one based on fragmentation, specialization and hierarchy. They suggest replacing it with a "process" paradigm which "implies a morality of intimacy, intensity, community, balance, and connection rather than a morality of principles, dialectics, personalities, and objects" (p. 152).

In one of the most comprehensive treatments of the results of the power-over paradigm I have read, psychologist Anne Schaef (1981) has identified two belief systems that seemed to be operating in the psychology of the clients with whom she has worked. These seem to provide a good overview of the assumptions that maintain the power-over system that kids experience in schools today.

First, Schaef defines the current system as one in which "the power and influence are held by White males." She says that she is not speaking of specific men, but, rather, of a belief system that has dominated our thinking for hundreds if not thousands of years (probably those years corresponding to patriarchy, see Eisler, 1987; and others). This patriarchal system is hierarchical, individualistic and based on domination (power-over). She also describes another system of beliefs that she has observed in many of her female clients. This system seems to be based more on a cooperative, holistic paradigm. Finally, she points out that many marginalized cultures share beliefs with this alternative system.

Thus, in my discussion, I would like to compare Schaef's patriarchal system based on power-over with her emerging system based on cooperation (which I will call "the other system" to stress that these beliefs are often found among those thought to be other by the dominant culture). I would like to contrast these psychological systems in terms of how differing beliefs relating to time, process and product, human relationships and communication, nature, knowing, morality, love, caring, leadership, and difference have resulted in the educational system we have today. My purpose in contrasting these systems is not to suggest that we simply replace the patriarchal system with the other one, but, rather, to suggest that our current educational system is dominated primarily by the patriarchal system and that it behooves us to look at the other alternatives. We may find that a synthesis of the two systems that retains some of what each has to offer is our best choice.

Time

In the patriarchal power-over system, time is thought to be linear and measureable; it corresponds to the time on the clock. It is divided into discrete units, and our activities are structured around the measured units. In the other system, there is a respect for what we might call "process time." According to Schaef, "time is perceived as a process, a series of passages, or a series of interlocking cycles which may or may not have anything to do with the numbers on the clock" (p. 100). Cultures functioning on process time are often seen as irresponsible because their members do not always show up "on time" according to the clock. This is because these people are respecting the time it takes to complete each process. The "on time" participants are not seeing that once these process-oriented people are present, they are ready to stay until the process is over, unlike the linear-time participant who has scheduled the meeting for 2–3 p.m., process completed or not. "A central assumption in process is that time is intrinsic to the occasion" (Oliver and Gershman, 1989, 195). (See also Hunt and Hait, 1990, if you would like to change your own orientation toward time.)

We can see conflicts between notions of absolute and process time everyday in our teaching decisions. In the elementary school, the time for certain subjects is constrained by the scheduling of recess, specials, pull-outs, lunch and the end of the day. Moreover, teachers often feel even further constrained by the demands of the curriculum they must deliver in reading, math, social studies, science, health, drug education, and so on. Similarly, secondary and college teachers have limited periods, usually 45 minutes to an hour in which to "schedule" learning; and they often also feel constrained by an overburdened curriculum.

The real conflict is felt in those moments in which everything seems to "click" . . . something magical happens in the classroom and everyone is involved. Perhaps it is a discussion, a project, a sharing of feelings . . . but it is taking too long and the teacher feels that sinking feeling of falling behind in the curriculum or knowing that the bell is about to ring. What is he or she to do? No doubt, the students also experience such interruptions of real process as disempowering. Being constantly shifted from one activity to the next without any consideration of where I was in the process would drive me to distraction.

The conflict between authentic engagement and the fragmentary accomplishment of seemingly endless lists of objectives is expressed very well by Oliver and Gershman in their exploration of process teaching:

> When this genuine thirst for learning springs forth, the student is often admonished for not keeping up with the full range of activities or "subjects" required in a conventional educational setting. Again the culture of fragmentation dominates. There seems to be something dangerous about becoming fully engrossed. We wonder at the magic of requiring four or five subjects five times a week for thirty-six weeks. This kind of schedule seems least likely to move students from the fragmented moments of clock time to the deep involvement of grounded occasion. (Oliver and Gershman, 1989, 189)

Mikhail Csikszentmihalyi, a psychologist at the University of Chicago, has found that creativity, peak performance, talent development, productivity, self-esteem and stress reduction are all promoted when people engage in "flow" activities. These are activities which are challenging but within reach and *in which one can become totally immersed.* The problem with school scheduling is that it interrupts such flow experiences (Csikszentmihalyi, 1990, 1991).

Similarly, Allington (1994) has said that "small blocks of time foster small tasks; larger blocks foster larger tasks" (p. 208). In order to get away from our reliance on meaningless, unrelated tasks, we need to structure larger blocks of time:

The point is that the best way to read a book is not at the rate of 10- to 15-minute blocks per day. [Try it yourself! It is really frustrating!] The best way to write an essay, a biaography, a review, or a summary is not in 10- to 15-minute blocks of time. . . . Time is one of those things that really does matter. (p. 208)

With large blocks of time, kids can go outside and observe nature, make a sketch, come back in and read about their plant or animal, and finish by writing a poem about it. With large blocks of time, kids can write stories, share those stories with each other, and work cooperatively to revise and improve their writing. With large blocks of time, kids can get involved in processes worth doing.

Several years ago, I worked with inner-city teachers as they were implementing a reading program that was designed to teach reading as a holistic thinking process rather than as a set of isolable subskills. I monitored what they reported as presenting problems to them as they were changing their curriculum. These teachers had huge classes (some as large as 50), many different languages being spoken (one class had 40!), and few available materials. Though all these things were mentioned as problems at the beginning of implementation, by the end of the year the only problem mentioned was "time." By this they meant classroom time to involve the students in their reading in the context of a situation in which they felt they had numerous other isolated objectives to achieve.

So how do we reconcile the pressures of absolute, linear time with the time it takes to allow students to get involved in their own learning process? How do we accomplish hundreds of mandated objectives and still respect those wonderful moments that want to move on their own schedule as students and teachers are carried forward by a process in which they are both involved? I believe that the first step is to recognize the tension. Currently, most schoools are organized almost exclusively around clock time. We need to insist on the space to respect process time when we, as teachers, believe that quality learning is taking place. We need to carve out spaces for true involvement with learning and look for linear schedules that maximize this by assuring that large blocks of time can be found.

As we focus more on process and less on atomistic objectives, and as we break down the fragmentation of the curriculum so that math and reading and science and social studies can be integrated and learned together, we will have more space for process time. For the past three years, I have been working with a school district that has been trying to increase the amount of writing instruction in its elementary schools. The biggest problem the teachers were having was finding the time. Many of them were trying to schedule in yet another half-hour or one hour period for writing and were then running out of time for other subjects. What many have realized is that writing can be a part of all those other subjects. It need not be a separate subject every day. By integrating writing with the other subjects, the teachers have found that learning in those areas increased as did the students' ability to use writing for meaningful purposes.

Many schools are experimenting with new structural arrangements of time that allow for more engrossment with learning. Some junior and senior high schools have "double periods" several times a week for different subjects. Sometimes double-length periods are created by the team teaching of an interdisciplinary course. Many elementary schools are moving pull-outs, announcements and other interruptions into a limited part of the day. These are laudable attempts to allow kids some process time.

Process/Product

So our exploration of the definitions of time in the patriarchal and other systems leads us to issues of process and product. Our current patriarchal metaphor for the educational enterprise is the machine (see Oliver and Gershman, 1989). We view the school as a huge machine in which "educated" students are turned out as our products. We measure our success by measuring discrete learnings through testing and other quantifiable measures of product. We order our curricula through measureable objectives or products expected. Our focus is on the ends rather than the means, and kids are objectified and expected to all be the same. They experience this process as one in which they are to be created and changed by someone else's actions.

An alternative is to focus on the process of education and the process being learned, to recognize that the means often become the ends, that children learn what they do. Teacher, student, curriculum and materials all come together into unique meaning-making community experiences that can only partially be prespecified. The students are actively making the meanings they take from these experiences, and these meanings are shaped by the cultural capital as well as the intention they bring to the experience. Learning involves activity and creativity on the part of the learner, and what is learned is always partially unique to the learner and the situation. Possible metaphors for this process suggested by Oliver and Gershman are the organism (the classroom as organism in which the parts are each part of an interrelated whole that is propelled to grow naturally and through its own unfoldment) and dance (the events are unique, aesthetic, potentially life-changing interactions that may or may not produce measureable products left after they are over). When learning is viewed in this way, the teacher is removed from a constant power-over position and the students are returned to their "power to" grow in mutually satisfying ways. (I will explore these metaphors in more depth in chapter 4.)

In a wonderful instance of reality check, Kreisberg (1992) shows how the teachers in the steering committee of the Boston Area Educators for Social Responsibility that he was studying did resort to power-over strategies when it was necessary to advance the power-to/power-with potential of the situation. He concludes that it may be that teachers in our society must sometimes resort to power-over strategies to accomplish their empowering goals. Similarly, I suspect, "products" will not and, perhaps, should not lose their potency as one measure of the educational enterprise. So again, what we are looking for here, perhaps, is the space to value the process as much as the product; to look at how involved students are in their own learning; to enable them to learn that reading and writing and thinking and communicating and knowing are ways to achieve personal and community empowerment, not just ways to satisfy external demands that we make of ourselves a product to be measured. We can respect both the means and the ends of our educational endeavors.

Knowing

For the patriarchal and the cooperative systems also view knowing very differently. In the patriarchal system, feelings and intuition are thought to be inferior modes of knowing when compared to logical, rational thought. In our society, men are encouraged to attempt to develop "pure" rationality, while women are encouraged to be the keepers of the "inferior" intuitive and emotional side. (Pure rationality is impossible anyway. See chapter 2.) Actually, many other cultures acknowledge the intuition and the emotions as powerful channels for both learning and assessing new information, and some have suggested that it is our overemphasis on ungrounded, abstract logical thought that has resulted in our current cultural malaise. (See Gallegos, 1990; Oliver and Gershman, 1989; and others.)

In a powerful study of the "ways of knowing" used by academic and working-class women, Belenky, Clinchy, Goldberger, and Tarule (1986) found that women may go through very different stages in their epistemological development when compared to men. Whereas men have been found to develop cognitively from (1) dualism (either/or, black/white thinking) to (2) an awareness of a multiplicity of points of view to (3) a logical, analytic approach to (4) relativism (Perry, 1970), Belenky and co-workers found that the women they studied seemed to go through a subjective stage in which everything was filtered through a personal subjectivity. Though some of the women they studied then proceeded to a objective, rational stage, the most advanced stage in their taxonomy was a "constructed knowing" stage in which subjective and objective procedures are integrated in the creation of knowledge.

Since girls and women often do value the subjective, intuitive and firsthand mode of learning, it is little wonder that they become increasingly alienated from themselves as they go through school. Indeed, one study has shown that self-esteem actually decreases for women as they go further in higher education (Arnold, 1987; Arnold and Denny, 1988). Belenky and co-workers (1986) tell a wonderful story about a women who identified a paper she wrote about her firsthand experience as her best though it was disliked by the professor. Yet "when she pasted together a mess of undigested, secondhand information he was satisfied" (p. 200).

Our schools attempt to teach the rational, "thinking" side of knowing separated from the other forms of knowing . . . intuition, emotion, imagination, sensation (see Gallegos, 1990). Our purpose in restructuring education is probably not to replace rational knowing with these other forms, but, rather, to understand that in the fully functioning human, all these modes of knowing work together. In chapter 4, I will explore the possibilities of extending our concept of education to include all the ways of knowing, those respected by the patriarchal system and those respected by other systems as well. (I have tried to encourage you to engage all these forms of knowing in your own empowerment process through the activities provided in this book.)

Relationship and Communication

Of course, systems of domination and alternative systems also view relationships and communication in those relationships differently. Central to the patriarchal paradigm is hierarchy. As a result, this system treats all relationships as "being either one-up or one-down" (Schaef, 1981, 104). When two people relate to each other, the patriarchal assumption is that one of them must be superior and the other must be inferior. (This is obviously related to the myth of the variability of human worth that I discussed earlier as one of the major supports for an educational system that promotes inequality.)

In the other system, relationships are seen as "peer" (Schaef 1981, 105), equality is assumed, and relationships are viewed as central to one's concerns rather than secondary to self and work. Code (1991) has suggested that friendship provides the best model for human relationships because it implies equality among autonomous individuals who are also deeply connected to one another. I like this model because in such relationships it is possible to focus on the needs of the other as well as those of the self in a mutually caring way.

Of course, communication will look very different depending on what relationship model is being played out. If our purpose is to stay "one up," then we will argue, confuse or assert. If our model is to understand, accept and care for each other, then we will explain, reflect and suggest in ways that can "bridge" our experiences (Schaef, 1981, 134).

Remarkably, these distinctions are reflected in studies of boys' and girls' learning styles. For example, in a wonderful example of teacher research, Aloise (1992) looked at the communication styles of students engaged in cooperative learning in her class. In the example she provides of a girls' discussion of a poem on knighthood, the participants build on each others' statements and affirm them. For instance, we see openers like . . .

> Student 1: The poet sees . . .
> Students 2: So it's not that . . . (expands on others' point)
> Student 1: Personal strength, yes! yes! . . . (expands on group theme)
> Students 2: And that's why . . . (expands on group theme)
> Student 1: (Writes and says) The knight is seen . . . (summarizes)

Students 2: So their nerves . . . (expands on theme)
Student 1: He's like locked . . . (clarifies)
Students 2: Yes. He needs someone . . . (expands)
Student 1: Right
Students 2: (continues)
Student 1: Right
Students 2: (continues)
Student 1: Yes, the constraints . . . (expands)

Note how often they say either "right" or "yes" to affirm the other's statements.

In contrast, in the example of a boys' discussion Aloise provides, there is more of a sense of argument and proving your point, a debate style where one of the boys is clearly the leader of the group. He does most of the talking (in this exerpt, 300 words to the other students' 56) and the function of the other boy who talks (there is one who doesn't) seems to be to either agree, disagree, or challenge. The openers looks like this:

Student 1: All right. We're going to . . . (sets purpose for the group)
Student 2: Yeah . . .
Student 1: Not reallly the . . .
Student 2: Yes.
Student 1: (Checking for agreement) I think we all agree that . . . in my opinion anyway. What do you think Tarek? Do you still think . . . ?
Student 2: You're probably right. . . .
Student 1: Okay, so we can all agree . . .
Student 2: I don't know about reversed. What do you mean about reversed?
Student 1: (explains at length)
Student 2: Okay. It sounds good.
Student 1: Okay, so we agree . . .
Student 2: Yes. Agreed. Agreed. Transformed.
(discussion continues)
Student 1: I think it is. I think it starts there.
Student 2: Prove it.

In the latter group, a hierarchy is quickly established. Interactions are then directed by the one higher in the hierarchy and disagreements are handled as competition. In the other, the two participants seem to be thinking together, as equals in pursuit of insight. Schaef's interpretation would be that the males are operating in a power-over system of rules and the girls are operating in one based on cooperation. (See also Weikel, 1995.)

I think it is important here to make clear that this is not to suggest that girls are the ones who know how to implement a power-to/power-with system and boys don't. In truth, neither group has been socialized for this. Girls are generally good at power-with but only in the sense that they often suppress their own needs in order to work for the group. Did both of the girls in the above example really agree so strongly with each other or were they trying to be cooperative? The power-with we are discussing in this book is connected to the power-to actualize one's true beliefs. This is not a type of power with which girls are always comfortable. Thus, we are not really talking about replacing the boys' system with that of the girls. We are saying that the "female" ability to cooperate with others is a valuable part of a new system we might create . . . but so is the "male" ability to exert power to get things done. Neither male domination or female subservience is appropriate in a power-to/power-with system. Mastery of both communication styles as well as the invention of a combined style is probably the ideal.

For underlying differences in beliefs about relationship and communication seems to be a basic emphasis on separation and autonomy versus an emphasis on connection and community. Belenky and co-workers (1986) distinguish between separate and connected knowing. In the former, knowing results from the application of impersonal procedures. In the latter, it comes from relationship, from an attempt to understand another, to care, to empathize, and to collaborate. The examples above illustrate these two styles fairly well. In the study reported in chapter 9, I found that teachers seem to be empowered when they have *both* connection/community *and* individual autonomy. This suggests again that we might best look for a synthesis of these two systems rather than for a choice between them in order to develop a power-to/power-with system.

It is easy to see how the patriarchal definition of relationships has dominated education. Everyone in the school, district (and community) is defined in terms of "one-upmanship." Obviously, we have the overt hierarchy; the superintendent over the principals over the teachers over the students. We also have a hierarchy among teachers; some are acknowledged as having more influence than others. We also have a hierarchy among students according to at least two scales; there is the academic hierarchy . . . who is smartest? There is also the social hierarchy . . . who is "in"? My guess is that everyone finds this constant ordering to be oppressive, from superintendents to students, and both males and females. Sometimes it is effective and even necessary to get things done. But wouldn't it be great to be able to move outside of it for large amounts of time?

To provide an alternative to this hierarchical ordering of persons, we can begin to look for relationships of mutuality and reciprocal influence. Teachers' views can be respected by administrators, and teachers and parents can be included in the district decision-making. (See chapter 4.) Students can be provided with opportunities for classroom interaction that foster mutual respect. (See chapters 4 through 6.) Debate need not be the only method of discussion in either classroom or faculty meeting. All students (and educators!) can be taught how to work collaboratively at least some of the time.

Relationship to Nature

A central part of the patriarchal paradigm as it has played itself out for hundreds of years has been the attempt to dominate nature (Balbus, 1982; Griffin, 1978, 1981; Merchant, 1980; and others). Feminist theorists have argued that this is closely aligned with the domination of women and certain racial groups, both of which are closely aligned with nature in this paradigm (Griffin, 1978, 1981; and others). Ecofeminist theories similarly stress the connections among all oppressions, including that of the earth (Diamond, 1994; Diamond and Orenstein, 1990). Diamond (1994) suggests that this connection is the logic of domination and control, whether it be of people or of resources.

In schools, I suppose this has played itself out in the higher grades in the dissection of frogs and the classification of plants and animals to the exclusion of the joys of having pets and growing plants, for instance. (I still remember being forced to dissect the frog in biology. I am sure that he jumped, and I felt that I was profoundly denying my true caring nature.)

Cooperation with nature seems to be the paradigmatic alternative to our present system (see Roszak, Gomez and Kanner, 1995). Balbus (1982) has hypothesized that humankind is now moving into the third of three major stages: (1) being dominated by nature (primitive), (2) attempting to dominate nature (instrumental-patriarchal), (3) working cooperatively with nature (post-instrumental). (Also see Havel, 1995.)

Certainly, given the global ecological crisis, there is a need for eco-logical education. Many curriculum materials on ecological living are becoming available. (For an example, contact the Global Action Plan in Woodstock, New York.) But teaching a new relationship to the earth probably requires more than adding isolated units to the curriculum, though this is certainly important. Nature can be brought into our sterile school buidings and children can be taken out into nature. (One parent group in Woodstock, New York recommended a retractable roof!) Schools can be proactively antipollution. Science can emphasize obser-vation of life as much as or in place of practices like dissection. (See Code, 1991 for an excellect discussion of scientist as caring participant rather than detached observer.) Reverence for life can replace attempts to control it.

Morality

Similar differences related to separation versus connection can be found in the area of morality. In the power-over system, morality is a public affair based on agreed upon rules and principles. Rules exist to limit the free-dom of supposedly self-centered people who are assumed to need regula-tion. Rules are sacred and can take precedence over the needs of persons (Schaef, 1983, 129). In the other system, rules are developed to increase freedom and facilitate growth. If a rule does not fit a paraticular context, it can be modified according to the needs of the individuals involved.

Gilligan (1982) found similar differences between the responses of women and men in her study of the development of morality. Whereas studies of men (Piaget, 1965; Kohlberg, 1981, 1984) found that boys and men relay on abstract laws and universal principles to make moral deci-sions, regardless of the context, women operate within a framework of caring and relationship, one that requires that they look at the context and the needs of the individuals and relationships existing in that context before making a decision on a moral issue. Indeed, Noddings (1984) suggests that caring provides a model for "a feminine approach to ethics and moral education" in the subtitle for her book Caring.

Clearly, the "rules and regulations" approach dominates in our schools as in most of the institutions of our society. Because there is little room for looking at the individual circumstances or altering a rule to preserve dignity or community harmony, students often feel disem-powered by these rules. Perhaps if there were a shift toward emphasizing community values and mutual respect, it would be possible to begin to approach issues of discipline and organization with a more "situational ethics" approach. This is not to say that having a basic set of rules and regulations is not important. It is only to suggest that these be tempered by considerations of caring and community.

For instance, students could be involved in thinking through the complexities of various situations that natually arise to arrive at the most "moral" solution, one that reflects a true caring about the individuals involved as well as an awareness of the rules. Many schools now have systems of mediation in which student teams mediate disagreements and problems involving other students. This sort of responsibility empowers students to define morality for themselves.

Love, Friendship and Caring

For the patriarchal and other systems also view the whole area of love, friendship and caring through very different lenses. Whereas the patriarchal system sees love and its expression as a series of rituals, the other system sees it as a mutual exchange of energy. Whereas the patriarchal system sees a friend as one who can be relied on to contribute to a group effort (teamwork), the other system thinks of friendship as a mutual sharing of one's being with an expectation of being understood and accepted. Whereas the patriarchal system sees caring as the fulfilling of one's commitments and moral principles, the other system sees caring as the giving of support to the other in terms of his or her needs or wants or goals (Schaef, 1983; Noddings, 1984).

The patriarchal beliefs about love, friendship and caring are manifested in many positive and negative ways in our schools. Ritual expressions of caring, teamwork and fulfillment of one's commitments are all positive values not to be abandoned. However, the dominant discourse of "being nice" is sometimes played out in empty routines and dogmatic rules. Children are sometimes encouraged to listen to each other not out of empathy or caring but because "it might be on the test" or because there will be a punishment if they do not. Morning rituals such as the pledge of allegiance are rarely understood by students to be an affirmation of their commitment to each other and to their community. The morning sharing time in many elementary classrooms is more of a ritual of one-upmanship than an experience of empathetic understanding.

We can add empathetic listening, and such things as accepting others' feelings and supporting others in their goals, to our list of objectives for social development. Many schools already do this by emphasizing community, cooperation and sharing. Noddings (1984) has provided an ethic of care to be used as an organizing principle for schools. (See chapter 4.) We need not throw out the patriarchal values of ritual expressions of caring, teamwork and fulfillment of commitments. We need only to combine these with relational values of mutuality so that students understand their true meaning.

Leadership

Predictably, the two systems we are discussing also model leadership in very different ways. The patriarchal system, based on a power-over paradigm, sees a true leader as one who leads the group by "having all the answers and presenting a strong, powerful, and all-knowing image" (Schaef, 1983, 128). The other system, based on a power-to/power-with paradigm, sees the leader as one who facilitates the groups' process by encouraging each individual to use his or her unique gifts. "Leadership means nudging people from behind rather than leading them from somwewhere ahead" (Schaef, 1983, 128). (To change your own leadership style, see Heider, 1986.)

These two definitions play themselves out in schools most dramatically in two very different sets of assumptions about the role of the teacher in the learning process. In the traditional model of teacher, the teacher is expected to tell the students what to do and how to do it. The teacher knows all the answers, judges the students' performance according to his or her own criteria and generally fills the students' empty heads with the knowledge that only he or she knows. Obviously, this can be disempowering to the students.

In the emerging concept of teacher as facilitator, the teacher is thought to collaborate in learning experiences in which the teacher and students collaboratively make meaning, select goals and evaluate progress. Students are empowered by participating actively in their own learning process. (This will be discussed in much more depth in chapter 4.)

It was amazing to me how clearly the teachers I interviewed (chosen because they seemed to exemplify personal empowerment) articulated this power-with model, both as teachers and as teacher-leaders. For instance, one teacher said, "The power to learn and make choices is theirs [the students], not mine, to control." Another said, "My goal as a teacher is to have them not need me." Another said, "Now I believe that you can trust the kids. They'll come up with the program and the way of evaluating it— they're better than we are." In terms of leadership, I heard things like:

> I think it's really important to allow people to continue to have access to what they know and what they feel has worked because it may work for them and it might not work for you or me but we're not in a position to make that decision.

> But, basically, they have to operate in their own comfort zone too. So you have to be really careful not to make someone feel that they are less worthy. Their opinion/style might be different, but they're not less worthy.

> I think that I don't [see myself as a change agent]. It's not something that I deliberately try to be. . . . I see the impact that we all have on one another and I think we all change one another. . . . I think of myself as a supportive person.

It was clear to me in these interviews that there are teachers out there who think of teaching as nudging students to take responsibility for their own learning and who think of leadership as nudging colleagues to grow in a collaborative environment that supports all.

Difference

Finally, and perhaps most importantly, power-over and power-with systems differ greatly in their views on difference; where the former system sees difference as threatening, the latter sees difference as an opportunity for growth (Schaef, 1981, 144). This is clearly reflected in the structured discrimination discussed in the first half of the chapter. In the classrooms we have now, we try to treat everyone as if they are the same, and we track students in order to preserve this illusion. We structure our curriculum so everyone learns to same thing at the same time. Students are thereby disempowered by a lack of respect for their individuality. Even our art classes, which are supposed to foster creativity, often engage all students in making the same product at the same time. Indeed, because difference is viewed as a threat in the patriarchal system, creativity is often stifled (Schaef, 1981).

Of course, even in our current tracked classes, homogeneity is always a total myth. Students differ in abilities, interests, cultural backgrounds, prior knowledge, attitudes toward school, learning styles and numerous other factors. Integrating a power-with philosophy into our schools will require that we make space for individual differences, that we celebrate them. Suggestions for making our schools multicultural in a way that goes beyond mere acceptance of difference are provided in chapter 5.

Activity 3.5
CHANGING PARADIGMS

For each of the following, daydream about ways that you could show students that these are also valued in your classroom. Record your ideas for future use.

process time

mutual respect

subjective knowing and intuition

feelings

situational ethics

repect for and connection to nature

caring

cooperation

difference

Note: If you are going through any of the changes suggested in this book, you may be having strong feelings of sadness, anger, fear and/or happiness and excitment. You may be feeling one primarily or you may be feeling them in succession. Strong feelings during periods of change are normal!! The process of change involves our whole being and reading about these ideas will not bring about the changes we are looking for unless we also honor the feelings that they engender. As you work with this book, take time to let these feelings carry you where they want to go. Write about them or speak to a friend. Talk about your feelings in a support group, if you have one (see chapter 8). Your feelings are an important part of the process of empowerment.

Summary

If we are to truly empower ourselves, then we must liberate ourselves from administering an educational system that disempowers our students. The system that we have now reproduces inequality and alienates students by devaluing their cultural backgrounds and their achievements. Students resist this devaluing in ways that are self-defeating. This resistance needs to be understood and rechannelled through truly counterhegemonic work by teachers, students and others in the community.

The system we have now previleges patriarchal values associated with a power-over paradigm to the exclusion of others based on more democratic values in which each person has an equal voice. Concepts of linear, absolute time, hierarchical relationships, competitive communication, separated, objective knowing, domination of nature, rule-based morality, ritualized caring, directive leadership and fear of difference need to be balanced or synthesized with concepts of process time, peer relationships, cooperative communication, connected, subjective and/or intuitive knowing, situational ethics, empathetic caring, facilitating leadership and the embracing of difference as an opportunity for growth. Whereas the power-over procedures have been and will continue to be useful when our purposes center on efficiency and order, we must recognize that they can be disempowering to our students when they deny their essential humanity. When our goals involve human growth and community development, we can emphasize procedures that reflect power-to/power-with values. Then our schools can become empowering communities in which students are supported in relationships of mutuality and connection that do not require the suppression of individuality. In part 2 of this book, I now turn to the task of envisioning this empowering educational system.

PART TWO

Envisioning a System of Empowerment

CHAPTER FOUR

An Empowering Education

In the first three chapters of this book, I looked at what empowerment might be for educators and students and what blocks that empowerment in our current educational system. This leads me directly into beginning to envision a truly empowering education. In part 2, I would like to share some of my ideas about the possible process (chapter 4) and content (chapter 5) of this empowering education, using literacy education as one example (chapter 6).

Clearly, these chapters cannot be exhaustive in describing what an empowering education would entail. Indeed, that would be contrary to my belief that each educator must decide these matters for him/herself. Instead, I would like to use these chapters to open up new areas of thought, stimulate open-ended thinking, and to speculate about the educational impact of changing from a power-over to a power-to/power-with paradigm emphasis.

In part 3, I will look at ways educators have empowered themselves. Among these are techniques for creating communities that support us in this process. But it is important to feel that we have something we want to be able to do before we can be motivated to pursue our own empowerment. Thus, my purpose in part 2 is to encourage you to examine your own beliefs about the content and process of education and your part in it.

Persons as Subjects

One of the first things we need to do to switch to an empowering pedagogy is to redefine how we see our students. In the power-over model, "other" in a relationship is objectified and viewed as an object of manipulation and coercion. If we are honest with ourselves, we will see that this is pretty much the way we have come to see students. "Motivation" really means getting them to do what we want them to do. "Discipline" means punishing them when they do not do what we want them to do. In the system that currently dominates education, students are objects that we are supposed to control.

Moreover, in our current system education is seen as one big machine in which students are the "raw material" pumped in at one end. They are then expected to come out as "products" of our machine (Oliver and Gershman, 1989). We talk about "expected outcomes" and "objectives" but rarely about people. When students do not respond to our "procedures" by producing the appropriate responses on "objective" measures, we label them as low ability and plug them into a different machine, one that has fewer "expectations."

The scientific rationality discussed in chapter 2 has contributed significantly to this objectification of students. Nowhere is this more blatant than in the numerous research studies in which the "subjects" of the study have X and Y "mean (average)" responses. The "subjects" report X and Y, and so on. Just read some of the research reports that I published early in my career and you will get a sense of what I mean. In this kind of quantitative research, the focus is on the average, on washing out differences. The "subjects" are not viewed as individuals, and all "variables" except the one being studied are assumed to be "randomly distributed."

So the machine metaphor and the language of science have left us with an objectified student whom we are expected to control. What happens if we begin to see this student, not as an object to be dominated, but as a fully human subject with his or her own subjectivities that deserve recognition? Subjects are people who create their own lives. . . . What happens if we see students as unique individuals with their own paths to self-actualization, their own lives to create, their own meanings to discover? What happens if students see each other this way and become a community of mutually-respecting, self-affirming individuals bonded in a community dedicated to their mutual empowerment? When we refuse to objectify people, we can affirm the uniqueness of each person within a community of "co-agency," characterized by co-action, collaboration and equality (Kriesberg, 1992, 120). (See also Balbus, 1982 on postinstrumental symbolization.)

Activity 4.1
OBSERVING SUBJECTS AND OBJECTS

Since some have suggested that our relationship to nature reflects our relationship to each other (see Balbus, 1982), let's try an experiment with nature. Go out into a natural environment and choose a plant or animal or tree or rock to interact with. Or, if it is winter, choose a plant or pet inside. Now, think of yourself as a scientist. Carefully, and objectively, record what you see. Note colors, shapes, lines, movements. Be scientific. Keep an "objective" distance. Record your notes here.

Now, think of your "subject" as having an independent life of its own. Think of its experiences. Close your eyes and let it speak to you. Communicate with it. Empathize and listen closely. You may be surprised to find some wisdom here. Record what you feel and observe below.

Now, think about these experiences. How has your relationship to this object/subject changed?

What are the results of this shift from seeing students as objects to respecting them as subjects who can create their own lives? First, tracking seems even less appropriate. If all students are unique persons, with unique interests, goals, cultural backgrounds, and paths in life, then why would we privilege test-taking ability as the only way to group them? Any way we would attempt to form homogeneous classes would be doomed to failure in a world of fully human subjects with myriad exciting differences. In addition, if all are fully human subjects, and thus of equal value, then how can we justify providing a better education to one group than to another (see chapter 3)?

The realization that students are fully human subjects will also lead to the questioning of our attempts to totally dominate and control them. Grumet (1988) has said: "In order for curriculum to provide the moral, epistemological and social situations that allow persons to come to form, it must provide the ground for their action rather than their acquiescence" (p. 172). In an empowering education, students must be allowed to participate fully in the decisions that affect their lives. This includes curriculum decisions. Involved in this way, they could learn to make and evaluate decisions, to select goals and means, and to think actively about their own development.

The empowering classroom, therefore, would be student-centered, but need not be permissive in the laissiz-faire sense. Neither the teacher nor the students would have complete control. Rather, the process would be negotiated and would take into account pressures outside the classroom as well as student and teacher abilities, interests and beliefs.

Of course, if yours is the only classroom in the school in which authority is shared, you will have to change very slowly from the more common power-over procedures to these power-to/power-with ones. You will have to give the students guidance all along the way. Students who are used to being anti-authority and who do not have skills in effective planning and evaluation are hardly ready to make all decisions for themselves.

Indeed, the way this general principle of shared authority would work itself out will vary tremendously from situation to situation, from one age group to another. Obviously, you would not expect a group of first-graders to be able to specify everything they wanted to learn or how they wanted to learn it. You would want to provide them with the limits and structure that allow them to function comfortably. Your shared authority could range anywhere from allowing them to choose the books they read, the animals they study, and the class projects they publish, to allowing them to have input on grouping procedures, classroom rules of conduct, and the consequences of rule violations. Secondary students who had had previous experience with shared authority would be more able to set classroom goals and to decide on appropriate methods for reaching those goals. They would be able to monitor their progress and to make changes as the program progressed. (I will discuss the possible content for such programs in chapter 5.)

Shor (1992) calls this a "participatory" pedagogy: "Participatory classes respect and rescue the curiosity of students" (p. 16). Of course, this harks back to the earlier philosophy of Dewey:

> There is, I think no point in the philosophy of progressive education which is sounder than its emphasis upon the importance of the participation of the learner in the formation of the purposes which direct his activities in the learning process. (1963 [1938], 67)

Dewey believed that it was essential in a democratic society for individuals to be able to construct their own purposes and meanings. He defined a slave as one who carried out the wishes of another.

Similarly, Shor (1992) suggests that nonparticipatory education "corresponds to the exclusion of ordinary people from policy-making in society at large" (p. 19) and leads to "endullment" defined as "the dulling of students' minds as a result of their nonparticipation" (p. 20). In contrast to this, Shor suggests that a negotiated curriculum can give the students sufficient control of the learning process to enable them to perform at peak levels by actively participating. Interestingly, recent research on motivation verifies the observation that having some control over the learning process increases motivation (see Spaulding, 1992a, 1992b).

All this discussion of seeing students as subjects and sharing authority with them also gets us directly into the issue of whether children are persons in the first place. I truly believe that there is a large segment of our society that sees children as nonpersons. Just look at the legal system and the limited rights of children. Children are often treated as property to be distributed along with other assets. Respecting children as fully human subjects who can participate in decisions regarding their lives affirms them as persons in their own right.

Activity 4.2
SHARING AUTHORITY WITH STUDENTS

Make a list of all the things the teacher decides in your classroom (or in the classrooms of people with whom you work if you do not have a classroom of your own). This should include everything from seating arrangements, timetables, assignments, organizational procedures, to topics being studied, books being read or essays being written, testing procedures and forms of homework. When you have thought about absolutely everything, go back and put a check by anything that you would be comfortable having the students decide or at least have input on. Select one or two and speculate on how you might do it, or talk to teachers who might be able to give it a try.

Of course, there are many specific ways that we can see the workings of power-over and objectification in classrooms. Even the traditional arrangement of the classroom into rows with the teacher sitting in the front of the room reflects a psychology of domination. Foucault (1979) has pointed out that this structure was developed in prisons in which the emphasis was on strict surveillance and control of prisoners. It is a basic premise of mine (and yours, I hope!) that schools should be nothing like prisons whose primary function is punishment and domination, not human growth and actualization. If students are involved in co-action and collaboration, then they should probably be sitting where they can see each other. If a variety of types of activities are going on in the classroom at the same time, then there should be different areas conducive to these different activities.

Old methods of teaching relying on group lectures, programmed activities completed in unison, and whole-class competitive testing can also be questioned as we move away from power-over objectification. Instead, methods such as cooperative learning, individual projects and presentations, and whole-class projects like newspapers and community action programs make more space for each individual to contribute according to his or her own abilities and interests.

Sapon-Shevin and Schniedewind (1991) have suggested that competitive school practices are based on myths, like the myth that competition is motivating (which is only true when everyone has an equal chance), or the myth that all the world loves a winner (when in reality many students have to choose between success and popularity). Instead, more cooperative activities build exactly the kind of classrooms we would think of as empowering. The learning is more democratic, students must take responsiblity for themselves and learn to care for the people they are working with, diversity can be valued, and multiple learning styles can be accommodated.

Of course, just changing our activities does not guarantee that domination and power-over competition will disappear from our classrooms. Students often get quite domineering during cooperative activities and quite competitive during individual assignments. Our classrooms are embedded in communities in which domination and competition are still valued, though this is changing (see Montouri and Conti, 1993). Thus, it might be quite useful to discuss these issues openly and involve the students in setting standards for supportive interaction.

Again, this will differ according to the situation. In the younger grades we can model responding supportively to our peers' work by saying what we valued and liked about their work before offering our suggestions for change (for example, see Tompkins, 1990, 85–88). We can even provide students with openers for response: "What I got out of this was . . ." "What I liked was . . ." We can suggest that they summarize the previous student's suggestion before providing one of their own in order to promote good listening. We can suggest that they ask questions of each other. As students get older, they can evaluate their own discussions and classroom interactions according to the cooperative or competitive tone set.

I should also note that collaborative activities do not necessarily preclude our having universal objectives which each student eventually masters, especially if these are goals with which the students are comfortable. In collaborative communities the autonomous individual is not lost; s/he is just embedded in a synergistic and supportive community. (See Kriesberg, 1992.) Thus, we can simply keep records for each student individually and allow him or her to master agreed-upon skills and knowledge in a variety of ways and in a variety of group or individual settings.

In such nonobjectifying classrooms, evaluation need not be used as a form of power-over that humiliates all but the brightest students. In a classroom of mutually respecting individuals, each would be helping the other to learn, rather than each trying to outdo the other. Goals that are chosen by the individual can be monitored and adjusted as the individual develops. There is no need for comparison among students. (See Atwell, 1987 for an excellent example of a reading/writing program that uses this form of evaluation.)

For self-evaluation is the process most likely to lead to self-empowerment. Instead of seeing students as objects to be measured and labelled, we can see them (and they can see themselves) as self-actualizing subjects who can determine their own goals (yes, within limits) and evaluate their progress and achievement. A variety of questions and formats can be used to help the students develop their ability to do this in ways that are appropriate to their age and level of self-awareness. Tierney, Carter and Desai (1991) have provided an example of how this can be done with language arts portfolios, for instance. (See also Camp, 1990; Carter and Tierney, 1988; Howard, 1990; Levi, 1990.) Allowing students to assess their own progress at least partially frees teachers from their roles as managers and allows them to enter into mutually respectful relationships with students.

Finally, if our students are fully human subjects, then they are more than brains. They have bodies (sensations) and feelings and intuitions and imaginations and impulses. They have dreams and hopes. They have personal histories and futures full of potential. This is not the education of the "whole child" as in earlier theories in which subjects like art and creative writing were added to the curriculum. Instead, it is a recognition that thought and feeling and intuition and imagination are mutually constituative ways of knowing anything. (See Gallegos, 1992.) Thus, they can be acknowledged as part of the curriculum *at all times.*

To exemplify this mutual interdependence of ways of knowing, let's imagine a fifth-grade class studying city government. The students begin by reading about how city governments are organized (thinking). They arrange to visit a local town council meeting to see decision-making in action (sensation). While there, they intuit that a lot has gone on behind the scenes (intuition). They begin to speculate on what that might have been (imagination). They each select city council members to interview based on their intuition about who might be able to provide more information (intuition). They prepare questions, conduct interviews, and report back to the class (intuition, sensation, thinking). They are so upset about what they have found out about political trade-offs that they write poems to express their outrage (feeling). They form a watchdog committee to keep an eye on the city council (impulse to act; moral outrage). They pull their learning together with essays about how city government could be improved, and they send these to the city council members (thinking, feeling, imagining, intuiting).

Activity 4.3
INTEGRATING WAYS OF KNOWING

Think of a topic your students always study, one that they do not particularly like because it has always been dry and boring to them (limited to thinking). Now, next to each of the labels below, write some ways to stimulate these ways of knowing related to this topic. (If you are not teaching, you may wish to do these activities with students you know in mind.)

TOPIC:

Sensing (seeing, hearing, smelling, tasting, or touching):

Imagining:

Feeling:

Intuiting:

Thinking:

Often, this integrated knowing can lead to the impulse to act or to change. What might that impulse be in this case?_____

_____

POSSIBLE ACTION: _____

Try the new unit that has emerged!!

Dance and Organism as Metaphor

One way to reconceptualize what is going on in our classrooms is to shift our attention, at least sometimes, from the machine metaphor to others with more life-affirming implications. Oliver and Gershman (1989) have suggested that "positive culture could begin with a vision in which there is a balance among three complementary metaphors: the dance, the living organism, and the machine" (p. 19). Whereas the machine metaphor emphasizes objectification and products, the dance and the organism metaphors suggest subjectivity and process. Whereas the machine metaphor suggests linear, absolute time, objective knowing, predictable, controllable outcomes, radical individuality and separation, a hierarchical ordering of individuals, rigid, universal rules of conduct, and expectations of sameness, the dance and organism metaphors suggest other realities.

Let's begin by looking at what goes on in classrooms as a dance. A dance is a process in which the dancers or the observers may change, but no concrete product is left when it is over. It is, by its very nature, transitory. Though we may have general plans, no two performances are exactly alike. Moreover, it is often the most moving when it is improvised and allowed to emerge from the creative moment. It is a process of interaction in which dancers come together, move apart, move in unison, move independently. It is a flow, a movement involving body as well as mind, imagination and intuition. It is a beautiful event, complete unto itself, aesthetic, fulfilling, and mysterious. It can be performed by individuals, pairs, and groups of various sizes. Dancers are, in a significant way, responsible to each other for the dance exists as a totality involving the contributions of all. Dance exists in a universe of process time in which knowing is at once subjective and objective.

I recently had the opportunity to observe my daughter's first-grade class in their morning rituals. I have often looked back on what I observed as a beautiful dance . . . the movement among children, the movement of furniture, the interactions with teachers as the children performed their morning assignments. Then, as if by magic, they were all on the carpet, moving around parts of a calendar, counting, singing. Then up for the pledge, arrangements of children, interactions, constantly shifting, producing at various moments transformations for individuals and a renewed solidarity and sense of presence for the group. The process took its own time, the learnings were subjective as well as objective, and the exchanges often involved mutuality and support. Poetry, imagination and a sense of mystery were stirred in the participants, teachers and students alike. Was this not just as real and important as the "objectives" of the activities?

Using the dance metaphor to see the interdependence of students during an activity also leads us to the organism metaphor suggested by Oliver and Gershman (1989). In a living organism, all the parts contribute to the whole, and the whole is a part of a larger whole. There is an exchange between parts and the whole and "the language of exchange is laughter and conversation and weeping; it is the language of community of planting and harvesting, of bonding and living, of giving and taking" (Oliver and Gershman, 1989, 20). Oliver and Gershman further state that "Organism is the metaphor of mutuality, reciprocity, becoming, and dying."

One of the teachers I interviewed talked about the rewards of working with students in the drama club in these terms:

> Maybe it's just about being. It's about being open, just being, being there, being present and being involved in the creation of the moment in partnership with people so that it's like you're not controlling it and then what happens is you walk away from that moment feeling inspired, feeling fulfilled, feeling like you contributed and at the same time getting filled up like you were contributed to.

I can think of teaching experiences that felt just like this . . . times when the class was openly discussing something important, when we all felt like we were part of something bigger than our individual agendas, when we were co-agents, spontaneous, whole feeling/thinking persons coming together synergistically for the moment. No product was created but something meaningful happened.

Thus, viewing the educational process as an organism rather than a machine may help to restore its possibilities for community and connectedness. It emphasizes the importance of the relationships among whole persons within the classroom and between the classroom and the persons in the larger community. The larger community can also be seen as an integral part of the nation and the world. This puts the emphasis back on the process, not only as group ritual and experience, as in the dance metaphor, but as an organic becoming based on the interdependence of individuals and communities. Learning is social. Difference is an asset; each person makes his or her own unique contribution. All parts (persons) are necessary to the whole, valuable. Rules are useful only insofar as they contribute to the growth and vitality of the whole.

Thus, I believe these metaphors are rich in their potential to balance the machine metaphor in our revision of schooling in America. They allow us to think about our classrooms in ways that legitimate imagination, community, interdependence and all the aspects of the human experience excluded from the process by a mechanical model. A balance, a synthesis, a "dance" among the three metaphors is needed.

This also gets us into the age-old question of whether teaching is a science or an art. Though the science model has been in vogue for some time, many continue to maintain that it is an art. Madeline Grumet (1988) suggests that this is threatening to some because art transforms the natural order, relies on having a community where all forms of expression are valued, and implies that emotions are as valid a form of knowing as are thoughts. I believe that we have reached the limits of what we can learn from viewing education exclusively as a social science and that we are ready to view teaching as a science *and* an art, and the process as a machine, a dance, *and* a living organism.

Activity 4.4
THINKING METAPHORICALLY

Perhaps it would be useful for you to think of your own metaphor for your class or school. Just play with this activity . . . let your subconscious do the work. Trust that anything you come up with will be useful to you.

Now, try finishing this statement four times:

Ideally, my classroom is like a _____
(food or meal)

Ideally, my classroom is like a _____
(activity or sport)

Ideally, my classroom is like a _____
(object in your house)

Ideally, my classroom is like a _____
(animal or animal group)

Go back to each of these metaphors and list the characteristics that are important in each.

1.

2.

3.

4.

Now, what are you learning about your deepest beliefs about education? Do these metaphors express all you would like education to be? If not, think of another metaphor for you to concentrate on for the next week, month or year.

Education is like a _____ .

___

Caring as an Educational Ideal

I also believe that caring provides the ideal around which we might organize our educational system. Much of the following discussion is based on the work of Nel Noddings (1984) who describes such an emphasis in this way:

> The one-caring has one great aim: to preserve and enhance caring in herself and in those with whom she comes in con-

tact. This quite naturally becomes the first aim of parenting and of education. It is an aim that is built into the process itself—not one that lies somewhere beyond it. (p. 172)

This caring can be about people or it can be about ideas and things. Caring is a fundamental, natural human response that we all experience as good. When we are cut off from this natural caring, we are not only cut off from the world of things and/or persons involved, we are cut off from ourselves. (See Noddings, 1984.)

In Noddings' model, caring involves "engrossment," or stepping out of our own reality to feel or empathize with that of one cared for, and "motivational displacement," or feeling a need to work toward the fulfillment of the other's needs. In the act of working on the other's behalf, we fulfill our own need to grow as ethical selves. If our own needs are too grossly ignored while we are working for others, the impulse to care will die. Thus, caring persons take care of themselves as well as others.

When we engage in caring, we simultaneously look at the situation from our own and from the other's point of view. Our goals are not imposed from our own agenda. "The one-caring sees the best self in the cared-for and works with him to actualize that self" (Noddings, 1984, 64). Mayeroff (1971) says that if we care, then our responsibiity is to "allow the direction of the other's growth to guide what I do." (p. 5) When we step out of ourselves and respect the world of the learner, the results can sometimes seem "miraculous" (Kaufman, 1994).

This emphasis on caring as the basis for teacher-student interaction fits exactly with our earlier discussion of nonobjectification. The teacher begins with the assumption that the student's experiences and goals have a validity of their own which must be considered as decisions are made. In this way, the inequality of the teacher/student relationship (which Noddings says is inevitable when a relationship is characterized with one doing the caring and one being cared for) is balanced by the teacher's attention to the needs and desires of the students.

One of the problems with the institutionalization of caring is that it can shift attention from the immediate involvement of the one caring (How can I care for this student in this situation?) to an abstract problem to be solved (How can we care about our students in general?). Then rules are designed which can take away from the uniqueness of each situation. This tension between absolute rules and situation-specific morality is exactly the one I discussed in chapter 3.

Caring is best actualized within a structure that allows for individual decisions apppropriate to the context.

Finally, as caring teachers our primary aim is the enhancement of the students' caring. "To help another person grow is to help him to care for someone or something apart from himself" (Mayeroff, 1971, 7). To do this, we must give the children practice in caring, and they must be free to discover those things for which they can truly care. We must also encourage interpersonal caring in our classrooms.

In such classrooms, there would be an emphasis on listening to each other and on social justice as an issue in the classroom and in the world. (See Wood, 1991.) Dialogue would be an essential activity in a caring classroom because it can develop interpersonal connections and provide opportunities for empathy. Subject matter would be related to the students' lives, and opportunities for learning that are not systematically evaluated would be provided (Noddings, 1984).

Finally, the entire school would be need to be restructured to allow for caring. New types of organizational structures, assessment procedures, and relationships among teachers as well as new rituals and new rites of passage would need to be developed in a way that would all emphasize the worth of each participant, student and teacher alike. (See also Kreidler, 1994.) Students would be involved in regular service activities, providing care to others, to the environment, to animals, and so on. The rest of the community could become involved in this "apprenticeship of caring" (Noddings, 1984, 187). We might want to consider smaller schools, with students remaining with teachers for longer periods of time. (See Meier, 1995.)

For we must remember that the teacher as the primary caregiver requires support and response. Many teachers burn out in their ability to care. This is because they are not sustained by the response of the cared-for. Instead, the cared-for views them as enemies. In such a relationship, it is impossible to continue caring. "Where is the teacher to get the strength to go on giving except from the student?" (Noddings, 1984, 181). (Teachers can also become burned out if they forget to care for themselves; this is an essential part of being a caregiver.)

All of the aforementioned changes are important to consider not only because they teach students to care for each other but because they may allow the students to perceive the teachers as caregivers rather than enemies. Students can then respond in such a way as to sustain the caring relationship by recognizing it, receiving it and growing. This would provide teachers with the motivation to keep caring.

When such a response from the student is not given, every resource in the school and community must provide care to the teacher until the appropriate caring relationships can be established in the classroom. Put simply, we cannot expect teachers to continue to care about unresponsive and hostile students without providing those teachers with ample support and validation of their efforts from some other source. Perhaps it is easier to change the classroom and school to a caring community so that students can become responsive and involved.

I have personally found that the more I attend to caring in the classroom, the more I like teaching. When I listen to students, respond to their needs with flexible requirements, discuss social justice and the need to care, encourage cooperation and mutual support, and encourage them to find that for which they can truly care, I am gifted with their enthusiasm and growth. When I ignore these things, I find that my students memorize and parrot back the content, grumble about assignments, and perform only minimally well.

Activity 4.5
CREATING A RITUAL OF CARING

As Wood (1991) has suggested, it is only when we have created new rituals and routines that the old regime of competition and power-over relationships will begin to crumble. However, these cannot be rigid rituals that take precedence over process-driven meaning-making. Instead, they must be open to change and individual expression.

Let's begin by creating at least one usable and flexible ritual or routine that will express the importance of caring in the classroom. This could be about the teacher caring for the students, the students caring for the teacher, or students caring for each other. It must be open-ended enough to be different each time, depending on the needs of the caregiver and the one cared for.

First, think about the ways that caring is already, at least sometimes, expressed in daily activities. Record some of those here.

Now, select one of these that might lend itself to being a regularly repeated activity. Design an activity that allows the participants to express caring on a more regular basis. (Remember, self expression need not simply be speaking. It could also involve writing or drawing.) Outline it here.

Try this activity, or, if you do not have a classroom of your own, ask a teacher you know to try it. Refine it so that it works as you would have it work. Is it flexible enough to allow new meanings and procedures to develop according to the needs of the situation? (I would love to collect these and put them together into a book. Please consider sending yours to me!!)

Talk with students about how they feel about this ritual or routine. What do they get out of it?

Voice and Dialogue in the Classroom

So the use of authentic dialogue in the classroom has the potential to promote empathy and caring. It can also be empowering to students because, in the process of being involved in authentic dialogue, students can develop their own voices. They can learn to speak their personal truths.

Dialogue as a teaching method involves talking with students rather than at them. It is usually somewhat structured and somewhat open-ended depending on the situation and the goals: "Balancing the teacher's authority and the students' input is the key to making the process both critical and democratic" (Shor, 1992, 85). Dialogic discussions make room for everyone's honest opinion, and students often respond to each other, rather than just to the teacher. Ideally, each student goes into the discussion with an open mind on the issue, or a willingness to change. The purpose of the dialogue is not to rehearse what someone thinks of as right or wrong answers, but, rather, to think critically and to hear what others think. It develops mutuality and empathy and is the fundamental basis for any cooperative community of learners.

Senge (1990), basing his work on that of Bohm (1991, 1994), has contrasted discussion and dialogue. In his model, the purpose of discussion is to air everyone's opinion and make a decision or come to a conclusion. The purpose of dialogue is, in contrast, more divergent—to find new approaches and increase the complexity of the thought processes. Because it is assumed that everyone has an important piece of the puzzle, participants are open to other's opinions rather than advocates of their own. The facilitator of such a dialogue can point out when it shifts to a discussion (debate?), make sure everyone has a chance to participate, and model dialogic language that includes the questioning of one's own assumptions.

Bruckerhoff (1990) calls such a dialogue a "conversation." He points out that it is most appropriate when the content is emergent (vs. predetermined) and the teacher and student share ownership. Other types of lessons include direct instuction when the teacher controls predetermined content, process lessons which put more of the process in the hands of the students and expressive lessons in which students engage in artistic or creative personal expression. I would argue that teachers need expertise in all these lesson forms so that they can be used when appropriate, but that they should be embedded in an overall structure of dialogic communication. That is, content is seen as problematic (open to new points of view, unfinished) and ownership is shared, and *within that context* direct instruction, process teaching and expressive lessons can be chosen by the students and teacher to facilitate their dialogic exploration.

Unfortunately, research on the use of dialogue in the classroom has shown that it is all too rarely used. Goodlad's (1984) research on schooling revealed that less than one percent of the questions asked required open-ended responses. Sizer (1984) also reported that in his study the typical exchange was only one or two sentences long. Gambrell (1987), in a study of elementary teachers' questioning during reading period, found that teachers rarely asked questions that required more than one word in response.

We can only speculate on the reasons for this lack of dialogue. First, an emphasis on static knowledge and right/wrong answers puts teachers into a "question-response-evaluation" mode (see Heath, 1978). Also, the need to control students may make dialogue seem threatening. Finally, few teachers have had any training or experience in facilitating effective dialogues. (For an excellent structure to begin to use dialogue in your class, see Sorenson, 1993.)

Shor (1985) has presented a list of teacher behaviors that either promote or discourage active participation in honest dialogue. I have condensed this into my own table designed to begin to describe teacher behaviors that empower or disempower students during dialogic discussions (see table 4.1). All of the empowering behaviors encourage students to find their own voices, whereas the disempowering ones silence the students' voices. (If you are currently teaching, you may wish to have someone use this table while observing you facilitating a dialogue among your students.)

You may have noticed that in all this discussion about dialogue, I have not addressed the issue of the content of such discussions. So what should these discussions be about? This is a thorny question that I will leave mostly for chapter 5 in which the content of the educational process is examined. However, one critical point to make now is that the topics must relate to the real subjectivities of the students.

> If dialogue is to occur in schools, it must be legitimate to discuss whatever is of intellectual interest to the students who are invited into dialogue. God, sex, killing, loving, fear, hope, and hate must all be open to discussion. . . . The attempt to separate that which may be spoken into legitimate domains strengthens those who would control our children and wrenches them away from lives of attachment and caring. (Noddings, 1984, 183)

Table 4.1. Teacher Behaviors That . . .

Disempower Students . . .	*Empower Students . . .*
Present analysis	Involve students in analysis
Interrupt students	Listen carefully
Use jargon	Use vocabulary familiar to the students
Ask right/wrong questions	Encourage students to respond to each other
Ask questions requiring one-word answers	Ask open-ended questions
Give safe, uncritical responses	Be authentic and critical
Correct students' speech style	Accept students' speech style
Call on white or male students more often	Encourage girls and students of color to speak
Dissimulate personal bias	Be honest about sociocultural contexts and biases
Limit choice of topic	Allow students to generate topics
Speak often and for extended times	Tolerate silence while students think
Evaluate discussion without student input	Encourage student evaluation of the discussion itself*

*Sorenson, 1993 suggests that student use self-evaluation questions like the following:
1. Did I contribute to the discussion?
2. Did I encourage others to contribute or clarify ideas?
3. What would I like to do in the next discussion?
4. Who encouraged me the most in the discussion?
5. Did I participate with an open mind?

In schools, if we think about it, there are many unstated rules about what we can speak about in classrooms and what would be "inappropriate" to discuss. Foucault (1980) has discussed how certain "discursive practices" define what can be said and how it can be said in particular social institutions and settings. For instance, in classrooms, we avoid potentially emotional or explosive subjects. Silences in the curriculum often include racism, poverty, sexuality, and human emotions.

Does it seem odd to suggest that we should talk about happiness and grief, about what makes life worth living, about conflicts of loyalties? Or does it seem odd that we do not talk about these things? (Noddings, 1984, 184)

But students cannot find their voices if what they can talk about is limited to that in which they have no interest. Fine (1991), in her study of one inner-city high school, has carefully documented how the school silences the real voices of the students. Students there (and elsewhere, I suspect) are discouraged from discussing the real conditions of their lives, and content is presented in a right/wrong format, always from the point of view of the dominant culture. Fine also found several examples of teachers who allowed students to find their voices. For instance, in one discussion of suicide in a health class, the socioeconomic class biases of the participants were openly acknowledged. She also found examples of open, honest communication in a multilingual English class, a co-op work program class, a history class (Paul Robeson discussion), a hygiene class (discussion about school violence), and a remedial English class (process writing).

The concept of "voice" is difficult to define. It is speaking honestly from a particular cultural and historical moment. It is articulating our own experience of the world. It is how we define ourselves. It is the student's "voice" as poor or black or female or disabled or Spanish-speaking or whatever that helps to define his or her subjectivity. It is not the "voice" that the teacher or the dominant culture would train us into. It is telling it in our own words. It is our authentic expression.

But voice and dialogue can be oppressive ideas if we approach them naively, without an eye to the multiple identities each person brings to the situation. Weiler (1988) has provided moving examples of how, in the complex interplay of subjectivities based on race, class and gender, different voices are alternatively nurtured or silenced. In her study of feminist teachers trying to raise issues of sexist oppression, she found these feminist teachers frequently came into conflict with their male students who were offended by their teachers' explicit identification as feminists. These teachers were often accused of "siding" with the girls. In one example, however, the teacher also delegitimized the voice of the working-class girl for whom feminist ideas were foreign. When this girl suggested that a girl who was raped might have brought it on herself, the teacher, who felt strongly that this was a dangerous attitude, used her knowledge to argue with the student who was thereby effectively silenced.

But for Marie, the working-class girl, once again middle-class discourse has controlled the classroom. For her, the issue was not only sexism, it was also classism. (Weiler, 1988, 139)

Thus, when conducting discussion in the classroom it is difficult and, perhaps, sometimes impossible to equally privilege every voice in the classroom. I would still suggest that we try, and that we name the problem when it occurs.

We also must avoid the assumption that encouraging student voice is automatically empowering. (See Ellsworth, 1989.) If we respond to statements of outrage and pain with rational argument rather than compassion, we may well disempower students who are not ready to objectify their feelings in that way. Moreover, teachers *are* in a more powerful position than students are and yet their subjectivity is shaped by their race, class and gender identifications. We must all be clear about our own place in the complex web of power in our society and in our classrooms if we are to dialogue honestly with students.

Moreover, in a classroom in which the students differ in their access to power, asking them to "share" equally is also problematic. Not all the students will feel equally safe. We can first work to increase the safety of the classroom by encouraging personal trust and commitment among the participants. Affinity groups may need to be developed before students feel able to speak with their own voices. All must acknowledge that we can never fully know the experience of another . . . that our hearing of their voices is partial. Finally, in some situations, even the term currently in vogue, "sharing," can be seen as slightly obnoxious. Depending on the topic, a student's voice may be raging or defiant or wailing or sobbing or exuberant or paniced. These are not things we "share" like a child's toy or a piece of cake (Ellsworth, 1989).

Redefining the Teacher's Role

It is probably clear to you from the above discussion that all these changes will require that we rethink the role of the teacher in the classroom, school and community. First, in caring, intersubjective classrooms, teachers will no longer be dictators, managers or technicians. They will not be involved in transmitting information into the empty minds of children. Instead, they will be collaborators, facilitators and mentors.

First, as collaborators, they will work with students as they attempt to solve problems, learn information and create products. As such, they might help with seeking out resources, contacting sources and organizing information. They will collaborate in the meaning-making process by sharing their own feelings and opinions when appropriate. They will interact with the students about their work, giving them feedback as requested. As members of their classes, they will use their knowledge, thinking, intuition and imagination to contribute to the group's or to an individual's efforts.

As facilitators, teachers will monitor discussions and decision-making processes. They will suggest rules for involving all students and intervene when some students' voices are being silenced. They will guide the students in setting goals and in evaluating their success in reaching those goals. They will also constantly monitor the needs of individuals during ongoing processes, intervening when necessary to involve or assist individuals with such things as autonomy within the classroom community, feelings of efficacy, appropriateness of behavior, and so on.

Finally, as mentors, teachers will sometimes "teach" by sharing their knowledge with the students who may be novices in the area. For instance, it is entirely appropriate, in my opinion, for a teacher to conduct short lessons on such things as punctuation and grammar when the students are involved in writing a class newspaper that will be published. The difference between this and traditional direct teaching is that in this case the topics arise from the meaningful activities of the students, and the students have the opportunity to use the knowledge in practical ways almost immediately.

Activity 4.6a
CHANGING CLASSROOM ROLES

If you are a teacher, it is time for you to involve a colleague in your change process. (If you are not a teacher, see activity 4.6b below.) It is almost impossible for us to think about what roles we are playing in the classroom when we are involved in the thousands of momentary decisions that make up teaching. Find someone you trust and feel safe with. Discuss the various roles that you wish to play in your classroom. (There are many other than the ones I have discussed. You may prefer others.) Make a list of them here.

1.

2.

3.

4.

5.

6. Others?

Make sure that your colleague knows what each of these would look like in practice. Now, arrange for your colleague to visit your classroom for a morning or a whole day if possible. Have him or her write down everything you do and, if possible, label it according to the role that you are playing. Get together and discuss his or her notes. What have you learned? What might you want to change?

Activity 4.6b
HELPING TEACHERS TO CHANGE ROLES

If you are a parent, administrator or lawmaker, there are things you can do to provide the space for teachers to change roles in the classroom. For instance, supporting new open-ended curricula like writing workshop (see Chapter 6) or opening up holistic assessment options all make a difference. For each of the areas below that you can influence, list some changes you can support to help teachers change their role in the classroom.

Curriculum:
(Holistic curricula which do not specify atomistic objectives make group process and individual projects more possible . . .)

Assessment of students:
(Holistic assessments that allow students to work on those things they need to master provide space for the student and teacher to work together in planning . . .)

Evaluation of teachers:
(Teacher observation instruments should not assume that the teacher is presenting a lesson. They should make space for collaborative work with students, for instance . . .)

Providing materials:
(Teachers and students need constant access to a wide range of trade books and reference materials . . .)

School organization:
(Flexible time arrangements that allow classes to spend large amounts of time on one project are very helpful. Also, time for teachers to get together to share ideas and time for students to meet with students with similar interests in other classes, etc. could also support change . . .)

Much has been written lately about the teacher's new role in decision-making. Actually, we know that teachers already make innumerable decisions in the classroom each day. (For example, see Brophy, 1984; Clark, 1984; Deschl and Wright, 1989; Manly-Casimir and Wasserman, 1989; Putnam, 1984; and Smith, 1989.) The real difference is that now there are attempts to involve teachers in decision-making at the school and district levels. (For examples, see Faidley and Musser, 1991; Firestone and Bader, 1991; Maxcy and Caldas, 1991.) The idea is that teachers need more control over the decisions that affect their daily lives.

In the move to involve teachers in leadership roles in the school and district (see Fay, 1990; Firestone and Bader, 1991; Lieberman, Saxl and Miles, 1988; Peterson and Cooke, 1983; Wagner, 1986; and others), we must pay close attention to our process. From a power-over mindset, this would involve moving teachers up in a hierarchy so that they have power over other teachers. From a power-to/power-with mindset, it would involve teachers (and all educators) in collaboration, facilitation and mentoring in a mutually empowering community.

For instance, collaboration would mean working *with* colleagues on projects the group feels are important. It might mean planning teaching activities or curriculum or making important policy decisions. It might include seeking out resources or organizing information. It would definitely involve sharing one's feelings and opinions and listening to the feelings and opinions of others in the attempt to arrive at a collaborative product with which everyone feels comfortable. Dialogic journals in which participants respond to each others' reflections are an excellent way to facilitate this process (Robbins and Brown, 1991).

As facilitators in the school community, teachers would work toward the full realization of their colleagues' goals and abilities. They would also encourage the full participation of parents and others in the community. They would attempt to support parents, teachers and administrators as they worked through their own process of change. They would work to guard the autonomy of individuals within the collective group effort. They would encourage their colleagues to experiment, to grow, to feel free to fail. In short, teacher/leaders with a power-to/power-with mindset would put their energies into supporting the development of a truly synergistic community of co-agency and collaboration. And, again, these activities need not be limited to teachers.

Finally, as mentors, all educators can feel free to acknowledge that that they have something important to offer. We might make presentations to our colleagues on topics in which we have a special interest. We might agree to becoming an "expert" in an area of interest to us in order to help with the group effort. We can share our knowledge and experience in an attitude of caring based on empathy for others and a sincere desire to contribute to their growth.

Those of us who have been socialized as women have learned all too well how to subordinate our needs to those of the group. This is *not* what collaboration, facilitating and mentoring are all about. They are about asserting our own beliefs and needs in the context of a community in which others are free to do the same. They imply a self-respect and a caring for the self within the context of the group. When we truly care for others, we do it because it feels like a fulfilling expression of our true selves, not because we wish to appear cooperative. Caring, collaboration, facilitating and mentoring must be self-affirming, not self-denying. They must be grounded in a critical understanding of the workings of power in our schools as well as in a commitment to the empowerment of self and other.

For we are beginning to recognize again that teaching is a fundamentally moral enterprise. How we treat children who are different, how we deal with antisocial behavior, and how we decide what is to be taught are all essentially moral decisions. As moral agents, teachers must have enough control of their teaching to ensure that they cannot be forced to act against the interests of their students (see Sprague, 1992). To do so would go against the realization of their basic humanity. Similarly, all educators must also participate in the moral deliberations of the school and community (see Maxcy and Caldas, 1991).

Connecting School and Community

Moreover, as the one caring about our students, our caring must extend outside the boundaries of the classroom and school. Our students are deeply affected by the larger community in which they live. So what is the educator's role in the community in which the students live? This can be very problematic for the teacher or administrator who lives in a radically different community from the one in which he or she works.

I was vividly struck by this dilemma last night when watching Oprah Winfrey's presentation of *There Are No Children Here* (Kotlewicz, 1991). This is a book written by a journalist about the lives of two poor black boys growing up in the "projects" in Chicago. It is a story of pervasive violence and oppression experienced at an early age. One of the boys' teachers, as portrayed in the movie, was white and clearly did not live in the "projects" with the boys. When there was a shooting in the schoolyard and one of the students is shot, she helps with the rescue effort, but, then, one clearly has the impression that she returns to her suburban or gentrified home.

And why shouldn't she? Must she live the lives of misery shared by these boys in order to help them? I think not. I wish her a safe and clean home. But I believe that she had a responsiblity to work for the improvement of the community. How could she live with the daily reality of their lives without wishing to change it? To do so would be to deny herself as the one caring. But how could she find the time and strength to make a difference? Is not her work already so intensified that she has time for little else?

I do not know the definitive answer to this dilemma. One answer is that she could have brought the community into the classroom, allowing the children to write about their experiences and to investigate issues related to violence and social policy. She could have brought in issues related to gun control and gangs. She could have allowed them to write to the school board, the mayor and others with the power to effect change. She could have brought in successful adults who had come from similar circumstances to give them hope. She could have engaged them in speculation about how their community could organize itself to patrol the streets, to improve relations with the police, to resist drug trafficing, and she could have sought speakers with experience in these efforts. She may or may not have gotten involved in these community organizing efforts herself, but she would have presented herself as one who cares about their lives and their community. In the process, the students would have been involved in reading and writing and learning while also being involved in learning something about how to change their lives.

In response to similar concerns, McCaleb (1994) asked herself the following question: "How can educators create a partnership with parents and young students that will nurture literacy and facilitate participation in the schools while celebrating and validating the home culture and family and community concerns and aspirations?" (p. x). Her answer consisted of a program of co-authorship involving parents and children in writing books about their lives. Through co-authorship, sharing within the family and community increased, voice and personal histories were validated, identity and self-esteem were enhanced, children grew in appreciation and respect for their families and their community, and the teacher came to know those families and that community better.

Instead of deciding on the projects out of context, McCaleb (1994) conducted extensive interviews with parents first. Then she developed several themes for shared book projects that seemed to emerge from the families' concerns. These included telling about the parents' childhood friendships, engaging in a shared building activity (using blocks and other items), writing about families as problem solvers through struggle and change, writing fictional stories with families as protagonists, and responding to a picture integrating aspects of their community. Some of the projects were completed by students and parents at home, but book development sessions were also held at the school at convenient times for parents and children to come and work together. Books were laminated and bound and kept in the classroom library.

In a similar attempt to reach out into the community and respond to its needs, a teacher I interviewed has been working to get parenting classes offered in her school for first-time parents. She sees this naturally evolving into GED and literacy classes for these parents, with the end result of providing children in the school with homes in which their literacy learning is encouraged.

Finally, in the attempt to connect school and community, many districts are initiating procedures for shared decision-making involving students, parents and educators. Structures which allow for the voicing of concerns of all parties on specific issues are being developed. Charter schools responsible to the state but not to local school boards are also one of the latest trends resulting from the desire of parents and teachers to have more autonomy in the development of educational innovations (Wallis, 1994).

Of course, educators need to learn more about reaching out to parents. In New York State, shared school planning is mandated by state policy. While there, I participated briefly as a parent in one school's attempt to involve parents and teachers in developing a schoolwide philosophy and curriculum plan. This was a monumental effort. The school personnel seemed sincere and were quite convincing in their openness to input from parents. However, most of the parents I observed were quite overwhelmed by the task and aware (probably appropriately) of their lack of knowledge and pre-thinking about the numerous difficult issues they were confronting. In spite of early efforts, educationese was running rampant all over the plan. I came away from the experience with a renewed sense of the importance of providing parents with the information they need in order to participate. For instance, how many parents know what the whole language philosophy is? How many are aware of the inequities in most tracking systems? Such information is necessary in order to make informed decisions.

It seems to me that the media could do a better job of informing themselves and the public about educational issues. As educators, we need to reach out to our local media to involve them in reporting to parents about more than test scores and funding decisions. Of course, we can also take more responsibility in keeping parents informed about school issues.

Innovative ways to network teachers and parents are definitely needed. I recently heard a teacher say that when she heard that a parent wanted to speak to her, she expected to be attacked. Over the years, my attempts to become involved in my daughter's education have often been met by passive resistance in various forms. Many parents I know experience parent/teacher conferences as teacher lectures. The parent is expected to listen but not contribute.

In my daughter's current school situation, I do feel that my opinions are respected. Looking back on earlier experiences, I can see that the polarization of parents and teachers was a result of poor communication and feelings of surplus powerlessness in both of these groups. Change will require a focus on mutual empowerment, mutual respect, authentic sharing and co-agency. Parents who have been alienated from schooling will need to feel that their opinions will count and that their culture is respected in the school. Teachers need to feel that parents understand the difficulties they face.

Activity 4.7
CONNECTING THE SCHOOL AND COMMUNITY

Try brainstorming on the following questions . . .

1. What activities in your class or your school could help the students get involved in their communities? Interviews? Reports? Community service? Others?

2. What resources and people in the community could be brought in to enrich your program? artists? writers? elderly? others? representatives of different cultures?

3. How could parents be made more comfortable with participating in their child's education? (What are the barriers? scheduling? cultural differences? How can they be overcome?)

4. How much do you know about the community and its component cultures? How can you learn more?

5. How could parents and other community members be kept better informed about your school?

Summary

As I said at the outset, this chapter has not been an exhaustive description of what an empowering eduation might be like. Such a complete description is beyond the scope of this book and would undermine its basic premise—that each educator must decide this for him/herself. What I have attempted to do is to outline some of the more immediate implications of basing our educational process on a power-to/power-with paradigm. My purpose is to shift the terms of the debate to notions of power and its role in the educational process itself.

With that in mind, I have suggested that we stop objectifying students. This would result in accepting their diversity, involving them in the learning process, sharing authority with them, replacing passive lecture methods with participatory ones, teaching mutual respect, engaging students in self-evaluation and goal-setting, and encouraging all of the processes of knowing that make us human. Dialogue would be used to develop students' authentic voices, and silences about real conditions would be avoided. At every step of the way, parents need to be kept informed about the rationale for these changes.

I have also suggested that the metaphors we use exert a powerful influence on the teaching/learning process. The machine metaphor legitimates the objectification of students and an exclusive emphasis on the products students produce. Dance and organism are metaphors that can return subjectivity and process to their place as important dimensions of the educational enterprise.

Moreover, in the education of fully human subjects, it is possible to see caring as the central ideal. Schools can be organized as caring communities in which teachers can be responsive to students' needs in the present moment so that students can perceive teachers as caregivers rather than oppressors.

The educator in such a caring community would be a collaborator, facilitator and mentor in the classroom, school and/or district. He or she would extend caring to the community by validating community concerns in classroom activities, involving parents and community members in decision-making, and/or getting involved in community empowerment.

C H A P T E R   F I V E

Knowledge as Power

So what does an empowering educational system look like? In chapter 4 I suggested that it is one in which students are subjects rather than objects and participate in the planning and evaluation of their own education. Educators relate to students as the one caring in a relationship of mutual respect. Classrooms center on dialogue and the development of student voice. As part of various communities of learners, educators act as collaborators, facilitators and mentors. Control over the process of education is shared among students, teachers, administrators and community members.

Now it is time to look at the content of this empowering educational process. What should students learn? Since this is not a book on curriculum theory, I am not going to discuss all the possible alternatives that have been suggested. Rather, I would like to again focus on the shift from power-over to power-to/power-with in terms of how such a mindset might bring in content that has been previously shut out of the educational process. As in the last chapter, these speculations are meant to stimulate discussion rather than to answer this question definitively. It is up to teachers and students, in collaboration with others in the school and community, to decide on the content that would be most empowering for them.

Power/Knowledge

One of the primary things obscured in our current presentation of school knowledge is the relationship between knowledge and power. If we examine the history of knowledge, we can see that what counts as knowledge at any historical moment is a product of who is in power and what knowledge fits with the dominant value system. (Indeed, Foucault [1980] has suggested that power and knowledge are so constantly connected that it is more accurate to use the term power/knowledge.) Just look at the common "knowledge" about Native Americans and how it has changed in the last twenty years to see how this works. As mainstream American appreciation of the environment has increased, so has respect for Native American culture.

Knowledge is socially constructed at a given historical moment within a given context. I often think of the ninteenth-century diagnosis of "hysterical" for women who were not happy in traditional female roles. This was thought to be a scientific and verifiable decision, but it actually reflected a deep social prejudice. Loewen (1995), in a book aptly entitled *Lies My Teacher Told Me*, has provided numerous examples of omissions and distortions found in typical history texts. These seem to be a result of the need to perpetuate myths that support the ideology of the dominant culture. For instance, racism is mentioned rarely in history texts, except as it connects to slavery. Helen Keller is presented only as a handicapped person, yet she lived her life as a radical socialist, and so on.

Unfortunately, many educators see knowledge as something that is static and neutral. Suggestions such as those of E. D. Hirsch (1987) who gives us a list of what every educated person in our society should know, in his opinion, perpetuate the standard of bias in favor of the knowledge of white Western-educated men. Hirsch suggests that this is the knowledge of those in power and, therefore, anyone wishing to move up in society must know it. What a wonderful legitimation of domination: We must all assimilate into the dominant culture because that is the only way we will gain access to power!

The reality is, of course, that Hirsch is somewhat right. We cannot remain so completely immersed in nondominant cultures that we do not know how to function in the spheres of power that operate in our public institutions. Students do need to be able to use standard English, literacy, and so on in ways that will gain them access to resources and jobs. But they also need to understand how certain forms of knowledge serve others and how they can create knowledge that will serve them (see Banks, 1991).

Empowering knowledge begins where the students are and engages them in constructing knowledge that is useful to them. Knowledge is empowering only when the learner can see how to apply it. "Apart from the knower, knowledge has no intrinsic power; in interaction with the knower's desires and purposes, knowledge has meaning and power" (Sleeter and Grant, 1991, 50). Students must be able to connect their lives to the knowledge presented in school; they fail if they cannot (Cummins, 1986).

Unfortunately, in a study of an urban desegregated junior high school, interviews with twenty-eight students selected to represent the range of achievement and ethnicity in the school revealed that "the great majority of the students inteviewed considered most or all of what the school was teaching them to be unrelated to their lives" (Sleeter and Grant, 1991, 62). I believe that this would be a common finding if this study were conducted across the country in a variety of communities. But must this be so?

Unfortunately, most of the knowledge taught currently is "reified knowledge" which "while abstract, tenuous and problematic, is treated as if it is concrete and real" (Everhart, 1983, 86). Reified knowledge is knowledge that was created in a lived context but has become static, institutionalized, and empty of real meaning in the current situation. I think immediately of the "knowledge" that Columbus "discovered" America, yet we know that thousands of Americans in numerous complex cultures already lived here.

In contrast, empowering knowledge is the knowledge that grows out of everyday life, out of how students experience themselves and their communities and the larger society in which their communities are embedded. Empowering knowledge is alive, honest, socially constructed and culturally relevant. Observation of racism in the school and community can lead to discussions of slavery which can lead to the discovery that Columbus was not particularly humane with the native peoples he sought to enslave. Students can study the constitution in terms of how it is and is not enforced in their community. Then they can look at other communities and constitutions. They can study the plants and animals in their environment and/or in their diet before addressing issues of ecology and worldwide starvation. They can compare characters in literature to themselves and to the people they know before applying this understanding of human nature to the analysis of world events. Knowledge in schools can be grounded in students' lives, linked to the relationships of power that legitimize or deligitimize it, and constructed in ways that empower the learners to understand themselves and their world.

Critical Pedagogy

Critical pedagogy is a term that has been used to describe a form of teaching that makes the relationship between knowledge and power explicit. It engages students in analyzing the conditions of their lives in terms of the way they are historicallly created (see Darder, 1991; McLaren, 1989; and others). Its fundamental goal is to give students the knowledge they need to transform their own lives and the lives of others in the interest of social justice.

One example of a critical teaching method would be that presented by Shor (1987). He suggests that we can begin with the stuff of the students' everyday lives, a chair or a hamburger, for instance. Then we can ask, "What is it?" and encourage students to describe the object in some detail (observation). Then we can ask, "Whose interests does it serve?," involving the students in social criticism (critique). Finally, we can ask, "How could this object be redesigned to serve my interests better?" (possibility). I would also suggest that students be encouraged to think beyond themselves . . ." If this object were redesigned to meet my needs, would this also be in the best interests of others?" (caring). Another question I would suggest would be something like "How could I influence the conditions of its creation so that it met my needs better? Would this be worth my time?" (action).

Similarly, Shor (1992) has suggested that the curriculum could be arranged around "generative themes" that emerge from the students' own lives, for example, "why are so many students in this school dropping out?" I believe that the stages described above could guide such investigations (observation, critique, possibility, caring, and action). "Topical themes" brought in by the teacher to expand on generative themes, for instance, "how could more jobs be created in our community?," and "academic themes" that reflect the knowledge students are expected to acquire, for example, "What is a market economy and how can it be influenced?" and so on. Students would create generative themes and be free to accept or reject topical themes. Ideally, academic themes would be integrated with the others in such a way as to make them maximally empowering (see Shor, 1992).

Critical theorists also sometimes divide classroom knowledge into three catagories (see Habermas, 1972; McLaren, 1989). Technical knowledge is knowledge that can be measured and quantified. It consists of the basic facts and skills generally currently dominating our educational system. Practical knowledge is geared toward understanding social (and natural) systems historically or through observation. It is about how things and people actually function. Finally, emancipatory knowledge sees how all forms of knowledge are influenced by relations of power-over. It would also include the knowledge of how power-over relations can be modified to end oppressive situations. Critical educators would have us teach all three of these types of knowledge in the interest of em-powering students to improve their own lives and the lives of others.

For instance, students could study media at all of these levels. Tech-nically, they could learn how to plan and tape videos for the school broadcast system. In the process of doing their own shows, they could learn about advertising and ratings pressures and how these control the shows they see at home. Finally, they could look at whose interests con-trol the media and how these are evidenced in the programs they see. They can critically examine the values being promoted. They can look for ways to have an influence over the media in their community in ways that benefit the entire community.

This brings me to the issue of social justice. Surveys indicate that this is a concern that seems to come quite naturally to kids. From a very early age, they are quite interested in things being "fair." As adolescents, students become even more concerned about problems like war, homelessness, pollution and poverty. If they are not supported in dealing with their frustration about these problems (which they often blame on adult society), they can react wtih "despair, hopelessness, meaningless-ness, fear, anger, rage and guilt that they cannot do or are not doing more" (Whitmore, 1986, 154). Whitmore suggests that if we work with adolescents on their valid social concerns, we can avoid much of the self-destructiveness that we see in today's youth. Suggestions for helping kids work with social justice issues have been given by Banks (1991), Pang (1991) and others.

I should note here that I am assuming that environmental issues are also social justice issues. Clearly, if some lack clean air and water, or if half the planet drowns from global warming, this is certainly an issue of social justice! Moreover, ecological problems are inextricably linked to other economic and social concerns, most especially the workings of power-over. As has been previously noted, domination of nature is prob-ably not separate from other forms of domination. An examination of the interdependence of natural systems can be connected with a similar study of social systems and global connections.

It seems to me that all this is also about teaching students to care, creating the caring communities that I discussed in chapter 4. If students are actively taught to care about themselves and others, this should extend into the curriculum. Opportunities to express caring by transforming oppressive or dangerous situations observed in the study of the self or society can be provided. Then students will learn the technical and practical skills required by these emancipatory activities in a meaningful context.

A simple example comes to my mind related to me by one of the teachers in the study reported in chapter 9. As I remember it, her second-grade students became very concerned about some trees on their playground that were going to be cut down. They wrote letters and investigated the issue until their feelings were known by the town agency involved. As it turned out, the trees had to be remeeoved for valid environmental reasons, but new trees were planted somewhere else as a result of the students' efforts. In the process, students learned about city government, letter writing and their potential power in a democracy. One might imagine that the students could extend this experience into a study of the rainforest and possible involvement with the efforts to save it. In response to those who see such activities as too "political" for school, I would suggest that denying children the opportunity to engage in such activities is a political decision as well, one that teaches a political passivity not appropriate in a democracy.

Indeed, this sort of progression, from identifying a problem in one's own life, to seeing how it affects one's community, to seeing it as part of a national or global problem is a natural extension of caring. Too often, unthinkingly, we allow our students to stop their analysis within the narrow confines of their own race, class and gender identifications. Such an analysis will rarely provide information about transforming the society in a meaningful way. Students can be guided to the realization that we are an interconnected community on the planet. Empowerment and caring require that we care about the rights of others as much as about our own. Power-to is not about fighting others for scarce resources; instead it is about seeing that our own fates are bound up with the fates of others and that mutual empowerment and power-with is not only possible but necessary.

Direct teaching of community participation skills can help students learn to exercise power-to/power-with rather than power-over. Last year I spent a day observing in a small private progressive school in upstate New York. I noticed that several of the teachers had lists on their boards like

"Words of Peace," "Signs of Praise" and "Encouraging Words." The classes had brainstormed the words on the lists. One class was working on the "Rules for Fighting Fair" developed by the Graves, Contino, Abrams Peace Education Foundation in Miami, Florida. These included things like "We attack the problem, not the person." and "We care about each other's feelings." Such direct teaching of community participation skills can be extended into the larger community and the world. (A seventh-grade student who had just transferred into this school told me that she was very happy here because "in the public school there is more hate.")

Finally, Freire (1973) has spoken of three types of thinking in relation to teaching about social justice. First, intransitive consciousneess is the belief that human beings can't really change things. Semi-transitive consciousness is believing that things can be changed, with each thing being an isolated case. Finally, critical transitive consciousness sees the connections between the personal experience and the larger social structures and relates individual problems of social injustice to their historical context, their interconnections with other problems, and the possiblities for change.

I see these levels of consciousness in my students all the time. One group gets very angry with me for bringing up issues of social justice because "it's just the way it is and it will never change." Another group gets very excited and picks one issue to think about all semester. A third group increasingly looks for connections between small actions and larger issues and generally responds in classroom discussions in terms of connections between the current topic and other topics we have discussed.

Activity 5.1
CIRCLES OF CARING

Think of several forms of social outrage typicallly expressed by students you know. List them below. Don't worry if they seem excessively self-centered.

Now, think about how each of these problems is actually a small part of a larger concern, involving many more people. Then think about how that concern is actually about another social issue, involving more people and so on. Create concentric circles of caring to show what might be discussed as the students' understanding of their own concerns deepens. I have provided one example.

Multicultural Perspectives

If an empowering curriculum includes students' natural concerns for social justice and community empowerment, then this curriculum will also be proactively multicultural. Unfortunately, multicultural education as currently implemented in many schools is not synonymous with a concern for social justice. Much of what passes for multicultural education just teaches superficial aspects of various cultures without looking at all honestly at the inequities afforded to members of those cultures.

To the extent that it remains education to help students get along or to help them feel better about themselves or to "sensitize" them to one another, without tackling the central but far more difficult issues of stratification, empowerment, and inequity, multicultural education becomes another approach that simply scratches the surface of educational failure. (Nieto, 1992, 1)

Nieto (1992) has suggested that multicultural education must begin with the students' own experiences, and be proactively antiracist and antidiscriminatory, pervasive, affirming and seen as necessary for all students. Let's look at each of these characteristics to see whether or not they are common in multicultural curricula today.

Ideally, multicultural curricula begin with the students' own experiences in order to affirm their voices and experiences as valid and important. This would include experiences unique to their cultural background as well as concerns unique to their age and developmental level. It would include being honest about the effects of poverty, divorce, prejudice and other issues evidenced in their immediate lives. Fine (1991) and others have shown that such realities are often silenced, perhaps most especially in those schools where these problems are rampant.

Second, a multicultural classroom is proactively antiracist and antidiscriminatory. In this classroom, students would talk about experiences of prejudice in their own lives and examine the operation of racisim and sexism in their classroom and school as well as in the larger society. Literature and history would be read with as awareness of bias and culturally different access to resources. Too often teachers ignore issues of racism because they fear that it will make students angry or emotional. This sort of "fear of naming" (Fine, 1991) just serves to alienate students and undermine the empowering potential of schooling.

Similarly, schools that are proactively antiracist and antidiscriminatory carefully select materials that represent all cultural groups and both genders fairly and teach all ethnic groups similarly. (Research indicates that white teachers may have more frequent eye contact with white as opposed to other students, for instance [McDermott, 1977].) This is not as easy as it sounds. It would require careful vigilance by groups of teachers working together to constantly evaluate and reevaluate the messages being sent in materials and classroom interactions. It would require the reeducation of teachers to help them understand the cultures of their students as well as cultures not represented in their schools. Only then could teachers examine their own unconscious discriminatory behaviors. (One excellent discussion of two specific cultural styles that sometimes show up in classrooms can be found in Kochman, 1981.)

Of course, being antidiscriminatory includes being antisexist. In schools where relations among faculty mirror the sexism of the society, communication of nonsexist ideals will be futile (see Weis, 1991). Schools must commit themselves to nonsexist policies at all levels. Moreover, explicit talk with girls about issues such as conflicting feelings about success and media images of beauty have been shown to affect girls' self-confidence (Bell, 1991). Classroom practices in which boys talk more and interrupt girls can be discussed openly in classrooms so that the children can learn to be sensitive to its occurrence and to make proactive decisions to end it.

A related area that is rarely discussed is discrimination based on sexual preference. This is connected to sexism and the enforcement of gender roles—girls are expected to be feminine and boys masculine. A critical examination of the insidious nature of these gender roles might lead to a discussion of homophobia. Though I realize that many parents do not want the schools discussing homosexuality (some say that this is the last acceptable prejudice), the civil rights issues involved are coming up on ballots around the country. Complete silence on the issue reinforces discrimination and further silences gay and lesbian students.

For to be truly effective, antidiscriminatoroy multicultural education must be pervasive. This means that

> It permeates the physical environment in the classroom, the curriculum, and the relationships among teachers and students and community. It can be seen in every lesson, curriculum guide, unit bulletin board, and letter that is sent home; it can be seen in the process by which books and audiovisual aids are acquired for the library, the games played during recess, and the lunch that is served. (Nieto, 1991, 215)

Schools in which multicultural awareness is pervasive take a careful look at tracking, work hard to acquire a multicultural faculty, and involve the community in developing the multicultural curriculum that treats all groups as worthy of repect. There would be no subject or space that would be unaffected by such pluralism.

Multicultural education can go beyond acceptance to affirmation. Nieto (1992) has provided a wonderful description of this difference in table 5.1, on the following pages.

As shown in table 5.1, multicultural programs can really be arranged on a continuum from those that only tolerate differences to those that accept them, to those that respect them, to those that affirm them. To me, the last level seems like the most complete experience of the power-to/power-with paradigm. Most schools are probably somewhere in the middle of this continuum, hopefully striving to move to the next level.

In a wonderful example of multicultural community-building, Christensen (1994) describes a classroom in which she created a "curriculum of empathy":

> To become a community, students must learn to live in someone else's skin, understand the parallels of hurt, struggle and joy across class and culture lines, and work for change. For that to happen, students need more than an upbeat supportive teacher; they need a curriculum that teaches them how to empathize with others. (p. 14)

Christensen discovered that violence was an issue that aroused all her students regardless of their background. Using discussion of gangs to ground her selection of literature and writing activities, she encouraged students to make connections to their lives and to share those connections. As they began to see that their own experiences of isolation and fear were echoed in the experiences of students and peoples of other cultures, they changed: As one student said, "I started respecting my peers. My attitude has changed against homosexuals and whites." Another student wrote, "I learned a lot about my own culture as an African American but also about other people's cultures. I never knew Asians suffered." Truly, this is a curriculum that teaches caring.

Orenstein (1994) has presented an excellent example of an anti-gender bias curriculum in the gifted and talented education classroom of Judy Logan in San Francisco's Everett Middle School. As part of their study of African-American history, students in her class produce and present monologues by prominent African-Americans (past or present). Each student must do both a man and a woman. "To ask a group of boys, most of whom are White, to take on the personae—to actually become—black women forces an unprecedented shift in their mindset"

Table 5.1. Levels of Multicultural Education

Monocultural Education	Characteristics of Multicultural Education	Tolerance
Racism is unacknowledged. Policies and practices that support discrimination are left in place. These include low expectations and refusal to use students' natural resources (such as language and culture) in instruction. Only a sanitized and "safe" curriculum is in place.	Antiracist/antidiscriminatory	Policies and practices that challenge racism and discrimination are initiated. No overt signs of discrimination are acceptable (name-calling, graffiti, blatantly racist and sexist textbooks or curriculum, etc.). ESL programs are in place for students who speak other languages.
Defines the education as the 3R's and the "canon." "Cultural literacy" is understood within a monocultural framework. All important knowledge is essentially European-American. This Eurocentric view is reflected throughout the curriculum, instructional strategies, and environment for learning.	Basic	Education is defined more expansively and includes attention to some important information about other groups.
No attention is paid to student diversity.	Pervasive	A multicultural perspective is evident in some activities, such as Black History Month and Cinco de Mayo, and in some curriculum and materials. There may be an itinerant "multicultural teacher."
Ethnic and/or women's studies, if available, are only for students from that group. This is a frill that is not important for other students to know.	Important for all students	Ethnic and women's studies are only offered as isolated courses.
Education supports the status quo. Thinking and acting are separate.	Education for social justice	Education is somewhat, although tenuously, linked to community projects and activities.
Education is primarily content: who, what, where, when. The "great white men" version of history is propagated. Education is static.	Process	Education is both content and process. "Why" and "how" questions are tentatively broached.
Education is domesticating. Reality is represented at static, finished, and flat.	Critical pedagogy	Students and teachers begin to change the status quo.

Acceptance	Respect	Affirmation, Solidarity, and Critique
Policies and practices that acknowledge differences are in place. Textbooks reflect some diversity. Transitional bilingual programs are available. Curriculum is more inclusive of the histories and perspectives of a broader range of people.	Policies and practices that respect diversity are more evident, including maintenance bilingual education. Ability grouping is not permitted. Curriculum is more explicitly antiracist and honest. It is "safe" to talk about racism, sexism, and discrimination.	Policies and practices that affirm diversity and challenge racism are developed. There are high expectations for all students; students' language and culture are used in instruction and curriculum. Two-way bilingual programs are in place wherever possible. Everyone takes responsibility for racism and other forms of discrimination.
The diversity of lifestyles and values of groups other than the dominant one are acknowledged in some content, as can be seen in some courses and school activities.	Education is defined as that knowledge that is necessary for living in a complex and pluralistic society. As such, it includes much content that is multicultural. *Additive multiculturalism* is the goal.	Basic education is multicultural education. All students learn to speak a second language and are familiar with a broad range of knowledge.
Student diversity is acknowledged, as can be seen not only in "Holidays and Heroes" but also in consideration of different learning styles, values, and languages. A "multicultural program" may be in place. Many students are expected to take part in curriculum that stresses diversity. A variety of languages is taught.	The learning environment is imbued with multicultural education. It can be seen in classroom interactions, materials, and the subculture of the school.	Multicultural education pervades the curriculum; instructional strategies; and interactions among teachers, students, and the community. It can be seen everywhere: bulletin boards, the lunchroom, assemblies.
The role of the schools in social change is acknowledged. Some changes that reflect this attitude begin to be felt: Students take part in community service.	All students take part in courses that reflect diversity. Teachers are involved in overhauling the curriculum to be more open to such diversity. Students take part in community activities that reflect their social concerns.	All courses are completely multicultural in essence. The curriculum for all students is enriched. "Marginal students" no longer exist. The curriculum and instructional techniques are based on an understanding of social justice as central to education. Reflection and action are important components of learning.
Education is both content and process. "Why" and "how" questions are stressed more. Sensitivity and understanding of teachers toward their students are more evident.	Education is both content and process. Students and teachers begin to ask "What if?" Teachers empathize with students and their families.	Education is an equal mix of content and process. It is dynamic. Teachers and students are empowered. Everyone in the school is becoming a multicultural person.
Students and teachers are beginning a dialogue. Students' experiences, cultures, and languages are used as one source of their learning.	Students and teachers use critical dialogue as the primary basis for their education. The see and understand different perspectives.	Students and teachers are involved in a "subversive activity." Decision-making and social action are the basis of the curriculum.

Source: Nieto, S. (1992) Affirming Diversity: The Sociopolitical Context of Multicultural Education. White Plains, NY: Longman, 280–281.

(p. 249). Though there are problems with silliness at first, the teacher deals with these directly and all the students gain insights into the workings of prejudice and begin to learn to empathize with someone from another culture.

Activity 5.2
EXAMINING YOUR MULTICULTURAL PROGRAM

Study the information provided in table 5.1. As you do so, put a check next to the characteristics that describe your classroom and/or school. What level do they mostly fall into? Is this where you want to be? What can you do to move your classroom or school to the level at which you wish to be? List at least three things that you can do immediately and three things that you could involve others in doing over time.

IMMEDIATELY:
1.
2.
3.
Other:

OVER TIME:
1.
2.
3.
Other?

Finally, how do you deal with gender bias in your school or classroom . . . ? How do you deal with sexual harassment?

How do you deal with homophobic name-calling?

How do you deal with the ways teachers teach boys and girls differently?

How do you deal with gender discrimination in the curriculum?

Would you characterize your antidiscriminatory program in regard to gender as
experiential?
proactive?
pervasive?
affirming?
necessary for both genders?

If we are to move to a more inclusive society, then nonsexist multicultural education will be about mutual accommodation. Students of both the dominant and the nondominant cultural groups and students of both genders grow from learning to accommodate the needs and styles of the other groups. This is not just necessary for the "minority" kids. All students need to learn to live in a multicultural democracy. In one two-way bilingual program (English-speaking students learned Spanish and Spanish-speaking children learned English), the two-year evaluation found that it was the English-speaking children and their families who were the most affected. They were sensitized to the difficulties of functioning in a second language and proud of their ability to function effectively in the other culture (Nieto, 1992, 257). Similarly, in a classroom discussion on sexual harassment, Orenstein (1993) observed that it was the boys whose eyes were opened to the meaning of their own behaviors: "You hear all the girls talk at once and you realize it's kind of a big deal," said one boy (p. 264).

Finally, in order to become antidiscriminatory multicultural teachers, we must become nonsexist multicultural persons. This is a lifelong process of learning by listening, asking and being open to others' perspectives. It requires that we admit to our unconscious biases and to the unwitting mistakes that we have made. There are many pitfalls into which we can easily fall if we are not constantly aware, and it would be unrealistic to pretend that we can be prefectly aware of all cultures at all times.

Activity 5.3
IMAGINING AN IDEAL NONSEXIST MULTICULTURAL PROGRAM

Now, close your eyes and picture your classroom permeated by multiculturalism, antiracism and antisexism. Look at the walls and bulletin boards. What do you see? What are the students studying? What are they saying in their discussion? What are you saying? Take time to let this happen in your mind. Make some notes about what you are seeing or make a sketch.

Now, the class has ended. You walk down the hall to the teacher's lounge. Your entire school is permeated by a commitment to multiculturalism and antidiscrimination. What sorts of things do you see in the school that reflects this? Record you vision here in some way.

When you get to the lounge, listen to the talk of the other teachers. You are struck by how much good antidiscrimination work is being done in your school. What do the other teachers have to say?

In thinking abut how you can make this vision a reality, you may wish to answer the following questions:
1. Who would be willing to work with you on this? _____
_____
2. Where else would your support be in the school? _____
_____
3. Where else would your support be outside the school?_____
_____
4. How could you get all these people involved in this program of change? _____
_____
5. What is the best way to start? _____
_____

Healing the Mind/Body Split

It is also important to remember that when we are dealing with cultural differences, we are really looking at lived experiences, feelings and sensations. It is impossible to contain a true liberatory pedagogy that is aggressively multicultural within a straightjacket of rationality. The old paradigm of power-over emphasized a mind/body split, possibly because one has to cut oneself off from one's body and its feelings in order to accept situations of oppression. Schools were there to educate minds that were expected to be objective, that is, unemotional. The life of the body, including sensations, comfort and emotions, had little to do with it. Those needs were relegated to the home, to the private sphere. Thus, the mind/body split is accompanied by a public/private split, both of which have been criticized by feminists because women have been relegated to the body/private side of these dichotomies, thus isolating them from access to power in the public sphere.

In an educational system based on a power-to/power-with paradigm, the mind and body and the public and the private would be reconnected in the domain of knowledge (see also Maher, 1987). Knowledge would not always be seen as "objective," especially since, as discussed in chapter 2, it always involves some level of subjectivity. Students would be allowed to draw on their feelings and their private lives in the construction of public knowledge.

Psychologists have talked about the various psychological functions through which we know our world. This include things like thinking, feeling, imagining, sensing, intuiting and wanting (Assagioli, 1976), as discussed in the last chapter. We can teach children about these functions, about what they can do for them, and about how to work with them. For instance, Noddings and Shor (1984) suggest that students be taught about the intuitive mode of thinking; they can be helped to understand that it demands receptivity, commitment, familiarity and concrete engagement with the subject at hand.

Heretofore, these nonrational modes of thinking have been thought of as private, but it is entirely possible to imagine bringing them into the public sphere. Students can talk about where great artists, scientists, and explorers got their inspiration. They can read accounts of discoveries that show the role of imagination, intuition and impulse. They can read biographies and discuss the importance of the psycholoogical functions in the lives of people they admire. They can be asked where they get their ideas and guided to see the role that feeling, sensing, intuiting and imagining play in their learning and knowing and in the learning and knowing of their peers. As Steven Gallegos has said, "If the thinking mode were appropriately educated, it would also contain an understanding of its own limitations" (Gallegos, 1991, 10).

Moreover, the students' personal lives, including the experiences of their families and their friends, can be included in the "content" as important information. The connection between their lives and the larger issues studied can be made. Examples include the connection between their parents' unemployment and the changing economy, the connection between available low-cost imports and the exploitation of Third World workers, and the connection between racism in their own lives and historical and current holocausts around the world. This connection between the personal and the political seems essential for true empowerment and can be made in terms of all the psychological functions. Indeed, bringing in the relevance of students' lives greatly enhances their ability to use feeling, sensing and imagining to aid in their thinking.

Finally, spirituality and creativity are human experiences with which our current educational system has a very difficult time. This is intimately connected to the mind/body split. Since these experiences are not "rational," they have had no comfortable place in an educational system that focuses only on mind.

Of course, by spirituality, I do not mean religion. The separation of church and state provided in our constitution is an important protection of civil rights. Instead, I am talking about things like feelings of life purpose, awe, wonder, mystery, compassion, oneness and connection, delight in beauty and creative inspiration. (See Gang, Lynn and Maver, 1992, for a discussion of "transpersonal learning.") Whitmore (1986) suggests that children and adolescents have these sorts of experiences much more than we think.

Maslow (1968) calls these peak experiences. They are the moments in which we experience a profound sense of meaning, of deep joy and connection. They can occur through a whole variety of human experiences . . . experiences with nature, with loved ones, or even with the realization of the significance of small everyday events. Maslow believed that these were univeral experiences and found that they were often described with the same words: truth, beauty, wholeness, simplicity, effortlessness, playfulness and self-sufficiency. He also believed that these experiences were as important to our development as our obvious biological needs.

Oliver and Gershman (1989) speak of this as "ontological knowing" which they contrast with "technical knowing." Whereas technical knowing involves analysis and definition and a separation of the knower from the known, ontological knowing involves direct experience of the totality of events and their connection to a greater whole. Whereas technical knowing is usually expressed in "analytic/linear explicit language" (p. 15), ontological knowing is often expressed "through mystical experience, metaphor, poetry, drama, liturgy, dreams or music" (p. 15). An empowering education would have room for both.

A sense of beauty and sense of wonder and reverence for all life can be encouraged in classrooms. We can include aesthetic experiences in our curriculum; experiences of great art for the sake of the experience rather than for the sake of learning information, and aesthetic experiences of nature to balance scientific ones. Poetry, dance, music and painting can inspire peak experiences and ontological knowing. Drama can integrate art, movement, music, voice, myth and symbolic meaning-making.

For creativity is often the way that humans express these peak experiences of connection and clarity. Though much has been written elsewhere on the subject of creativity in education, I would be remiss not to at least mention it here. Creativity is central to what makes us human, what makes our lives fulfilling, and what connects us to ourselves and to others, yet opportunities to be creative are missing from many children's school experience. Creativity is not just something for art, music and poetry class; every subject allows for student creativity in the posing and solving of problems, the analysis of novel situations, the selection of materials and ideas to create a new product, and the exploration of their personal reactions to the content. Brainstorming, doodling, visualizing and free association are activities that can help students tap into their creative process (see Rowe, 1994a, b).

Like the nonrational psychological functions and ontological knowing, creativity is difficult to schedule, measure and grade. In a system based on competition and "objective" assessment, this poses a problem. Thus, we are faced again with the reality that the pieces of an empowering pedagogy cannot be implemented in isolation. An empowering educational process requires an empowering curriculum which also requires an empowering assessment philosophy (see chapter 4) and so on. Thus, all of the suggestions made in this chapter really assume that the suggestions made in earlier chapters will be connected to them!

Making Knowledge Whole

Finally, there is a way in which this entire chapter is about making knowledge whole, authentic and empowering. When we reconnect knowledge with power and culture and body and mind and public and private and mystery and awe and wonder and beauty, what will happen? I suspect that we will find that new questions are being asked, that students are engaged in new ways. *Big* questions like, what makes me happy? Why am I here? What can I do for my community? What should society be like? How are people alike and different? How can we best get along with one another? Why are so many people so unhappy? How do developments in science affect history and literature? What is the significance of pop culture? What is the significance of my life? What is the connection between the personal and the political in my life? How can I learn to accept death and change? What do I really value?

These are all the kinds of questions that we carefully eschew in our present educational system. We are afraid they are too emotional, personal, that kids will become too engaged, that sensitive issues related to personal religion will surface, that sensitive issues related to love and life and sexuality will surface, that someone will ask us for the answers. They fly in the face of our present bias toward rationality, compartmentalization, technology and objective measurement. But how can we justify denying our children the right to freely explore those things that give their lives meaning?

For knowledge that is meaningful is alive and honest. It is not reified and static and it is not dull. Kozol (1985) has talked about how historically significant men and women studied in school are "tailored" to make them safe. Their passion, their spirit, their courage, their revolutionary zeal, their complexity, including their faults, are covered by "incredibly dull stories" about them. Kohl (1995) describes one such example in a children's book on Rosa Parks. The book says she was a seamstress but neglects to mention her involvement in NAACP. The book suggests that Mrs. Parks did not move to the back of the bus because she was tired, rather than because she was indignant about segregation. The book suggests that the boycott that followed resulted directly from this action, yet the African-American community had been planning it for several years. Mrs. Parks is labelled as stubborn rather than courageous, and so on.

I have seen the same thing done to characters in literature; students are asked to memorize definitions of literary terms and examples in the novel rather than to respond to the very real passion and the very real prejudices expressed by the author. Knowledge that is alive is complex and ambiguous and open-ended. It is historically and culturally located and it empowers the learner.

In such a context, it is quite possible that the academic subjects as we know them will disappear. It is impossible to keep knowledge alive and honest and open-ended and also bounded into artificial catergories called disciplines. In a wonderful study of the rise of geography as a discipline, Goodson and Dowbiggin (1991) have demonstrated how, in response to pressures for funding and legitimacy, its scope and definition mimicked that at the university. To gain access to resources and credibility, school subjects attach themselves to university academic disciplines. As a result, the content is determined more by the narrow career interests of academics than by the needs of students in the schools.

If we want to restore students to their natural curiosity, we will help them to look for the valuable connections between history, science, math, art, music, sports and literature rather than obscure them. The current trend toward interdisciplinary units may provide a beginning structure for finding these connections. If implemented with an understanding of the purpose of reconnecting knowledge, if students participate in planning the direction of such units, and if connections are made to the students' immediate lives, then these units can provide a setting for making knowledge whole.

Activity 5.4
ASKING IMPORTANT (BIG) QUESTIONS

Think about a *big* question that you would like to answer about your life. It may be one of the ones listed above or it may be another that is on your mind. Write it here.

Think about that question for a minute and then let a picture of the answer come into your mind. It may be a symbol, a person, a word, an object or anything else. Draw it here.

Now, think about that symbol or drawing. What information does it give you about the answer to your question?

Now, think about all that you learned in school and in life. What has had relevance for that question? What has not?

Summary

So how can the knowledge that we presently teach in school be made more empowering? What happens to knowledge when it is based on a power-to/power-with philosophy? Knowledge that is empowering is openly embedded in the power relations that created it. It is situated in a historical and cultural context and is therefore not viewed as immutable or absolute. Social reality is seen as changeable, and multiple cultures are invited to participate in that change process. The students' immediate experience is used to understand the larger community and world. Multicultural perspectives are pervasive and explicitly antidiscriminatory. Students are allowed to follow their natural impulses toward social justice.

And this is not purely a rational process. Students are taught about all the ways that they construct their reality, including feeling, thinking, intuiting, imagining, sensing and wanting. Their own lives are valued as important content with important connections to the subjects being studied in school. Spiritual feelings like feelings of oneness and reverence for life are accepted, not as they relate to specific religions, but as natural parts of human experience. Students are encouraged to be creative and to ask important questions about the meaning and purpose of their own lives. Content is alive, honest, complex and open-ended. The connections between subjects are as important as the divisions, and knowledge is presented as whole and fluid and open to analysis and construction from multiple points of view.

CHAPTER SIX

Literacy as Power

Education can be a process in which decisions about learning are shared among teachers, students, parents, administrators and interested community members. It can focus on empowering knowledge that builds on the real lives of students and facilitates ever deeper levels of caring and personal and social awareness. Perhaps the one area of the curriculum in which these ideas can be most clearly embodied or disembodied is literacy.

In this chapter, I would like to look at the various ways that we define literacy and how these definitions of literacy affect instruction. Recent developments in instructional methodology do put some control in the hands of students and teachers, but it is my belief that these methods could go even further in empowering students and teachers to take control of their lives.

Defining Literacy

What is literacy? The most common definition would be that it is the ability to read and write. On its face, this looks like a harmless enough definition. The problem with it, however, is that it obscures the important connection between literacy and power.

There are at least three popular misconceptions about literacy that contribute to this (Lankshear, 1987). First, people believe that it is a unitary trait that you have or don't have. Actually, it involves a variety of abilities that one can master at a variety of levels. One can be good at reading words but unable to understand complex meanings. One can be good at filling out forms and unable to write persuasive prose, and so on.

A second misconception is that literacy is independent of the social context. Actually, literacy takes on different forms and different meanings depending on the social context in which it is taking place. Reading the Bible in church is different than reading it for a college course, for instance.

Indeed, students learn different uses for literacy depending on their cultural background (see Heath, 1983; Snow, 1983; and others). This often puts them in a difficult position in school. Children who have been taught not to question authority will need to doubt their culture to become critical readers. Children whose culture values colorful, imaginative language will need to become bicultural to write terse, objective prose. Asking children to adopt certain uses of literacy can be similar to asking them to change cultures.

Finally, the most dangerous misconception, in my opinion, is that literacy is politically neutral, the same for everyone independent of the use to which it is put. The reality is that "literacy is the use to which it is put" (Lankshear, 1987, 49). For some students, the literacy they learn in school is reading and writing to fill out forms and guess predetermined correct answers. For other students, school literacy is reading and writing to draw conclusions and think creatively and critically. These are very different forms of literacy with different political implications. One is empowering and one is not.

Lankshear (1987) has (based on the work of O'Neil, 1970) called these proper and improper literacy. Proper literacy allows one to have genuine control over one's life by using it to facilitate effective decision-making and an understanding of social relations that can enable one to transform oppressive realities. Improper literacy reduces reading and writing to rule following and accepting things as they are presented.

Even if we speak of functional literacy, we come up with different definitions. Studies of adult literacy programs (See Lankshear, 1987) show that the official definition of functional literacy includes such things as consumer economics, occupational knowledge, health knowledge and knowledge of community resources as well as other essential skills required to cope with the demands of today's world. The goal is to participate in the world as it is, not to criticize or change it. In contrast, Lankshear (1987) sugggests that notions of optimal functional literacy will ask questions like, functional for whom? for what? If we are talking about being critically aware of the world and in control of our own lives, we are talking about something very different than the official version.

Indeed, there are at least three different models for literacy in our society (Scribner, 1984). All three seem important for optimal literacy. They are (1) literacy as adaptation (the official definition of functional literacy described above), (2) literacy as personal growth in which the literate person is believed to have special powers of self-improvement (the liberal, individualistic definition), and (3) literacy as political power (critical or proper literacy). (Also see Knoblauch and Brannon, 1993.) In a classroom focussed exclusively on literacy as adaptation, one would expect to see lots of real-world materials, that is, magazines, newpapers, pamphlets, and so forth as well as textbooks focussed on the superficial learning of culturally valued information. In a classroom focussed on literacy as personal self-improvement, one might also see novels, classical literature and philosophy and lots of personal writings. In a classroom based on literacy as power, one could see any of these materials but they would be discussed in terms of whose interests they serve and how they can be appropriated to serve the interests of the students and their community. The major differences among these classrooms would probably be seen in an accepting versus a questioning ethos and an individualistic versus a community orientation, and many classrooms represent a blending of these models.

Every time I ask my students to describe classrooms based on these definitions, the same unconscious assumption emerges without any direction from me. They envision literacy as adaptation in the lower academic tracks, literacy as personal growth in the middle tracks, and literacy as critical thinking about society in the upper tracks. I do not know how closely this resembles true differences between tracks, but Oakes' (1985) data indicate that it may be fairly accurate. The fact of the matter is that all tracks are perfectly capable of engaging in all three forms of literacy, so where does this assumption come from?

This is clearly one way that schools reproduce social inequities. Accepted practice legitimates teaching different literacies to different students. The "bottom" track students are alienated by the attempts to teach them a passive form of literacy. Students in the "middle" track are not given a literacy that they can use to participate actively as members of a larger society. And students in the "top" track may need some time to grow personally and affectively from the books they read.

Thus, all students deserve to spend time in school engaging is each of these forms of literacy. I have seen classrooms in which students as

young as first-graders use literacy to adapt, to grow and to think critically about their world. Age need not be a factor. In the second-grade
classroom I visited as part of my work for chapter 9, the students in one
work station were discussing the impact of television on their lives. After
discussing guiding questions, they were to write their opinions. In the
senior high classroom I observed, the students were taking surveys on
social concepts of romantic love to prepare for their reading of *Romeo
and Juliet*. Though neither of these classroom were "top track," these
teachers had found ways to involve kids in using literacy skills to think
actively about the world in which they live.

Emancipatory definitions of literacy seem to embody many of the
forms of empowerment I discussed in the last two chapters. For instance,
Elasser and John-Steiner (1977) have argued that literacy instruction will
only be effective when students see themselves as subjects rather than
objects, as creators of culture rather than victims of others' decisions. For
Freire (1973, 1978, 1987), literacy is critically "reading the word and the
world" so as to engage in praxis (action based on reflection). In this way,
one can be actively involved in creating the world in which he or she
lives. Materials include words and issues that are central to the lives of
the learners.

We can continue this application of educational empowerment to
literacy: In an empowering literacy, authority is shared between the
reader and the text. Readers feel empowered to think critically about
what they are reading, especially in terms of the agenda of the writer.
"Whose interests does this serve?" would be a common reading question. So, too, would be "What possibilities does this open up for me and
my community?" Writers would be aware that their work would be read
by readers with a variety of backgrounds and agendas. They would be
able to effectively communicate their own message while adequately
considering the point of view of their audience. Reading would be a
kind of dialogue between reader and writer. Writing would involve finding and using one's own unique voice, contextualized historically and
culturally. Moreover, in an emancipatory literacy, readers and writers
would know how to use reading and writing to understand their world
and to transform it.

An empowering literacy would also be multicultural. Empowered
readers/writers would be consciously aware of the assumptions and
norms of their own cultures and how these affect their interpretations.
They would also have a basic knowledge and understanding of other cul-

tures. This would include an understanding of the differential access to power afforded different cultural groups along with a lived sense of how these different experiences affect the members of these groups.

For empowered readers/writers engage in these processes with more than just their rational minds. If reading and writing are to be living, authentic acts of communication, then they will often involve feeling, sensing, imagining, intuiting and wanting. The messages expressed would both comuunicate and stimulate these things, and the readers/writers involved would understand and even appreciate the benefits and limitations of these modes of perception, as well as their relationship to different cultures and communication purposes. Reading and writing would be creative/critical acts of communication among fully human subjects engaged in making sense of and transforming their world.

Activity 6.1
DEFINING LITERACY IN YOUR CLASSROOM/SCHOOL

Watch the children in your classroom or school as they engage in reading and writing activities. In which subjects or activities are they using reading and writing to empower themselves? List them below. In which subjects or activities is this not the case? List these as well. Below are some questions you can use to guide your observations.

Literacy as Empowering	Literacy that is not Empowering

1. Are they learning proper literacy? Is it emancipatory? transformative? critical?
2. How much opportunity is there for critical thought about self and society?
3. Is literacy multicultural?
4. Are they engaging multiple psychological functions?
5. Are they having opportunities to find their own voice?
6. Are there opportunities to speak up against silences in the curriculum?
7. Are they using literacy to function in the world, grow as individuals, and transform the life of the community?

So, what is the definition of literacy that they are learning in your classroom? Is this the definition of literacy that you want them to learn? List three changes you want to make in your literacy instruction:

1.

2.

3.

4. Other?

Teachers and Literacy Instruction

Teaching an empowering literacy requires empowered teachers. Unfortunately, teachers focussing on literacy instruction have been disempowered by all of the factors I discussed in chapter 2. Indeed, the history of literacy instruction provides excellent examples of how scientific rationality, technical control, bureaucratic control, surplus powerlessness and sexism have limited and defined reading and writing instruction in the twentieth century (see Shannon, 1989).

In our postwar experience, we can think immediately of the basal readers, their endless subskill lists, their controlled vocabulary and their careful teacher scripts. Though the subskill lists seemed "scientific," the actual research support for any one list was scanty (Rosenshine, 1980). Indeed, the justification for subskills probably goes back to research like that of Davis (1944), who was working with the Cooperative Testing Service of the American Council on Education. After compiling a probable list of subskills and devising items to test for them, he concluded, because the items seemed statistically to measure some different factors, that they must have some instructional validity. (See Blachowicz, 1983, and Johnson, Toms-Bronowski and Buss, 1983 for critiques of this research and how it has been interpreted.) The real reason subskills became the bedrock of reading instruction for forty years was probably more because they lent themselves to the types of individual lessons and objective testing that dominated the scientific rationality popular in curriculum design (see also Luke, 1988).

Indeed, many teachers have reported to me that they are primarily controlled by the tests that are used to measure their students' progress. For instance, the state of Connecticut gives a "Mastery Test" in literacy periodically during the elementary school years. Teachers feel that they will be judged by how their students do on this test. The greatest changes in the literacy curricula across the state seem to have come each time the mastery test has been redesigned.

Similarly, the traditional basals were designed in such a way that teachers felt that they had to complete every lesson exactly as specified. Teaching scripts were provided in order to make the lessons "teacher proof." The assumption was that many teachers were underprepared to teach something as important as reading. The end result was technical control in the extreme and the deskilling of teachers; college courses had only to teach the teachers how to implement the materials and manage prepackaged programs (Shannon, 1987; Winograd and Smith, 1987). (Perhaps the most insidious result of this deskilling has been that teachers have been denied a critical literacy of their own. How many teachers have been given opportunities to use reading and writing to critically examine and possibly change the conditions of their lives? How can teachers teach critical literacy if they have not experienced it themselves?)

Moreover, in order to handle the students who do not succeed using these prepackaged methods, a large bureaucracy related to reading has developed. Reading or language arts curriculum coordinators, reading consultants and reading teachers have taken over the business of making decisions about reading instruction. I am not suggesting that these people, who have graduate degrees involving years of study of the reading/writing processes, are not useful; what I am suggesting is that their existence has taken more and more control out of the hands of the classroom teacher, who has been increasingly deskilled.

Probably as a result, many elementary school teachers (who have the bulk of the responsibility for introducing most kids to literacy) have little self-confidence related to their ability to make decisions about literacy instruction (see Duffy, Roehler and Putnam, 1987). In preparation for the in-service work I conducted in 1986, I surveyed the teachers involved in terms of their attitudes about reading instruction. What I found was that their self-concept related to their ability to teach reading was very low. I would relate this to the concept of surplus powerlessness I discussed in chapter 2. These teachers are isolated and thus fall into self-blaming when the methods they have been given do not work as well as they believe they should.

Perhaps more illustrative of this is the fact that teachers may believe that they have less control than they actually have. In a study comparing teachers' and administrators' responses in terms of their impression of the pressure to implement basals as written, Shannon (1983) found that teachers felt they were much more constrained than the administrators reported that they actually were.

Finally, I do not know how much the lives of individual teachers of reading have been affected by sexism. I do know that when I attended national conferences on reading early in my career (late 1970s), the attendees, who were teachers, were women, and the "expert" presenters, who were generally college professors and curriculum coordinators, were, with few exceptions, men. Though this is changing and is less of a problem in reading than in other educational specialties, it sticks in my mind as a kind of symbolic warning.

Activity 6.2
CONTROLLING LITERACY INSTRUCTION

Who controls the literacy instruction in your district? _____

_____

Are you sure? _____

_____

What evidence do you have?_____

_____

Would you and your colleagues like more influence? _____

_____

How could the control be transferred to the teachers? _____

_____

_____

Sample Ideas: Participate on building-level or districtwide curriculum committees; get flexibility in the curriculum clarified; look for training to help you get away from your basal; collaborate with peers on new kinds of literacy lessons; design a new vision and speak to the school board; request that there be teacher/leaders for language arts in every school building; and so on!

Methods for Teaching Literacy

The methods available for teaching literacy follow from the available definitions. In functional classrooms, students complete worksheets and answer right-or-wrong questions. In personal growth classrooms, students read books of interest and write personal stories and journal entries. In critical literacy classrooms, students read critically in areas of special interest to the community, though, quite frankly, I have seen little of this going on. Most classrooms use some combination of these approaches, but I would suggest that none of the methods in widespread use, even the most student-centered, go quite far enough in the effort to enable students to gain a truly empowering literacy.

If we look at the basals and textbooks used postwar to present, we will again see examples of the kind of power-over educational process and content I described in chapter 3 as disempowering. First, students are commonly "tracked" into ability-level groups, and research indicates that the "bluejays" and "robins" are not given equal opportunities to learn. As stated in chapter 3, research indicates that the lower-group students are interrupted more often (Allington, 1980), read less (Allington, 1977) and are taught with less emphasis on meaning (Allington, 1978), even though we know that a meaning emphasis is beneficial (Anderson, Mason and Shirey, 1983).

Secondly, in both reading and writing instruction, "skills" are separated instructionally from their meaningful use. Students practice finding the main idea, making plurals, organizing paragraphs and so forth on worksheets designed by textbook publishers on topics of little interest to specific students. The emphasis is on getting the items "right" rather than on being able to use these skills in everyday life (see Durkin, 1978). This is a classic example of emphasizing product over process. The process of reading and the process of writing are lost in a plethora of activities.

The end result of this emphasis on activities designed by someone else and assessed by someone else as being right or wrong is that students acquire an amazingly passive view of literacy. For many students, reading and writing are something you do for someone else, not for yourself. No wonder we seem to live in an aliterate society. Moreover, passivity in literacy can be so extreme as to cause complete failure. It is impossible to read or write successfully in a fully passive way. They are inherently active processes. This phenomena of passive reading has even generated a term in the remedial reading literature: "passive failure in reading" (Johnston and Winograd, 1985). The irony is that it is the students, not the programs, that are blamed for this passive failure.

Assessment of progress in such programs continues to be quantitative and to emphasize right/wrong questions. Using multiple-choice questions and short passages, these tests usually measure mostly lower-level reasoning and recognition of facts. Scores are strongly affected by the students' prior knowledge, thus inevitably biasing them toward the more middle-class students (Johnston and Pearson, 1982). (The general disadvantage of certain cultural groups in most prepackaged literacy programs cannot be dismissed. For instance, most activities are completed individually, thus promoting competition and putting those that work best cooperatively at a disadvantage. Moreover, only certain cultural groups get practice at home with answering questioning the answer to which the adult already knows [Heath, 1989].)

In response to these and other criticisms of traditional basal programs (see Durkin, 1978; Duffy and Roehler, 1983; Irwin, 1991; Irwin and Baker, 1989), many have shifted their emphasis from teaching skills to teaching strategies (Duffy and Roehler, 1983; Irwin, 1991, for example). This is not as subtle a change as it sounds. Rather than being taught to do things like finding the main idea or drawing conclusions or detecting the author's purpose to complete a workbook page or other abstract assignment, students are shown how they can use these things to achieve their own, sometimes self-selected, purposes. Students are taught to be strategic, to think about what they are doing and why, and to actively select strategies that will best help them to accomplish their goals. This puts the students more in charge of their own learning and could possibly integrate functional, personal growth, and critical literacy learning, depending on the self or community orientation of the goals the students choose.

Other new methods are also now being used in many schools (see Willinsky, 1990). One of these is teaching reading through literature (Bromley, 1991; Cooper, 1993; Cullinan, 1987; Galda, Cullinan and Strickland, 1993; Norton, 1992; and others). In fact, this method is so popular that many basals are currently being rewritten with real literature and formats that enable them to be used in this way. (The real issue is not whether a basal is being used, but how it is used. I can envision a basal being empowering or disempowering based completely on how it is used.)

In these programs, students read real literature, either individually, in groups or as a whole class. Various activities are designed to promote their understanding and, in some cases, to promote critical thinking and individual response. These programs offer numerous advantages in terms of empowerment, not the least of which is that they usually put more control back into the hands of teachers (though one can easily imagine a district adopting a strict "reading though literature" curriculum that dictates what will be read by whom and when and how). They provide opportunities for using multicultural literature and multicultural interpretation. Activities often involve integrating feeling, imagining and intuitive responses and are often cooperative and dialogic. Moreover, in many of these programs, students have the opportunity to self-select the literature they will be reading, thus giving them some input into their own learning experiences and avoiding the grouping of students by ability.

I do have a couple of concerns about these programs, however. First, though many teachers take advantage of the empowering opportunities available when they use literature to teach reading, many just use the same disguised ability groups, isolated right/wrong worksheets and competitive individual assessment that they used with the basal program. Just changing from basal stories to real literature does not ensure an empowering educational process.

Moreover, what type of literacy are these programs emphasizing? Though in some programs students do read some nonfiction tradebooks, the emphasis in many classes is almost exclusively on fiction. The activities, then, mostly stress what I would call reading for personal growth.

What about reading to get information necessary for one's life (the functional literacy described above)? What about reading critically and using information to understand and transform the circumstances of one's community (critical literacy)?

Some might suggest that "reading in the content areas" would be a solution for this (see Vacca and Vacca, 1992; and others). This usually means that students are given help with using reading to meet the demands of their content-area classes (usually science, math and social studies). Such programs often include things like using resources and assembling information to make a report, following directions, summarizing and organizing information and thinking critically, but these skills are applied to predetermined information, rather than to self-directed goals. An empowering context in which students are actively involved in naming issues and investigating their relationships to other issues might help students to see how such literacy strategies could be used in an empowering way.

Another promising development in literacy instruction that has arisen in response to criticisms of traditional subskill textbook-based writing programs, is what is now being called "process writing." In these programs, teachers use writers' workshops (see Graves, 1983, 1994; Atwell, 1986; Hansen, 1987) in which students write independently on self-selected topics. They go through a series of stages, prewriting, drafting, revising and publishing at their own pace. (Publishing takes a variety of forms: sending, putting in school paper, making into self-published book, etc.) Writers conference with the teacher and share writing problems with their peers as their work proceeds.

Again, this approach has numerous advantages over the traditional punctuation worksheet or Christmas vacation essay. The most important of these is that the student is given the opportunity to experience writing as something that he or she can do for his or her own meaningful purposes. Also, the writer is allowed to go through all the stages that an adult writer would probably use. Because students are writing about their own experiences and concerns, they can include feelings, images and intuitions much more easily. Each can write with his or her own unique voice with all of its ethnic, gender and socioeconomic particularities.

Though there is much to recommend such programs from an power-to/power-with point of view, there are still a couple of problems to be worked out. First, the isolation of the writing workshop from the other subjects and from other classroom activities often results in an

undue emphasis on what has been called creative writing—stories, poems, plays and letters. This is probably because the content being studied
by the students in the other subjects is not meaningful to them, so they
do not choose to write about it when given the chance. Then writing
workshop becomes synonymous with the personal growth definition of
literacy in its emphasis on the individual.

"Writing to learn" is the term given to programs that integrate
writing into the teaching of the content areas. (See Thompkins, 1990;
Vacca and Vacca, 1992; and others.) Students are encouraged to use a variety of writing strategies, like journals, notes, and creative response, to
help them learn predetermined content material. Developing one's ability to use writing to learn material is empowering, but it would be more
empowering if the students were sometimes using the writing to learn
material they wanted to learn for a meaningful purpose and if that purpose involved a struggle with real issues in their community. Then they
could then see how an empowered writer might use these skills.

A second problem with empowerment in the writers' workshop
approach (and, indeed, all these new approaches) results from the fact
that its proponents have not fully developed their critique of school discourse. As long as the classroom climate upholds silences in the curriculum about racism, poverty, sexuality, sexism and oppression (see chapter
5), then the students will play this out in their writing. If their voices are
not valued throughout the school day, then it is unreasonable to expect
them to "find their voice" during the writers' workshop. I guess what I
am suggesting is that the empowering potential of any isolated instructional approach is limited by the total context in which it is embedded.

This brings me to mentioning the term "whole language." (See
Edelsky, 1991; Goodman, 1987; Routman, 1991; Weaver, 1990; Vacca
and Rasinsky, 1990; and others.) I have worked in the field of literacy for
almost twenty years, and never have I seen such a muddle over a term. To
some extent, the confusion is solved when we remind ourselves that
whole language is a philosophy, not an approach. It is, simply put, the
belief that language skills are best learned by participating in whole,
natural, meaningful activities. Seen in this way, developments like process
writing, teaching reading through literature and reading and writing in
the content areas reflect the whole language philosophy (depending on
your definition of meaningful).

There is one more method in current use, which some people call
whole language, that involves integrating the aforementioned techniques

with the other school subjects, using thematic units. This has the advantage that reading and writing instruction are not isolated from the multiple contexts in which they might be useful for the students, and the disciplines are not artificially isolated. But this promising development has suffered the same fate as the others mentioned above; namely, an unproblematic acceptance of the silences in the curriculum and a lack of opportunity for student choice. Thus, students are often encouraged to choose themes like "chocolate" (the theme I have seen most often), if they are given the opportunity to choose the theme at all. This is ironic since a theme like "civil rights" is much more likely to lead to study of the standard curriculum on things like the Constitution, the American revolutionary war, and the Civil War than is a theme like chocolate; a theme like "saving the planet" is much more likely to lead to study of the standard curriculum on botany and biology and so on.

Finally, all of these more empowering programs (as compared to traditonal basals and writing textbooks) also have the advantage that they often incorporate the use of portfolio assessment. In portfolio assessment, a student's growth is assessed over time by collecting and examining real evidence of daily work. In many cases, students are involved in selecting the pieces that go in their portfolio, and in assessing their own strengths and weaknesses as evidenced in the portfolio and setting their own goals based on this assessment (see Farr and Tone, 1995; Johnston, 1992; Tierney, 1991). If used in this way, this is evaluation for empowerment as discussed in chapter 4. We might also speculate that it need not always be individual. Could the class also assess itself periodically as a group? Could it develop a class portfolio? Would caring or mutual respect be promoted by such a portfolio?

Toward a Philosophy of Literacy Instruction

So what is the ideal empowering literacy instruction? What do you think? What kind of instruction can prepare students for economic survival, encourage them to use literacy for personal growth and develop a proper/critical literacy that can enable them to use reading and writing to change their lives and their world? What kind of literacy instruction can allow students to read and write with their whole selves, including sensations, feelings, images and intuitions? (Grumet [1988] calls this "bodyreading," a term that is useful in getting us out of our heads.) What kind of literacy instruction connects students to their communities, their country and the world? What kind of literacy instruction allows them to see opportunities for and disruptions of social justice in the literacy materials that surround them? What kind of literacy instruction makes room for an authentic struggle with their lived reality?

Activity 6.3
DESIGNING YOUR OWN LITERACY PROGRAM

If it is appropriate for you, take this time to design your own literacy program.

If you are an *elementary school teacher*, this would involve reading and writing and the content subjects.

If you are a *secondary school teacher* of a content subject, you may still wish to do this activity. What kind of literacy are the students learning in your class? How could this be improved?

If you are an *administrator*, you can look at the program across classes. How could the school and district set a tone for proper literacy?

If you are a *legislator*, look at how the current bureaucracy encourages literacy as adaptation and personal growth only. How can legislation promote empowering literacy development? Finally, if you are a *parent*, look at the literacy that your children are learning. How could you influence school policy to improve the literacy program?

Summary

In this chapter, I have attempted to illustrate some of the ideas about empowerment suggested in earlier chapters by looking specifically at one area of the curriculum, literacy. I found that, as with any other "subject," literacy cannot be clearly divided from the rest of the curriculum. Moreover, though there have been many promising developments in the field as the idea of empowerment has come into vogue, I have tried to point out that the total effect of these is limited by the generally empowering or disempowering climate of the classroom and school in which they occur.

I have also attempted to illustrate that, again, what we do in the classroom has to begin with the question of the purpose of education, in this case, literacy education. What is literacy? What kind of literacy do we want to teach? The answers to these questions suggest that reading and writing instruction are by no means politically neutral. Literacy for what? for whom? The answers to these questions suggest that current methods must be embedded in a more general critique of classroom discourse if they are to be maximally empowering for us and for our students.

PART THREE

Empowering Ourselves

CHAPTER SEVEN

Self-Empowerment

Whether you agree with any of my suggestions for change or not, you are probably interested in empowering yourself to transform your school or classroom or policy in some way. One obvious step is to find ways to overcome the internal forces that cause us to conform to others' expectations. This will involve rejecting practices that go against what we believe, revisioning education in a way that reflects our deepest beliefs, and reskilling ourselves so that we can act in an informed manner. We will also have to work on other internal blocks to empowerment like low self-esteem, surplus powerlessness and negative thinking.

Though this chapter focusses on things that you can do for yourself, remember that we cannot expect to empower ourselves in a vacuum. We need other empowered persons to support us. The next chapter will deal with creating an empowering community that will help us sustain the growth we achieve as individuals and promote growth that we could not achieve on our own. As Steinem (1992) has said, "We make progress by a constant spiraling back and forth between the inner world and the outer one, the personal and the political, the self and the circumstance" (p. 8).

Identifying Empowering Experiences

Perhaps it would be useful at this point to review what we mean by empowerment. In chapter 1, I suggested the following description of empowered educators:

Empowered educators believe in themselves and their capacity to act. They understand systems of domination and work to transform oppressive practices in society. They respect the dignity and humanness of others and manifest their power as the power to actualize their own unique humanity. They are strong, practical and compassionate as they work individually and with others to support the self-realization of all persons in their classroom, school and community.

This description reflects some very simple truths about empowerment. An empowered person is automatically supportive of the empowerment of others. An empowered person feels efficacious and self-aware. An empowered person has integrity and expresses his or her beliefs and values in action. An empowered person works alone and with others to develop a community that supports the growth of all its members.

For an internal sense of empowerment also rests on a sense of connection to something outside of ourselves. Piero Ferrucci (1990) has described what he calls the seven paths to the self. These paths include things like beauty, action, illumination, dance and ritual, science, devotion, and will. He proposes that each act on each of these paths either "reinforces separation or affirms unity" (p. 1). It seems to be in the latter that we experience empowerment. During these experiences, which he characterizes as transpersonal, we often feel things like amazement, rightness, knowledge, unity, universality, and social relevance. They often involve such things as creativity, being oneself, acceptance, imagination, intuition, service, and respect for self and others.

When we are feeling empowered, we feel energized rather than drained. We feel centered, rather than off balance. We feel strong and clear, rather than weak and confused. We feel connected to others, rather than alone and isolated. We feel that we are being ourselves and doing something useful.

Let's begin by naming our experiences of empowerment or disempowerment. Often, the empowering or disempowering nature of an experience is dissimulated under other labels like "efficiency" or "supported by research." The key, I believe, is to go inside and see how it feels to you. Then name the experience honestly.

Activity 7.1
NAMING EMPOWERING AND DISEMPOWERING EXPERIENCES

In the two columns below, list experiences in which you felt either empowered or disempowered. Include books you have read, educational experiences you have had, and experiences you have had as a teacher in the classroom and with your colleagues.

Empowering Experiences	Disempowering Experiences

Now, go back to the empowering column. What are the key characteristics of these experiences? List these below. How can you get more of these experiences in your life? What are the key characteristics of the disempowering experiences? Can you avoid any of these in the future?

Characteristics of Empowering Experiences	Characteristics of Disempowering Experiences

Gawain (1993) has suggested that there are seven steps on the path of personal transformation. These are:

1. Making a commitment (to follow your truth)
2. Following inner guidance
3. Finding support
4. Using tools [reskilling]
5. Allowing healing
6. Expressing creativity
7. Sharing with others (p. 185)

You may wish to go back to your list of empowering experiences to see how they fit with this list. They probably involved a combination of several steps. Taken together these steps describe a process of discovering what you believe and getting the support and information you need to creatively share your discovery with others by teaching in a new way or by helping others in your school and community.

Similarly, Steinem (1992) has listed what she has called the normal stages of empowerment:

1. Seeing through our own eyes
2. Telling "secrets" [breaking silences]
3. Naming problems
4. Bonding with others with similar problems
5. Achieving empowerment
6. Bonding with others with similar power
7. Achieving a balance between independence and interdependence (pp. 44–45)

This list also tells us a lot about empowerment. It suggests that it has something to do with knowing ourselves; that it has to do with bringing the forbidden out into the open; that it involves naming the unknown or unspeakable; that it involves bonding with others; and that it involves both independence and interdependence. Indeed, both of these lists balance getting in touch with our personal truth and finding a supportive community.

I wonder if this process is ever finished for anyone. We may go through these stages several times in our lives for different issues. Many of us remember these stages in the "conciousness raising" of the seventies. At that time, we were dealing specifically with our lives as women. But there are many other problems that can be confronted with naming, connecting

with others, and empowering ourselves . . . and one of those is the pre-
dominance of power-over practices in the institution of schooling.

Activity 7.2
REFLECTING ON OUR EMPOWERMENT PROCESS

Think about the process of empowerment that you have been going
through as an educator. What were the critical turning points? For example, working with another teacher helped me to . . . or taking a course
in X helped me to . . . You may wish to look back over the lists provided
by Gawain (1993) and Steinem (1992).

1.

2.

3.

4.

5.

(If you are having trouble, think of times when you followed your own
truth, found support, learned new information, made a commitment, expressed yourself openly, acted with integrity, . . . and so on. Think back to
when you felt empowered emotionally and physically.)

Now, what do you think the next steps are? In what ways are you ready to
grow at this point in your experience as an educator? (Again, you may
wish to refer back to the lists of possible steps.)

1.

2.

3.

4.

5.

Reflective Action

In order to empower ourselves to act, we must clarify what we really believe. What practices reflect these beliefs? What practices make us uncomfortable? Why? What beliefs do they reflect? In the previous chapters, I included many activities which were designed to encourage you to explore these questions in terms of the processes and content of schooling. You may wish to take a minute now to go back through your notes in this book and list what you learned about the practices you do or do not believe in.

Activity 7.3
SAYING WHAT I BELIEVE

Make lists of school practices that you do or do not support:

I am comfortable with . . .   I am *not* comfortable with . . .

Now it might be useful to go back through this list and think about the myths that support the practices you feel are inappropriate. In previous chapters, I talked about power-over beliefs in such things as the variability of human worth (some people are worth more than others), scarcity (that only some can succeed), meritocracy (we get what we deserve), scientific rationality (that scientific results are not affected by the biases of the researchers), objectification (that it is appropriate to think of students as objects to be controlled), linear time, hierarchical relationships, friendship as ritual, rules as absolute, product over process, thinking as the only way of knowing, individualism, control of nature, and diversity as threatening. Which of these are reflected in your list?

Now, can you summarize your philosophy?

Of course, our educational philosophy must always be open to change based on reflection on our experience. This reflection can include questioning the underlying assumptions of our practice, understanding that our practice is historically conditioned and can be changed, and openly examining the results of our practice in terms of our overall values and goals. Then we can connect reflection and action (praxis).

The Boston Women's Teacher Group (Friedman, Jackson and Boles, 1984) has provided a wonderful example of how we can examine educational practices in terms of underlying assumptions. They identified four central conflicts in which the rhetoric of the school did not match with practice.

1. Teachers are supposed to prepare students to be adults but the teachers are not treated like adults themselves.
2. Teachers are supposed to develop the "whole child" but only in ways that are acceptable to an institution that expects order and discipline.
3. Teachers are supposed to provide equal opportunities to children but the system promotes competition.
4. Teachers are supposed to develop students who can think for themselves but they are often pressured to use increasingly technical and right/wrong approaches.

In uncovering these conflicts, these teachers are naming the real philosophy of the educational system rather than believing superficial rhetoric that is not actually supported by practice. (See also Powell and Solety, 1990.)

Contextualizing our practice in terms of the larger historical situation that it is reflecting can also help us determine what we wish to promote. Mills (1959) has called this having a sociological imagination; it is seeing the connection between what is going on in the world and what is going on in our own lives. For instance, competition for grades in schools is not just an attempt to motivate students. It is also a reflection of the competitive individualism in the larger society. We feel trapped and powerless when we fail to see this connection. Seeing it often provides the insight needed for making changes.

In the case of our own empowerment, we are stymied when we see things only in terms of specifics. For instance, we may think the problem is the obnoxious personality of one administrator, or the rigidity of our colleagues, or our own inadequacy. We may think the problem is that our students are uncooperative and spoiled. All of these things may reflect some sort of truth but they are not contextualized in a way that gives them deeper meaning. Why does this obnoxious administrator have so much power? How can this power be controlled? Why is he or she so obnoxious in the first place? Why are our colleagues so afraid of change? Why do we feel inadequate? Why are our students acting this way? If we answer these questions with a sociological imagination, we will often see that these problems are a part of a power-over system that perpetuates specific practices of domination. This is naming the problem in a way that empowers us to act.

For teachers, this is the part of our practice that has been called reflective teaching (Henderson, 1992; and others). This is teaching not by simply implementing curricula and procedures given to us but by continually reflecting on our practice in terms of its origins and outcomes and adjusting our actions according to our conclusions. Zeichner and Liston (1987) talk about attempting to prepare teachers "who are both willing and able to reflect on the origins, purposes, and consequences of their actions, as well as on the material and ideological constraints and encouragements embedded in the classroom, school and societal context in which they work" (p. 23). Ross, Bondy and Kyle (1993) define a reflective teacher as one who "makes rational and ethical choices about what and how to teach and assumes responsibility for those choices" (p. 3).

Two of the teachers I interviewed specifically mentioned the moment of beginning to reflect on the "why" of their practice as a turning point in their career. Another pursued graduate school because "I was going to have some answers about why or why not it was a good idea." All these teachers had obviously reflected on their practice as evidenced by the ease with which they explained the rationale for their decisions.

Schon (1983) has talked about three levels of reflection: technical, educational, and moral or ethical. Technical reflection asks questions like "Will it work?" in the limited context of this situation. Educational reflection asks questions like "Is this the best objective for this curriculum?" Finally, moral reflection asks "Is this the most ethical decision in terms of what is best for the individual and the society?"

Again, I saw evidence of all of these in the interviews I conducted, though reflections at the technical level were limited. (All of these were experienced teachers, however, and it may be reasonable to assume that they were more concerned with technical questions earlier in their careers.) For this group of empowered teachers, the ethical level seemed predominant. Practices were tested against criteria like having students "look at issues beyond their community" or "One of our roles as humans is to care . . ." or helping students to "find their own voice" or "to give people the power to change their own lives."

For it is impossible to avoid moral and ethical questions in education. Not to deal with questions of multiculturalism is to decide for uniculturalism. Not to deal with questions of power is to decide for power-over. Not to look for ways to connect to the real lives of students is to decide to shut them out of their own educational process. Each of these involves moral questions about social justice. Reflective teachers address such issues in their philosophy and in their practice.

Michelsen (1991) has pointed out that reflection is most valuable when it is carried out in community. This is an important point to come back to again and again. Carrying on reflection in groups will help us to build an empowering community that can support us in our own self-exploration. Indeed, it is probably impossible for any one person to step back far enough to see all the implications of each of his/her decisions. A teacher I interviewed who was involved in a "Teacher Portraiture Group" in which teachers visited each other and wrote "portraits" said that such involvement helped her to reflect on her own teaching in new ways.

Thus, developing reflective skills and attitudes may be a necessary part of empowerment. Ross, Bondy and Kyle (1993) state that teachers need to be able to see the dilemmas that arise in classroom teaching, to interact with other teachers and with professional resources, and to conduct action research in their own classroom. (This consists of planning, acting, observing and then making judgements about various procedures that are being tried out. I will discuss this reflective implementation more in the last section of this chapter.) All empowered educators need to be introspective, open-minded and willing to take responsibility for their own actions. They need to be able to view situations from multiple perspectives, seek alternative explanations, use evidence to support their positions and evaluate their own decisions based on their own personal set of values. How reflective are you? That is the subject of activity 7.4.

Activity 7.4
DEVELOPING REFLECTIVE SKILLS AND ATTITUDES

For each of the following skills and attitudes, rate yourself on a scale of 1 to 3:
    1 = Not very true of me
    2 = True of me most of the time
    3 = True of me all of the time

___ Sees conflicts and problems in classroom practice
___ Interacts with other educators to solve problems
___ Seeks professional resources to solve problems
___ Tries new ideas by carefully planning, observing and evaluating results
___ Introspective
___ Takes responsiblity for actions
___ Open-minded; listens openly to other points of view
___ Looks at situations from multiple perspectives
___ Looks for alternative explanations and ideas
___ Uses evidence to support opinions
___ Evaluates decisions based on coherent set of values

Now, which of these characteristics would you like to improve in yourself? Select one: _____

List at least three ideas for developing your ability in this area.

Reskilling

At least two of the reflective skills listed above, seeking professional resources to solve problems and looking for alternative explanations and ideas, result in what I would call "reskilling." You may remember that in chapter 2 I discussed the deskilling of teachers that results from the belief that there can be "teacher-proof" materials. Because the technical control of materials and procedures has been so strong, the preparation of educators has often consisted of little more than learning to implement someone else's ideas.

This deskilling has led to disempowerment, the feeling that one does not have the knowledge or expertise to make decisions. In some cases, this may be true, but *it need not be.* You are perfectly capable of getting the knowledge you need to make educational decisions. If your university and district have failed to provide you with the information you need, it is not your fault! You can take control and go out and find the information that you need.

Maeroff (1988) lists knowledge as one of the essential elements of empowerment. He found that as teachers got more knowledge, they also got more confident. He also found that "teachers are hungry for stimulating educational experiences" (p. 41). (See also McDonald, 1986.) This has certainly been my experience as well. My reading comprehension in-service programs are loaded with technical information and new terminology and they are very well received. Teachers and principals often say things to me like, "Why didn't anyone tell us all this before?" During a year-long in-service I conducted in Chicago, the teachers took control of their reading instruction. When I discussed this with them, they said things like, "Now we know what we are doing." "Now we have the knowledge to make our own decisions."

Spaulding (1992) has discussed motivation in terms of perceived competence and perceived control. We are most motivated to do something if we feel able and in control. I believe that these factors are also the essence of empowerment. We will feel empowered as teachers if we feel that we have the knowledge that we need along with some control over what we do. Control will not help if we do not have the knowledge we need.

All of the teachers I interviewed for the case studies in chapter 9 mentioned getting knowledge as a part of their empowerment process. Some mentioned specific books; some mentioned college courses and professors; some mentioned professional in-services. All of these are ways to get important information.

Of course, getting knowledge is not important for teachers only. Administrators, parents and lawmakers all need to take to time to investigate current knowledge before making decisions. I believe that much of the pressure from parents to "go back to the basics" and from administrators to "maintain order" and from lawmakers to be "accountable on standardized tests" come from ignorance about the alternatives, rather than a commitment to a power-over mentality.

I would be the first to say that some books, courses, and in-services are not empowering, however. Indeed, I have seen some that are disempowering. How will you know the ones that will serve you? Well, you can probably apply some of the same criteria you would use in your own classroom and school. Does it connect to your lived experience? Does it address a problem about which you have concern? Will you be an active participant or a passive learner? Will it provide opportunities for you to interact with other teachers? Will it be intellectually stimulating? Will it give you the complex knowledge you need to make decisions, or will it simply give you recipes and formulas devised by others?

My own bias is toward books and courses and in-services that provide theory along with practical suggestions. Ask others about the experiences they have had with various programs and books. Do they seem like they were empowered by the experience?

Educators often find that they are empowered by simply continuing their own education. This may be the time to take that graduate course in literature or biology or women's history. When was the last time you read something for the sheer enjoyment of learning? Now is the time! As you liberate yourself to study the things that interest you, you will probably find yourself promoting the same experience for students.

If you are not presently involved in a stimulating reskilling experience, it may be time to find one. I would suggest that you go back to your philosophy as you wrote it on page 170. Where could you get more information on alternatives that reflect where you want to go? Get started!

Revisioning Alternatives

Once we know what we value and we have gathered information about available alternatives that others have discovered, we can go about the business of envisioning new alternatives that best actualize our beliefs about education. "How could it be different?" is the question we now ask. I call this "revisioning" to stress the fact that it is a recursive practice that happens over and over. As we grow and learn, our vision will develop and change. Just as it is important to get a vision to work toward, it is equally important to hold that vision lightly, to let go of the parts that are not serving us or our students and to revision again.

Utopian thinking seems invaluable at this stage. When we worry about what is "realistic", we hold ourselves back from the full creativity of which we are capable. We can test our vision against reality when we are in the process of change. Worrying about possible problems with implementation at the stage of revisioning will only stimulate negative thinking.

Senge (1990) has developed the concept of "personal mastery" as a cornerstone of the development of organizations. This personal mastery begins with a personal vision and is based on a belief that one can change the future. "It means approaching one's life as a creative work, living life from a creative as opposed to reactive viewpoint" (p. 141). It requires that we we live with the dissonance between our vision and reality, by "continually clarifying what is important to us" and living "in a continuous learning mode" (p. 142). According to Senge (1990), such people

> have a special sense of purpose that lies behind their vision and goals. *For such a person, a vision is a calling rather than simply a good idea.* They see "current reality" as an ally, not an enemy. They have learned how to perceive and work with forces of change rather than resist those forces. They are deeply inquisitive, committed to continually seeing reality more and more accurately. They feel connected to others and to life itself. Yet they sacrifice none of their uniqueness. They feel as if they are part of a larger creative process, which they can influence but cannot unilaterally control. (p. 142)

Creative visualization is a wonderful process for getting in touch with intuitive insights. This is simply the process of getting a mental image of what it is that we really want. According to Gershon and Straub (1989), visualizations are more effective if they evoke feelings, use a single image instead of a whole series, include you in the image, are either literal or metaphorical, and are physically depicted as through drawing. I have also found that images are more powerful if I take the time to engage all my senses; I try to feel, smell, see, hear and sometimes taste as well! Many find that visualizing is much more powerful than thinking in words because it brings up things that we have not yet completely thought through on a rational level.

Activity 7.5
VISUALIZING WHAT I WANT

Find a quiet place and plan to spend at least 30 minutes on this exercise. It is probably one of the most important in the book. (It is also one you may wish to repeat several times in your career.) Have pencil and paper (or journal) and crayons or markers ready accessible. (Space has been left below as well.) There will be four visualizations all together.

If you like, keep your eyes closed or half closed as much as possible. This will help you move back and forth between your imagination and your rational thought (Gershon and Straub, 1989). Finally, even if you are not a teacher, you may wish to do this from a teacher's point of view to get a sense of how your vision of education would materialize.

1. Imagine yourself five or ten years in the future. You have found that ideal school to work in and you are teaching in the ways you had always hoped. It is a bright, sunny spring day and you are going back to your classroom after a quick cup of coffee or tea during recess or free period. The students are already in the room getting ready to work. You are looking forward to getting back to this classroom. As you walk in, look around the room. What do you see? How is the furniture arranged? What are the students doing? What sorts of things are in the room or on the walls? Interact with the students. What are they saying? What are you saying? Hear the noises in the room. What are the students studying? How was this selected? How are they feeling? How are you feeling? Spend some time visualizing yourself in this situation. Before you leave the image, look around the room and find some symbol that can represent the experience for you.

When you are ready, open your eyes and draw a quick sketch representing what you visualized in your classroom and/or the symbol that you found. Don't worry about using stick figures or drawing badly. The purpose is to record.

Now, what do you see as the key elements that emerged for you? How are these represented in the symbol?

2. When you are ready, close your eyes and get settled for another visualization. Class is over and you are heading back to the teachers' room. Look around your school as you are walking in the hall. There have been many changes and you feel very happy and proud of what the school has become. You are especially happy to be in a school that reflects your own beliefs and dreams about what education can be. What do you see on the walls? In the other classrooms? What sorts of things are happening around the building? What do you smell? What sounds do you hear? What kinds of talk do you hear as you enter the teachers' room? What are the relationships among the teachers like? Take time to experience and enjoy this school and your colleagues. Is there a symbol here that is meaningful to you?

Now, when you are ready, open your eyes and draw a quick sketch representing your school and what you saw. Or, focus on the symbol that you found at the end.

What did you learn about yourself from this visualization?

3. Finally, visualize the community in which you teach. (If you are teaching, use that community.) You are driving to school and looking around you at the houses, stores, city services, and so on. What do you see? Look beyond the surface—What needs do you see? How does your ideal school help? Your school is such an active part of the community. It is so rewarding to be connected to the community in this way. As you drive around, you see several people that you know from their involvement with the school. Stop and chat with them for a while.

When you are ready, draw a picture or describe the community members that you have met and their involvement with the school.

Now, go back over your visions and try to list the most important things you learned about yourself, your goals and your values.

Make a list of the changes you want to begin to implement immediately.

You can do parts of the above activity whenever you feel that you are losing touch with what you really want. Or, you may wish to design a variation that works for you. Keeping in touch with our visions is an important part of being empowered to manifest them. You can use symbols that came up for you during the activity to reactivate the vision and the feelings of commitment and joy that may have accompanied it. You may even wish to find a physical object to represent the vision for you. I once got a clear image that my life needed more color. After doing a visualization to get a sense of what that meant for me, I went and bought a new box of 48 crayons and put it on my mantle to remind me to think about this as I went through my daily life.

Clearing Core Beliefs

Now it is time for us to begin to make it happen. How does that make you feel? Excited or nervous? Enthusiastic or discouraged? For most of us, there is still the problem of overcoming other internal blocks to empowerment as well as working to change the external context (see chapter 8).

We can begin this process by clearing out self-limiting beliefs that are keeping our other beliefs from becoming actualized. According to Gershon and Straub (1989) there are five categories of core beliefs that are important in the process of self-empowerment: self-responsiblity, self-esteem, trust, positive thinking and flowing with change. Let's discuss each of these in turn.

Self-responsiblity

Do you take responsibility for what happens to you or do you blame others? Do you take responsibility for what happens to you or do you blame yourself? It is very important to distinguish between accepting blame and accepting responsibility. Responsibility means responding . . . what might I have done to contribute to this situation and what might I do differently? What can I learn from what has happened? It does not mean blaming yourself, seeing yourself as inadequate or as having failed. It is not about whose "fault" it is.

Teachers who take responsibility for their teaching do not go around talking about things like "those lazy students who won't cooperate." Administrators and parents who take responsiblity do not talk about "those lazy teachers who don't care." This is futile; we can't change others but we can change ourselves. We can think about what we can do differently to motivate those who are not responding. Teachers who take responsiblity may say, "I am having trouble motivating some of my students." Administrators who take responsiblity may say, "I am having trouble helping my teachers to care." Parents who take responsibility say, "I am having trouble helping my child's teacher help my child." This is not self-blaming; it is naming a problem in terms of something that they can do to make it better.

And let's not go around blaming teachers who do blame their students or administrators and parents who blame teachers. Instead, let's look at the environment in which all are working. Our best guess is that teachers are blaming the students because they feel that to do something else would mean admitting failure. They evidently feel this to be very threatening. Administrators and parents often blame teachers for the same reason. They can't quite see what they can do to help. They don't want to see how they contribute to the problem. How can the environment be changed so that educators can look for alternatives and take responsibility without feeling badly about themselves? (See chapter 8.)

Remember that it is self-blaming and isolation that create the surplus powerlessness discussed in chapter 2. When we are isolated from others having similar problems, we often feel that our problems are due to something inherently wrong with us. We think everyone is doing just fine. You may find yourself doing this . . . looking around at others and thinking that they are not having the problems that you are having. But this might not be true. Have you asked them? Usually, when we connect with others, we will find that certain things are not just our problems. There is nothing wrong with us. Many others are struggling with the same things.

Another way to confront our sense of surplus powerlessness is to use affirmations. Many self-help books out these days suggest affirmations as a way to change the self (See Gawain, 1986; Gershon and Straub, 1989; and others.) These are short, positive statements about yourself that you can write down, repeat silently as often as possible, and put on your desk, your bathrooom mirror or anywhere else where they can remind you to change old habits of thinking. Some affirmations for self-responsibility listed by Gershon and Straub (1989) are:

I take the responsiblity to create my life.
I have the power to change my life.
I make the choice to grow. (p. 70)

Of course, the best affirmation is probably one that you construct yourself based on what you know about how you limit yourself with the blaming of self or others. Remember, it is not a question of fault. It is a question of what we can learn from the situation.

If you decide to use such affirmations, remember that affirmations repeated in private can never take the place of being supported by a community and overcoming our isolation. Don't let affirmations lead to another cycle of self-blaming if you find that they are not effective without support from others. In my own experience, such affirmations can help to provide temporary support, but they do not substitute for the encouragement of others.

Activity 7.6
TAKING RESPONSIBILITY

Close your eyes and imagine a teacher other than yourself who is having problems in her classroom. It can be someone you know or a fictional figure. Imagine that she has a very difficult class this year with numerous special needs. She has not had all the preparation she needs to deal with the problems that are coming up. She is trying very hard but nothing is working. She is tired and frustrated.

Imagine yourself walking into the teachers' room and this teacher is in the corner chair crying. You go over to see if you can help. She just lets her feelings pour out. "I can't do this anymore. I'm just a lousy teacher and that's all there is to it. I'm never going to be any good at this."

What would you say to her. Write this below.

These are the messages you should give to yourself every time you are feeling discouraged because of self-blame.

Self-esteem

No book on empowerment can say enough about self-esteem. Indeed, as I have been reading the literature on self-esteem, I have begun to think that self-esteem and empowerment are almost synonymous. Put simply, self-esteem means feeling competent and worthy. Empowerment includes this as well as knowing what you want and need, knowing how to go about creating it, and actually going through with it.

Nathaniel Branden (1971, 1987, 1992), one of the foremost writers on self-esteem, has defined it as:

the experience that we are appropriate to life and to the requirements of life. More specifically, self-esteem is . . .

1. Confidence in our ability to think and to cope with the basic challenges of life.

2. Confidence in our right to be happy, the feeling of being worthy, deserving, entitled to assert our needs and wants and to enjoy the fruits of our efforts. (1992, vii)

These two characteristics can be called self-efficacy and self-respect. The former helps us to feel in control of what happens to us and the latter helps us to connect with others without fear of losing ourselves in the process.

Real self-esteem cannot be tied to the judgements of others or even to external accomplishments. The greater our self-esteem, the more respectfully we interact with others. Thus, in our current world, as we move toward power-to/power-with rather than power-over, we need self-esteem more than ever. Moreover, "the greater the number of choices and decisions we need to make at a conscious level, the more urgent our need for self-esteem" (Branden, 1992, 13). Clearly, self-esteem is necessary for empowerment.

But how do we get self-esteem? We all know that early experiences we have in life have a powerful effect. Parents that love their children unconditionally can raise their self-esteem. Parents that respect the child's feelings, and provide structure and honest feedback, will help to build their self-esteem. In similar ways, teachers can affect the self-esteem of their students. Studies show that self-esteem tends to plunge for just about everyone during the school years (Steinem, 1992, 130). Also, the more higher education a woman has, the lower her self-esteem (Steinem, 1992, 124–25). But we cannot change our childhood or educational history now. What if we still feel that we need more self-esteem? What can we do now?

One of the most fascinating of Branden's findings is that our self-esteem can be affected by the choices we make in the now. One of the paradoxes is that self-esteem is self-perpetuating. If we have high self-esteem, we will seek and perservere in the face of demanding goals. When we reach those goals, it positively effects our self-esteem. If we have low self-esteem, we may cling to the safe and undemanding, which ultimately weakens our self-esteem. He has found that we can raise our self-esteem by choosing such things as active thinking, honest self-expression, open awareness, clarity, facing reality, respecting truth, acting congruently with our beliefs, fulfilling our responsiblities, and remaining independent.

In our everyday lives, then, self-esteem has everything to do with responsibility, consciousness and integrity. When we make our own choices and set our own goals, we strengthen our self-esteem. When we turn those choices over to others, we weaken our self-esteem. If we want to help others build their self-esteem, we need to work toward environments in which they can make their own choices, seek understanding and new knowledge, take risks, set goals, and be honest. (See chapter 4 for ways to do this for our students. Chapter 8 deals with establishing such an environment for our colleagues.)

If we want to build our own self-esteem, we must make sure that our actions reflect our values and make choices that reflect our concern for honesty, caring and commitment. We must have the courage to think independently, persevere in the fact of obstacles, and accept, express and assert ourselves when appropriate.

Of course, this is not to say that external structures do not affect our self-esteem. Cultural stereotypes of teachers as less competent than other professionals and stereotypes about various cultural groups to which we belong make it more difficult to build self-esteem for ourselves. Also, it is much more difficult to be independent and assertive when you are likely to be denied access to resources because of your race or gender. We cannot always change these assaults on our self-esteem, but we can name them and build relationships with people who help us to resist internalizing them. We can also give ourselves empowering messages and consider our self-esteem when we make our choices. All persons have a right to self-esteem.

For instance, I don't think I need to quote extensive evidence to convince you that females are often taught to think less of their abilities than males (self-efficacy) (e.g., woman as object rather than agent, as when I worry more about how I look when I teach than about what I am going to say) and to give up their own needs for the sake of others (self-respect). As Anne Schaef (1981) discovered in her psychotherapy practice, many women struggle with this, sometimes for all of their lives. Some women cope with this by focussing on the details of events, some by becoming very "good," some by embracing fairness as a strategy, some by singlemindedly following all the rules, and some by becoming incredibly understanding of others. The bottom line is looking for validation from men in power. Instead, we can see the gender-role system for what it is and reclaim our power both individually and collectively. This will lead to increased self-esteem.

In their study of women in leadership positions, Cantor and Bernay (1992) found that these powerful women had heard certain empowering messages as children. These messages seem to be very much related to self-esteem. They are

1. You are loved and special.
2. You can do anything you want to do.
3. You are entitled to dream of greatness.
4. You can use and enjoy your Creative Aggression.
5. You can be courageous and take risks.   (p. 256)

If we didn't hear these messages in childhood, we can still give them to ourselves. For "You are loved and special," for instance, we can pamper ourselves and keep lists of our good qualities. We can use positive affirmations like: "I know that I am a good _____." "I feel good about myself when _____." "I have many talents and abilities that make me special." We can pay attention when others show that they care about us.

The best way to work on "You can do anything you want to do" is to begin to take small, manageable risks. Try something new you really want to do. Visualize success. Ask others to say this to you periodically. For the message "You are entitled to dream of greatness," you may wish to look around for other people who have achieved something you admire. You can begin to emulate these people and to use them as role models. Keep a record of your dreams. They will provide you with useful information about your aspirations. For "You can use and enjoy your Creative Aggression," you will probably need to work with learning to constructively express anger. This is a long process, but worthwhile. Many books are available to help you with this, or you may wish to get professional help. Assertiveness training can help here, too. Finally, for "You can be courageous and take risks," taking risks will be necessary. But start small so that you can build your confidence. You need not change overnight!! (Other suggestions can be found in Cantor and Bernay, 1992.)

Another block to the growth of our self-esteem can be the inner critic discussed briefly in chapter 2. All of us have this inner critic to some extent. It developed to protect us from making mistakes that might cause us harm. It may also be the part of us that has accepted stereotypes about our cultural identity. Thus, it is especially active when we are in threatening situations, that is, taking risks.

The first step in befriending this inner critic is recognizing it when it speaks, understanding that it is just trying to protect us, and assuring it that we will not take unreasonable risks (see Stone and Stone, 1993). My inner critic is very active; he/she is often saying things like: "That was a stupid thing to say." "No one is going to like this." "You are going to disappoint people when you give this workshop. You don't really know what you are talking about." When that happens, I have learned to recognize the inner critic as only one part of myself. I talk to the critic and explain why I am taking the risk that I am taking. I thank the critic for his/her concern and show him/her how I am really safe. I give myself positive messages and go on. Sometimes I check with the people who the critic says will say or think negative things about me, and, to date, they never have.

In summary, we can build our own self-esteem by (1) making choices to be true to our beliefs and aspirations, (2) naming and resisting negative stereotypes about ourselves, (3) giving ourselves positive messages, and (4) making friends with our inner critics so that we can take the risks necessary for (1) and (2). These are not things that can be achieved overnight, nor are they likely to be successful without a supportive community (see chapter 8). Moreover, though we can work to take control of our self-esteem, we must also realize that many of the assaults on our self-esteem result from structural forces outside ourselves that we can try to change.

Activity 7.7
BUILDING SELF-ESTEEM

Make a list of all the things that make you special...things that you are good at. Be sure to include things like honesty, caring, communication, listening, patience, organization, reflection, loyalty, and having fun. State them as affirmations . . . as in
I am happy.
I am caring.
I am honest.
I am a good listener.
Have the courage to share these in a group.

I am
I am
I am
I am
I am
I am

I am

I am

"

"

"

"

Now, make a list of some of your successes in life. Be sure to include things you did as a child, things you do at home, and things you have done professionally. Share these with others as well.

1.

2.

3.

4.

5.

6.

7.

8.

Finally, take some time to picture and experience yourself using all these talents in your professional life. See yourself as confident, worthy and valuable. (Some say that the more time you spend picturing this, the more likely it is to happen.)

Whenever your inner critic is particularly active and you feel down on yourself, remember your successes, your special characteristics and how much you have to offer others.

Trust

Another characteristic we need to develop in order to pursue our visions is trust. Though Gershon and Straub (1989) speak of this as trusting the universe to support us, we can easily be less metaphysical and speak of this in psychological terms. Trust is intimately connected with feeling deserving. It means that we generally expect things to go well for us. It also means that we generally trust other people, within reasonable limits. We expect others to support us. (The opposite of this would be the person who expects everything to go wrong and sees all people as potentially harmful.) Whenever we try something new there is a certain leap of faith involved. We jump off the cliff, so to speak, relying on our trust that everything will probably work out for the better one way or another.

People who have this characteristic say things like: "Every problem has a solution. Things always work out in the end. I can always learn from my mistakes. People have always been there for me. Most people are on my side." People who don't have this characteristic say things like: "The world is a very dangerous place. You are wrong to trust people. No one can be trusted. Things never work out for me."

These core beliefs about the world form very early in life. They may be defenses that we build up to protect ourselves or they may be scripts that we learn from our parents directly. The important thing is to understand our core beliefs in this area and to decide to change them if we wish. How much trust do you have? Do you expect to be supported? Do you expect things to go well? Do you generally trust people to help you?

There are several things you can do to begin to reestablish this sense of optimism. Some possible affirmations for developing trust include:

I expect things to go well for me.
I am supported in all that I do.
I believe in people.
People have always been there for me.

This is a very difficult area for me, one on which I am still working. What helps the most is watching to make sure that I don't overly focus on the negative things that happen and that I pay sufficient attention to the positive ones. I remind myself of all the times that things have gone right for me whenever I feel my trust wavering.

Another way to work through beliefs in this area is to go back to the time when they began. Where did they come from? How long have you felt this way? Imagine yourself back in the situation in which they began and make a different choice. Imagine yourself interpreting the situation differently.

Positive Thinking

Many have written about the power of positive thinking. This is closely tied to trust, as described above. Burns (1980) has had success with helping depressed patients by simply working to change negative thoughts to positive ones. His work, called cognitive therapy, is based on the premise that your thoughts create your moods. "You feel the way you do right now because of the thoughts you are thinking at this moment" (p. 11). Moreover, his research indicates that the negative thoughts that lead to bad moods "nearly always contain gross distortions" (p. 12). These distortions include all-or-nothing thinking (e.g. "I am perfect or I am a failure"), overgeneralizing from a negative event, mental filtering or dwelling on the one negative detail, disqualifying the positive experiences, jumping to negative conclusions, magnifying or minimizing the importance of things, reasoning emotionally (with negative emotions), making should statements, labelling and mislabelling (e.g., I'm a loser) or personalizing (i.e., thinking we are the cause of a negative event).

Burns recommends that every time we are in a bad mood, we can think about the thoughts we had immediately before and during this mood, looking for the jump to negativity and the possible distortion. Then we can think about how we can look at the situation more positively. Of course, sometimes bad things happen that make us feel sad. We should allow ourselves to feel sad when it is appropriate. But are we doing this more than we need to?

Whenever you hear yourself or others thinking negatively you can respond with a positive spin. Here are some typical negative statements I hear from educators and some possible positive thoughts to replace them:

Negative:	*Positive:*
It will never work.	It might work.
They will never let us.	Let's see if we can.
We're all too busy.	What can we do to make the time?
We don't have the space.	Where can we get more space?
It isn't in the budget.	Where could we get some more money?
It's never been tried before.	Let's try it.
Our students can't do it.	They might surprise us.

Activity 7.8
POSITIVE THINKING

On the following chart, keep track of the negative thoughts you hear yourself having for one week. Then, if you can, go back and identify the distortion that resulted in this negative thought. Finally, and most importantly, think of a positive thought with which you can replace the negative one.

EXAMPLE:

Thought:	Distortion:	Positive Thought:
I will never finish this book.	All-or-nothing thinking	I will finish it when the process allows.

Now, try a list of your own:

Thought:	Distortion:	Positive Thought:

Flowing with Change

Finally, to be really empowered, we need to be able to flow with change (Gershon and Straub, 1989). There seems to be something about the human species that makes change difficult. On stress measures, things like moving to a new place or even getting married or taking a vacation cause us stress (Selye, 1978). Yet change is ultimately what makes life interesting.

In a remarkable study of what people cite as enjoyable experiences, Mihaly Csikszentmihalyi (1990) found that we are happiest when we are involved in something that challenges our abilities and causes us to grow. If the challenge is preceived as too far beyond our ability, then we experience anxiety. If we have mastered the activity and we are no longer growing, then we become bored.

In terms of teaching, it would seem that if the curriculum and theory we were implementing always stayed the same, we would grow quite bored. Ideally, the changes we are faced with or sometimes choose for ourselves provide enough challenge so that we can enjoy our work. I know that if I did not change my courses regularly, I would become stale and ineffective.

One of the most surprising commonalities I found in the case studies summarized in chapter 9 was that the motivation to change was provided by the need for a challenge. One said directly that she "loved to do new programs because there is a challenge in it." Another, when asked how she took on projects that would frighten others, said, "I was scared before I did it . . . but I loved the challenge."

Some educators resist change because they perceive it as something that is being forced on them. Bureaucratic and technical control are realities to be dealt with constructively (see chapter 8). The trick seems to lie in finding a way to make the change your own. Find a way to adapt it to your style or belief system and you will be able to participate freely (see Senge, 1990).

Finally, you may also wish to support your own change process. We are all growing and changing and sometimes this can be disconcerting, especially if we are trying to do it alone. You may be trying to change your teaching style or you may be trying to become a leader in the school or district. Brown (1983) has provided the following questions as ones we can ask ourselves to help move us ahead:

Where am I now in my life?
What is emerging in my life right now? What is my next step?
What is getting in my way? What is holding me back?
What do I need to develop in order to take my next step and
    to move through my block? What quality do I need to develop in my life? (p. 69)

Activity 7.9 will help you apply these questions specifically to education.

Activity 7.9
SUPPORTING MY CHANGE PROCESS

How would I describe my teaching (or leadership) style at this time?

What changes are attacting my attention? In what ways do I see myself growing during the immediate future?

Is anything getting in my way? Is anything holding me back?

What do I need to develop in order to take the next step? How can I support myself as I make these changes in my teaching or leadership experiences?

You can ask yourself these questions on a regular basis to renew your commitment to your own personal growth.

Last night I had a dream that I was giving a talk to a large group of teachers. Actually, I think it was a dream about writing this section on overcoming internal blocks to empowerment. I ended that talk with a series of affirmations for the teachers to repeat to themselves whenever they needed to support their change process. I think it went something like this:

> I am a wonderful and unique teacher. No one else can teach quite like me. I am constantly looking for new and exciting ideas that will benefit my students. This helps me to love teaching every day. My students respond by learning more and more and this in turn energizes me. My class is becoming a learning community in which differences are truly appreciated. When things do go wrong, I can always see the positive side,

the opportunity for learning. I feel free to take risks and to try new things. I have wonderful relationships with my colleagues, who support me in my growth as a teacher and as a person.

Manifesting Our Vision

After developing a philosophy of education, a vision, and a positive core belief system, we are ready to work on the transformations we have envisioned. It is probably helpful to take one step at a time and to select enough of a change to challenge our abilities without causing undue anxiety. We can't change everything overnight! The next activity will guide you in choosing one action for getting started.

The best way to implement any change is to use a reflective procedure like the one suggested by Ross, Bondy and Kyle (1993). First, get clear about your goals and carefully plan the change you would like to make. Anticipate possible problems. If this is a classroom activity, make sure that you have provided enough structure . . . remember, this will be new for your students as well. Then try the activity or change process, carefully observing everything that happens. You may wish to take notes either during or immediately after the trial. Again, if this is a teaching situation the students will give you lots of feedback if you are open to it. Examine their work. Did the results match your goals? Why or why not? Finally, make some judgements about what happened. What did you learn? Is there something you would like to change? Are you ready to go further with this change process? Again, activity 7.10 provides you with a structure for such reflective implementation.

Reflection in such a process can include technical, educational and ethical criteria (see p. 172). For instance, teachers often first look at technical issues like: Were they able to do it? Did the class get out of hand? Did I finish the lesson? Also, they ask important educational questions like: What was actually learned—affectively as well as cognitively? How did this fit into their overall development as learners? Is this going to connect with other parts of the curriculum? Were there any students who were unable to benefit due to cultural or academic differences? Finally, reflective practitioners also reflect on the social consequences of their actions. Will this help our students to become active citizens able to promote social justice? Is this helping the students to feel empowered or was there a disempowering hidden curriculum? Will this lead to a greater sense of community and connection with others? Was the change adequately multicultural and antidiscriminatory? (Activity 7.10 provides questions based on each of these levels.)

Actually, this entire process of reflective implementation is what some have called action research, research done by practitioners usually in their own classrooms or schools, in order to answer questions about teaching. (See Kemmis and McTaggart, 1982; Ross, Bondy and Kyle, 1993) I have also seen teacher leaders do action research on their leadership activities. Generally, the emphasis is on teacher research, though there is no reason I know of to eliminate administrators and parents from doing their own research. I will discuss teacher research specifically more completely in chapter 8. Suffice it to say that the teachers with whom I have worked on teacher research projects have found it to be profoundly empowering.

Teachers with whom I have worked have also found that keeping a personal/professional journal is extremely helpful in supporting their reflective implementation (see Holly, 1989). This helps to structure private reflections about what has happened and allows one to deal with feelings and intuitions as well as thoughts. Just writing about an experience often brings us new insights, especially if we avoid blaming ourselves or our students. If you have some kind of support group, you may wish to begin each meeting with each person reading an excerpt from his or her journal. (See chapter 8.)

Activity 7.10
GETTING STARTED

At this point, you are probably ready to start some reflective implementation of your own. Go back to the list of immediate changes you created in Activity 7.5. Select one of these changes and make a plan. Be sure that this initial change is realistic. Don't try to change everything at once.

Part I. Planning

    A. Planned change:

B. Possible problems and solutions:

C. Structure and time line:
(list of separate steps and possible dates)

D. Alternatives (if problems arise):

Now, try it! When you are done, you may wish to use the following guide to structure your notes and reflections or you may wish to structure these in some other way.

Part II. Notes and Observations

A. What happened:

B. Participant comments:

C. Observations of work completed:

D. What was learned:

E. Hidden curriculum:

F. Observations of specific students or participants:

Part III. Reflection

    A. Technical

        1. What worked well?

        2. What didn't work?

3. Did they learn what was intended?

4. What would I change to make it go more smoothly?

5. Other?

B. Educational

1. Was this appropriate for their stage of development?

2. Was the hidden curriculum beneficial?

3. Will this tie in with other areas of the curriculum?

4. Was there anyone who was unable to benefit due to cultural or academic difficulties?

5. Was this an important educational objective in terms of what is needed to function and grow in school and in the world?

6. Other?

C. Ethical

1. Will this help our students to become active citizens able to promote social justice?

2. Is this helping them to feel empowered or was there a disempowering hidden curriculum?

3. Will this lead to a greater sense of community and connection with the world?

4. Was the change adequately multicultural and antidiscriminatory?

5. Other?

Summary

Because this chapter was about consciously beginning a process of personal empowerment, the focus of this chapter was on you, the reader, and your process. While reading this chapter, you clarified how to identify an empowering experience and thought about what experiences have empowered you in the past so that you can get more of these in your life now. You took a look at what you really believe about education, and you thought about how you might "reskill" yourself to know all that you need to know. You revisioned an alternative for your professional experience that uses all your creativity and imagination, and you worked to clear out any possible blocks to moving forward, like blame, low self-esteem, lack of trust, negative thinking and resistance to change. Finally, you began a process of reflective implementation involving clarifying goals, planning, trying, observing and reflecting on results.

But you cannot expect yourself to become empowered on your own. Empowerment is also a collective process in which we see that others have the same concerns, and we are supported in our power-to by others moving toward greater expression of their own power-to. We experience power-with when we are in a group that supports us in this way. As stated in chapter 1, this power-to/power-with connection is essential. In the next chapter, I look at how we might create an empowering community based on power-to/power-with values.

Creating Empowering Communities

Fortunately or unfortunately, we (educators) do not work in a vacuum. It is very difficult, if not impossible, to become empowered if we have no control over what happens in the classroom or if everyone around us is functioning from a power-over competitive mindset. Indeed, creating and being part of an empowering school community is probably the most important thing we can do to empower ourselves. All of the teachers I interviewed for chapter 9 mentioned having supportive relationships with colleagues as being especially empowering.

To build such a community we must question and reform the workings of technical and bureaucratic control when they promote power-over relationships. We can also reconnect with our peers, possibly by forming an empowerment support group or by getting involved with other projects in the school and community and by actively promoting power-to/power-with in these settings. Finally, in the process of working with others in supportive and collaborative milieus, we can find our voice as empowered educators.

> Teachers must act in an imperfect world. We have no choice but to risk ourselves. The choice is to consider the risk private or to build a community that accepts vulnerability and shares risks. Vulnerability is endurable in a community of care and support—a community in which members take time telling and listening to the stories of each other's journey. . . . We must begin to scrutinize and become intentional about the communities within which we teach. (Heubner, 1987, 26)

External Pressures in the Organization

As I mentioned in chapter 2, internal factors like internalized domination, surplus powerlessness, and low self-esteem are not the only blocks to our empowerment. Educators have also been routinely subjected to pressures of technical and bureaucratic control (see Shannon, 1989). Transforming these requires that we and our colleagues question them at every level.

First, technical control is most overtly represented by the tyranny of the textbook, that is, feeling that we have to cover all of it and/or use parts that we feel are disempowering and/or use it in ways that are disempowering. It is also sometimes represented by extremely rigid and overspecified curricula that leave little room for our own, our colleagues' or our students' creative self expression or process time.

The first step I would recommend is actually checking out whether our assumption that we must implement these mandates so rigidly is actually true. Shannon (1983) found that teachers believed that they were mandated to use a basal in a lockstep manner when that was not really the philosophy of the administrators with whom they worked. This suggests that we are so used to the technical control which has been exerted for several decades that we sometimes assume the expectation is there when it is not. Talk to your principal or curriculum coordinator. How much latitude do you really have? You may be surprised.

If you are uncomfortable with mentioning this as an individual, you may wish to assemble a group of educators to work on the issue in a nonthreatening manner. You can present yourselves as persons who are exploring options. Then you can ask the questions you need to ask without seeming to be challenging or defensive. This has the advantage of involving you with your colleagues at the outset. Then, if the technical control is real, you can work together to get it changed. Keep the discussion open in the general school community as well. Join curriculum decision-making committees. Keep parents informed. Make your rationale clear and, if possible, public.

Another form of technical control that teachers and administrators often mention is standardized testing. As I mentioned in chapter 4, teachers (and principals) in Connecticut feel that they are going to be evaluated on the basis on how their students perform on state mandated standardized tests. The results of the Connecticut Mastery Test, for instance, are published, community by community, in the local newspaper.

Administrators are forced to account to school boards and parents who don't necessarily understand all the factors that affect these scores. This situation is repeated throughout the country. Indeed, when I have been involved in districtwide curriculum reform, I have found that the revised curriculum is not fully implemented until the mandated testing is similarly changed.

Again, this is something that can be explored by an interested group of educators. This group could involve teachers, parents, administrators and lawmakers. Take a good look at the test. You may find that a whole variety of classroom procedures could result in good performance on it. If the test is worth anything, it will not require you to follow a single curriculum. If your district decides to adopt an objective not measured by the test, like encouraging students to enjoy reading, then you may wish to devise some other way to show that this objective is being met. Then you can communicate your goals and successes to parents and board members directly so that they can read the scores on the standardized tests more critically.

If the demand that teachers implement the textbook or a rigid curriculum or teach to the test is inflexible, then teachers have to make hard choices. Goodman (1988) lists these five strategies that teachers (and others) can use to resist technical control:

1. Overt compliance: comforming to expectations
2. Critical compliance: conforming but remaining critical
3. Accomodative resistance: conforming but supplementing the curriculum
4. Resistant alteration: making significant alterations
5. Transformative action: replacing the curriculum with a personally developed one

Luckily, parents are in the position to object openly to rigid curricula, since their jobs are not at risk. Educated parents can be a useful ally in the process of change!

In order to get policies changed, we need to learn to work effectively within the bureaucracies in which we find ourselves. Bureaucratic control is the other major external pressure we face. Working within the subsystems of school bureaucracies can be called micropolitics (see Ball, 1987).

Fortunately, school bureaucracies are not as tightly structured as some (see Corwin, 1975; Weick, 1976). There is relatively little direct supervision on a daily basis and most of the policies are open to interpretation (Ball, 1987). School organizations are based more on natural systems models than on rationalistic models (Corwin, 1975). This means that decisions are the outcome of competitions among subgroups rather than the direct orders of a central administrator.

To work within the system in a local school district, we need to listen and observe carefully to ascertain the informal networks that exist. Who has whose ear? How much does the principal support the teachers? Informal talk is probably the best way to get information. Listen to the stories that are told. What does this tell you about the distribution of power and how it can be influenced?

We also need to learn to be excellent communicators if we are going to get things changed (see Ross, Bondy and Kyle, 1993). Communication is not only about being understood; it is also about listening to and understanding the other's point of view. Clarification of differences is essential:

> The real purpose of communication is not to manipulate others so you can get your way (even if you believe your way is what is best for children) but to negotiate with others so that real understanding results and mutual respect and professional collaboration is more likely. (Ross, Bondy and Kyle, 1993, 312)

Gordon (1970) has suggested three communication strategies that help with this (see also Lappe and DuBois, 1994). First, passive listening is saying nothing while the other is speaking, using one's energy to nonjudgementally hear what is being said. This would involve hearing both the content and the feelings. (It is probably best to respond to the feelings first, e.g., "So you're really feeling worried about how the parents are going to react.") Second, active listening involves trying to repeat back to the speaker what he or she has said in your own words. We should avoid ordering, warning, preaching, advising, lecturing, criticizing, praising, ridiculing, diagnosing, consoling, questioning and distracting because they do not express acceptance. Finally, it is helpful to use door openers that communicate that we want to hear more. These would include responses like "I see" or "Interesting" and more direct invitations like "Let's discuss it." I also like to use mirror questions when they are natural. These are questions in which you repeat the speaker's words. Here is an example of an effective conversation:

Speaker: I just can't see how we can do this!

Listener: You don't see how we can do this? (mirror question)

Speaker: No—the parents will really complain if we don't correct all the spelling errors. I don't want to be thought of as someone who can't spell.

Listener: Oh, yes, you are concerned about what the parents think. (response to feelings) I wonder what we could do to avoid negative reactions from the parents . . . (etc.) (focussing on positive problem-solving rather than negative concerns)

In the above example, the listener has begun to explore her own ideas, but she has put them in the terms of the other person's perspective (see Ross, Bondy and Kyle, 1993, 314). This shows that respect for the other's concerns. Moreover, she chose to problem-solve collaboratively rather than to simply say "I think that we should send a letter to the parents." (You never know . . . the other person might have a better idea!)

I have also found that even the most negative concerns can be switched to a positive problem-solving experience almost immediately if the other person is at all open to it. Instead of being stymied when someone says "They will never let us do it," one can simply respond by restating this as a problem to be solved: "I wonder what we could do to involve the administration in this change so that they would feel comfortable with it." (Also, notice the lack of blaming in this sort of response. See chapter 7 for other suggestions for changing negatives to positives.)

Of course, when encountering blocks, it is important to stay positive and to look for ways around them. One good example of this occurred after I conducted a two-week summer institute preparing teachers to go back to their districts to share their knowledge. Two of the teachers with whom I had worked were told by the superintendent that he was not interested in having them present in the district. After getting over the initial shock, they simply contacted the local teacher service center, got themselves certified as in-service providers and offered the workshop there. Most of the teachers they wanted to reach attended, along with teachers from other districts.

Finally, it is important to note that both technical and bureaucratic control are currently undergoing drastic changes in many school districts. The movements toward teacher leadership and shared decision-making discussed in chapter 4 are examples of these changes. If done with an eye to transforming the hierarchy that puts teachers at the bottom, they can go a long way in enabling teachers to have input into the decisions that affect them. Unfortunately, however, neither of these movements insures a caring community or the overturning of power-over. Indeed, if done in a power-over mindset, they can divide the community by putting some teachers over others and by creating an illusion of democracy that promotes psuedo-community and hidden domination. In that case, energy will have to go into revealing the hidden power plays and engaging participants in examining the current arrangement of power along with options for distributing it more equitably.

Activity 8.1
ASSESSING TECHNICAL AND BUREAUCRATIC CONTROL

What are the sources of technical control in your situation? Do you feel controlled by a textbook or a test or another prepackaged program?

How real is this control? Are you sure that you have no other choices? Speak with others to assess the reality of your perceptions.

Describe the bureaucratic structure in your system. How tightly do others control what you do? Again, are you sure your perceptions are accurate?

Is there a policy that you think needs changing? If so, how might you go about building an alliance with others who feel as you do? What will be the blocks to change? How can they be overcome? Make a plan.

Goal: _____

Possible support people in district: _____
_____

How to get support from community: _____
_____

Who needs to approve this change? _____

How can you make this happen? _____
_____

Who is likely to misunderstand this change? _____
_____

How can you help them understand? _____
_____

If you wish, list your planned steps in order:

Action   Date completed
_____

1.
2.
3.
4.
5.
6.
7.
8.

Creating an Empowering School Community

Probably the most important thing we can do to support our own empowerment is to work toward building empowering communities in our schools and districts. Though we live in a society that values the individual over the community, many now think that the breakdown of community has gone too far and may be responsible for many of our social problems.

There is ample evidence that being in a community can actually improve one's health and extend life. Ornish (1990) has reported that patients in support groups have improved recovery from heart disease. Shaffer and Anundsen (1993) have cited numerous studies that link social support to things like longevity, recovery from cancer, and improved immune function. The key seems to be feeling connected and feeling that one has someone to turn to when problems arise.

Many of us have moved away from community commitments because we we have had experiences with communities that require conformity and are dominated by one or more powerful persons. But it is important to realise that communities do not have to be this way. Many people today are currently experimenting with new power-to/power-with types of communities.

Shaffer and Anundsen (1993) describe a "conscious community" as a community that nurtures each person's individual growth and encourages individuality and diversity. In a conscious community, members consider their own needs and the needs of the group when making decisions, because they understand that what is good for the self is good for the group and vice versa. Ideally, the conscious community is characterized by synergy, the growth of energy that comes from being together in mutual respect rather than the depletion of it by dominating relationships. Individuals gain power and freedom from belonging to the community. Every member is viewed as important and his/her views are considered. The group reflects periodically on its own process. Feelings are shared and honored. In such a community, individuals are empowered.

You can work toward building this kind of community in your school. Moreover, you will probably notice that, as I continue this discussion, what I am saying about the school community also applies to the classroom. The kind of conscious community that I am describing is very much the kind of caring community I described in chapter 4 as an empowering classroom. That makes sense. The kind of community that empowers people is the same for students and educators, and I believe that the one will filter down into the other. It would seem very difficult to maintain an empowering community in the classroom if one is surrounded by a disempowering community in the school. If the school community is empowering for all educators, this respect and caring will be carried back into the classroom. Similarly, empowering communities in districts will engender empowering communities in schools.

We can begin this process of switching to a conscious community by putting an immediate end to all but the most innocent competition among teachers. It's not about who is a better teacher than who, and leaders who set this up are heading for trouble. The result of this kind of constant comparison among teachers is surplus powerlessness . . . the retreat into isolation and self-blaming. I believe we should outlaw all talk that compares or ranks teachers in relation to each other. Each teacher is unique and has an important contribution to make to the school . . . period.

Of course, the tendency to rank people is not unique to schools. It is the dominant rationality of our society. We are always competing . . . who has on the best dress, who looks the best, who is the smartest, who is the most popular, who is the most successful, who has the nicest house, the fanciest car, the list goes on and on. This is all tied to the myth of the variability of human worth that I discussed in chapter 3. It reinforces the constant fear that some humans are more valuable than others . . . and so, we must fight for our worth by being better than others or at least as good as others on every criterion we can imagine. Once we really rid ourselves totally of that notion, it helps us to see that all educators are worthy of support and care as are all students.

Thus, if we are to have conscious communities in our schools, any sort of qualitative evaluation of teachers must allow for individual differences in goals and style. Evaluative feedback given to teachers can always include praise as well as suggestions for change and should be in the form of a two-way discussion between the evaluator and the teacher rather than a lecture from the all-knowing evaluator. All evaluative decisions can be made on the basis of multiple and varied examples of the teacher's work and can avoid comparisons with other teachers or expectations that all teachers teach alike.

Indeed, I would suggest that all negative statements about other educators stop immediately, even those statements said in confidence to a trusted colleague. When you put someone down, you are saying that it is OK to put people down, and, if you want a conscious community, it is not. Similarly, in our classrooms we want only positive statements made about our students. Even corrections or suggestions for improvement can be prefaced with praise and stated in a positive manner, and most of us already avoid all overt comparisons.

Connected to this, then, is the importance of supporting and affirming individual differences. Cohen (1990), in a study of teachers identified as excellent, found that almost every teaching style was present in this group. In other words, teachers are excellent when they do what they do well. Our constant search for the one right method of teaching completely denies our basic individuality. What works for you might not work for the teacher next door and vice versa. You have very different styles, personalities, and so on. It may be important to let others know that you respect the way they teach even though your styles are very different. Just as we value diversity in our classrooms, we can value diversity among the teaching and administrative staff.

Moreover, the decision-making and communication channels in the school must be inclusive if we are to have a truly empowering community. This means that dissenting voices are honored and heard. One usually finds that these dissenters have a hidden message for the group to consider. "Remember that the identified troublemakers are actually messengers revealing imbalances in the system as a whole. Look into the mirror that they hold up to discover the shadow of your community, then bring it into the light" (Shaffer and Anundsen, 1993, 239).

Peck (1993) has said that in order to move from a "pseudo-community" to a conscious one, members must go through a painful process of "emptying." They must shed expectations and preconceptions, prejudices and quick-fix solutions, the need to fix or solve and the need to control. Only after such self-examination will we be able to share and listen authentically.

For nothing overcomes isolation and feelings of powerlessness like authentic communication. Put simply, this is a discussion in which everyone speaks their truth. Unfortunately, we are so used to having to hide our feelings, especially if they are negative, that we have to work very hard to learn to speak openly. Yet, if a community is to have authentic communication, then it must be prepared for conflict and change. All groups go through natural stages moving from excitement with possibilities to a struggle for autonomy to a stable structure to synergy to some sort of transformation which may involve expanding, segmenting or temporarily disbanding (Shaffer and Anundsen, 1993, 210). Any group that tries to be in harmony all the time will quickly become a disempowering community in which real communication is blocked.

An empowering community is also a caring community. This includes the model of caring I discussed in chapter 4 . . . engrossment or empathy with the other's point of view and displacement of motivation or desiring to help the other get what he or she needs. This means that if one teacher feels she needs the support of a textbook when the rest of the teachers are abandoning it, that teacher's need is respected. Perhaps she continues with the textbook at hand, or, perhaps, her need for structure is met in some other way. It also means that if one teacher is really excited about trying a writers' workshop and the rest of the school is working on the math curriculum, there is some space made to allow her to go with her passion. It means that if the principal or superintendent is really excited about a new approach, some of the teachers will volunteer to try it.

Caring also means that if a teacher or administrator has a sick child or spouse or has suffered a great loss, the community comes together in support, perhaps with team teaching lessons, being with him or her in the teachers' lounge, or even doing something as simple as bringing him or her special lunches or making dinner for his or her family. Shaffer and Anundsen (1993) suggest that even work communities should have permeable boundaries between work and personal life that allow such support to develop (p. 120).

Finally, an empowering school community must support risk-taking if it is to support growth. This means that it must also be comfortable with failure. One of the most powerful ways to overcome surplus powerlessness is to share our failures so that others can move out of their own isolation and self-blaming. They can see that they are not the only ones who are having problems with motivating the students or finding time for science or grading creative projects or whatever. The administrative personnel can change the expectation that experimentation must always go well. There can be praise for trying something new with a healthy expectation that it will probably *not* be perfect the first time. If you and your colleagues can laugh when things go wrong, you are probably on the right track. I have found that laughter is an extremely powerful tool for dispersing the stress of change and uniting colleagues in a shared experience.

Activity 8.2
EXAMINING THE SCHOOL COMMUNITY

Think about the social climate in your school. What are its disempowering characteristics? Are there cliques? Teachers who are more supported by the administration than others? Teachers who are more respected than others? Competition? Isolation? Lack of support? Pressure to conform? List the disempowering aspects of your school community below.

What are the empowering characteristics of your school community? Good communication? Experimentation? Support and caring? Shared decision-making? Cooperation? Support for diversity? Support for risk-taking and failure? Authentic sharing? Laughter? List what comes to mind.

Now, what can you do to build on the empowering aspects of your community and discourage the disempowering ones?

List three things you can do immediately.

1.

2.

3.

Senge (1990) has provided a model for the "learning organization" which has been adopted by many corporations in the attempt to remain competitive in the twenty-first century. This model has much in common with the model for conscious community I have just described and perhaps provides some structural ideas about reorganizing schools. Senge postulates that only a "learning organization" based on (1) systems thinking (seeing how everything is related to everything else), (2) personal mastery (the growth of individuals in their personal goals—see chapter 7), (3) mental models theory (the awareness of assumptions and their limitations), (4) shared vision (the product of individual visions), and (5) team learning (learning in groups based on authentic dialogue—see chapter 4) can change fast enough to remain effective in the postmodern world. Enemies of such a system include identifying with one's position rather than feeling a part of a whole, blaming outside forces for problems, reacting to small events without seeing the big picture, and resistance to conflict and openness.

Senge puts great emphasis on the learning team as a basic unit for running the organization. In such teams, members must be open and open-minded. Individual visions must be merged into a shared vision not through capitulation but through dialogue and mutual understanding. These teams (1) think insightfully about complex issues by tapping into many minds rather than just one, (2) work together by acting with an awareness of each other's actions, and (3) have roles on other teams so learning can filter through the organization. The role of the leader is to create the conditions for such team learning. Decisions are made by teams rather than by management whenever possible.

I have described this in some depth because it seems to me that school districts organized around such learning teams would promote the development of conscious community. But this will only happen if sufficient attention is given to the nature of the interaction in these groups. We have curriculum planning committees, school improvement teams, and numerous other planning groups in many schools and districts now. Unfortunately, most of them operate on pseudo-harmony, competition for ownership, and defensive routines like aggression and avoidance of responsibility. School leaders can directly address such behaviors and set the tone for true learning teams. They can also work to provide such teams with ample time to meet during the school day.

Connecting with Others

Whether on a successful school learning team or in a schoolwide conscious community, you may also wish to connect with others in smaller, more focussed groups either inside or outside you school or district. Most of the teachers I interviewed for chapter 9 had been involved or were still involved in support networks or groups. Though these may have many purposes like discussion of research or the development of new programs, the deeper purpose of such groups is the experience of belonging to a community in which one's views are heard and respected and in which one is encouraged to grow and pursue one's own vision.

There are many already existing groups with which you may wish to connect, like TOWL (Teachers of Whole Language . . . look for a chapter in your area) or the National Writing Project groups or various special interest groups in national professional associations. A partial list of organizations focussed on school reform is provided at the end of this chapter.

If you are looking for a group not exclusively focussed on teaching, there are also many options. For instance, the Utne Reader (Box 1974, Marion, OH) has started a neighborhood discussion group project and can tell you if there is one in your area or send you a packet telling you how to start one. Global Action Plan (Woodstock, NY), a private, non-profit agency promoting environmentally conscious living, has a system of empowerment groups centered around developing ecologically sound living systems. Of course, many social agencies, religious organizations, community organizations, political organizations and the like also provide places for empowering support groups to form.

I have often found that it is useful to start your own group, especially if you want it to be centered on teaching or another specific kind of personal empowerment. That way, the purpose can be agreed upon at the beginning and you can have input into it. I have found that 4–6 people is a good number . . . enough to get good discussions going but few enough to allow everyone "air time" on a regular basis. I have also found that groups always need more time than they schedule, so I always begin with two- or three-hour meetings. I find it nice to have them at homes where informal breaks for eating can promote another kind of communication. (Some people think that food is the most important element in any communal gathering.)

If you decide to do this, the first decision you really have to make is whether you want diversity and want to include anyone interested or whether you want to limit the group to people with certain characteristics (all women, all progressive teachers, etc.). You may wish to have your group consist of people just from your school, or just from you district, or from all over. There are pros and cons to each of these decisions. If you keep the group within the school, then you will probably find yourselves working to solve specific school problems. It has the advantage of giving you support in your building as you implement new procedures. If you go out of your building or district, you have more privacy and more freedom to explore without reaching closure on any issue. However, you will also not have direct support in your school for things you want to do.

When you first meet, you will have to discuss procedures. Again, I have found that keeping personal-professional journals (see Holly, 1989) and reading them aloud at the meeting can be very powerful. This is a good way to begin the meeting. If you do not wish to begin with journals, it is still a good idea to begin with a "check-in" in which each person shares anything he/she needs to share (see Shaffer and Anundsen, 1993, 86).

One type of journal that may be particular effective for groups of teachers is a dialogue journal in which space is left for colleagues to respond. Thus, we may make a journal entry and then share it will another member of the groups who responds in writing. Then we respond and so forth as a dialogue emerges. Though it may take some time before we are comfortable sharing our journals with one another, it can be very powerful for generating group awareness of issues (see Miller, 1990; Nieman, 1988; and others).

As you work on developing your procedures, you may wish to develop an informal list of rules. I adopted the following list from a teacher research group in Massachusetts and found it very useful for the teacher research group in which I participated (see Evans et al., 1991). You may wish to tailor these to your needs, but everyone in my group agreed that it helped us to avoid needless conflict and to set a tone of inclusion and conscious community in which individuality and diversity are honored. Also, rules should be sufficiently general to allow the group to change over time.

Finally, you will have to deal with issues of leadership and authority. Though you may wish to avoid having a leader, this rarely lasts for long. It might be more useful to explore new models of leadership and try them out in your group. You may wish to have a "roving leadership" (DePree, 1989) in which each person steps forward to assume leadership in his or her area of competence. This requires a great deal of trust and flexibility but has the advantage of keeping everyone involved in taking responsibility for what happens in the group. You may also want to rotate various roles. Shaffer and Anundson (1993) suggest that these might be "focalizer, relationship minder, event organizer, peacekeeper, gadfly, dream holder" (p. 276). I like these roles because they avoid sounding like a traditional committee meeting (timekeeper, secretary, facilitator, etc.).

Ideally, decisions will be made by consensus. This means that everyone will agree to the decision. In order to have real consensus, everyone must speak up, be open to hearing each other's needs, and be patient and honest. Members must be willing to accept a decision that they can live with, not one that represents their ideal. Probably the most important thing a leader can do during such a decision-making process is to make sure that everyone is speaking up when needed and listening when appropriate. Also, a little humor goes a long way. (Consensus in large groups is much harder to achieve and those groups will probably need an alternative decision-making procedure for the times when they reach a stalemate.)

There are many kinds of teacher support groups that can be formed. As mentioned earlier, one of the teachers described in chapter 9 belongs to a teacher portraiture group. After observation, colleagues write a "portrait" of each teacher in the group. When they all get together to discuss the portrait, they are careful *not* to turn into an evaluation group. Their task is

Table 8.1. Participation Guidelines

The following guidelines have been used by a teacher/research group in Massachusetts and may provide a useful basis for beginning our work:

1. We seek to help each other obtain more information about our own classrooms, to better understand our classrooms. We do not attempt to suggest better teaching strategies.
2. When a teacher presents her work for discussion, we respond to her by trying to see the questions and issues from her point of view, and by helping her figure out what she wants to understand, not what we find most interesting or important.
3. We try to learn something, to answer some questions about our classrooms. In other words, we are task-oriented.
4. Each participant is asked to avoid extended discussion of issues or problems over which she has no control or influence.
5. Written notes of each session are regularly distributed to all participants and tape recordings made of each session are available to any participant on request.
6. Because teaching is personal and members of the group talk about some issues which are worrisome, discussions are confidential.
7. The "subjects" of the investigation are recognized as people too; they are respected and not treated as objects.
8. Each participant has "air time" on a regular basis.

Source: Evans, Stubbs, Frechette, Neely and Warner, *Educational Practitioners: Absent Voices in the Building of Educational Theory,* Working Paper No. 170, Center for Research on Women, Wellesley, MA.

---

to observe and describe nonjudgementally, to support each other rather than to criticize or make comparisons among members.

Peer coaching provides a similar kind of collaborative situation. Teachers attempting to try new things can work together, observing each other and providing helpful feedback about what is working and what is not working. There is often so much happening at such a rapid pace while we are teaching that it is impossible for us to observe everything. A colleague or colleagues that we trust can be an invaluable resource for providing alternative interpretations of what is going on. Ideally, the role of observer and observed is shared equally in the group and there would be lots of time for discussion and support. Again, the purpose is to support each other in our growth, not to criticize, evaluate or compete.

Acually, any kind of collaborative planning or problem-solving group can turn into a support group if set up appropriately. It would have to meet long enough to allow each member personal time to speak. It would have to begin with the agreement that mutual support is one of its purposes. It would also have to begin with the agreement that all the aspects of conscious community, like inclusion, consensus decision-making, respect for individuality, and the honoring of feelings, will be a part of its process. I think that if these planning sessions included teachers, parents and administrators, they would be very effective for overcoming the barriers that have grown up among these groups.

Sher and Gottlieb (1989) have suggested that "Success Teams" represent a useful kind of support group. These are small groups (they suggest 6–8 members but I think they can be smaller) that meet in order to support each member in reaching some goal in his or her life. Each person gets the same amount of air time and the other members respond to what the person is saying in a truly caring manner . . . by listening to what that person wants and why and by supporting that person in reaching his or her goals. It seems to me that these goals can be related to education or they can be more personal.

I have also seen both reading and writing groups function effectively as support groups. These have the advantage of not focussing so specifically on education that the rest of our personality is excluded. Reading groups can focus on reading professional materials selected by group members and then discussing one each week, or they can focus on other types of reading materials like novels or controversial articles. In my classes at the university, I have experimented with having students meet regularly in small groups to discuss their personal pleasure reading. We usually begin with a short reading period followed by time to write a response to whatever one has read. The group interactions begin with readings from these reading response journals. These educators have reported to me that these groups are remarkably powerful for bonding them to each other and for expanding the range of allowable conversation.

Writing groups can be even more powerful for creating bonds of support. Again, in my writing methods classes at the university, we simply begin with a writers' workshop (see Atwell, 1987; Graves, 1983, 1994). Each person writes whatever he or she wishes. In the writing group meeting, one person reads his or her writing, and the group responds. We begin by carefully modelling those responses with templates that reflect positive response. I have used the list provided by Tompkins

(1990, 86). It includes listener compliments like "I like the part where . . ." or "I'd like to know more about . . .". It also suggests that the writer ask questions like "What do you want to know more about?" or "What is the strongest part of my writing?" Finally, listeners can ask questions like "What part are you having trouble with?" and "What do you plan to do next?" After a brief period of time, such suggested questions are not necessary as each member begins to feel that he or she can trust the group to be respectful of his or her goals and feelings (see also Graves, 1995; Routman, 1991).

I am also envisioning some groups forming around the empowerment activities suggested in this book. Reading would involve this book as well as related references. Journal entries could center around the activities herein. Certainly, sharing your thoughts and feelings as you work toward a greater sense of personal/professional empowerment would provide support along the way. It can help to lessen self-blaming and isolation, promote risk-taking, and provide an excellent forum for practicing conscious community. If you decide to start such a group, I would love to hear about it!

Teacher Research Groups

One specific kind of group that deserves special mention is the teacher research group. I had the privilege of participating in a teacher research group for one year and found it to be one of the most rewarding professional experiences of my career. Though our research questions changed constantly and only one formal paper resulted (see Timion, 1993), we all grew from the experience. Questions ranged from "How do my students choose the books they read?" to "How do content area teachers use reading and writing?" to "How am I changing as a result of my work this year?" We met once a month for several hours (including dinner). At the beginning of the year we discussed readings, then we moved to discussing our journals and our developing questions and data. Finally, we had a "party" at the end of the year at which each member shared the results of her research with a group of friends and interested colleagues.

An excellent account of one teacher's experience during our group process is provided in Timion, 1990, and reproduced here in appendix B. As you will see from reading her account, being a teacher researcher can be an intensely personal experience with its many frustrations balanced by its many rewards.

In the most general sense, teacher research is simply research carried out by teachers. The idea behind teacher research, as I see it, is that the people actively involved in the teaching/learning situation are the best ones to know what needs researching and the best ones to observe real situations over a long period of time. Teachers who do research learn to observe and critically question daily events in their classroom. In this way, teacher research can lead to real change (see Goswami and Stillman, 1987).

Teacher research is revolutionary because it places the teacher in the position of authority as he or she writes up interpretations to be read by others. Many teachers find this very difficult. Every teacher in our group at some point said, "Who would want to listen to me?" It took a lot of courage for these teachers to realize that they were the ones with the fullest understanding of the context in which they worked. Bissex (1987) has pointed out that in a traditional context, university researchers "know" and teachers "do": "If teacher research had been on the horizon ten years ago, I might still be in a classroom myself rather than having been driven to choose between knowing and doing" (Bissex, 1987, 5).

Because the teacher is a participant in the situation and because things like random assignment to treatment, controlled environments, and so on are not available in such situations, teacher research generally relies on qualitative data involving things like observations and interviews rather than on statistical treatments. This is not always the case, however. There is no reason to limit teacher research to qualitative inquiry if another option is feasible and most appropriate. (For an excellent beginning description of qualitative research, see Bogden and Bilken, 1982, or Eisner, 1991. Also, Bissex and Bullock, 1987 have a very useful checklist for getting started.)

If you are thinking about doing teacher research, then it is probably wise to start looking for examples of the various kinds of research that can be done. (Excellent examples can be found in Bissex and Bullock, 1987; Irwin and Doyle, 1993; Olson, 1990; Pinnell and Matlin, 1990.) Do not feel that you have to study research design or statistics extensively. Typical data include observation notes, copies of student work, checklists, interviews, surveys, journals and records of meetings.

Much of good research consists of simply finding a good question and deciding how to best answer it. Your question could be as simple as "How do my students interact during writing groups?" and your research method could be to tape the group meetings and later devise categories for the types of interactions you hear. Then a simple count from each tape will tell you what you want to know. It may also lead you to another research question "How could I help the students to listen to each other?" or something like that and on and on. Moreover, as you can see, when you get involved in such studies, the students can often get involved, too. This can be a valuable self-study for them. (See Stevenson, 1988.)

Probably the most important element of teacher research, however, is the teacher research group. An early text that helped our group significantly was Mohr and Maclean (1987), and there are many others now available (see Cochran-Smith and Lytle, 1993; Hubbard and Power, 1993; Patterson, Stansell and Lee, 1990; Patterson, Santa, Short, and Smith, 1993; and others). In our group, we often observed with amazement that we always left more energized and awake than when we came.

> I continued to drag myself through the one-hour commute to my teacher-researcher seminar meetings twice a month. But once I got there, my energy level rose, for the isolation that I was experiencing as a teacher-researcher could melt away during our discussions. (See appendix B)

Miller (1990) has written an extensive account of two years in the life a teacher research group. In her group, the teachers struggled with feelings of being torn between what they believed and what they were expected to do. Realizing that they all struggled with this, however, helped them to face issues about authority and voice that they could not have faced alone. They were also able to reflect as a group on the anxiety and struggle necessary for real change.

This group used dialogue journal writing to deepen their self-understanding and to get responses from each other. (After writing, the journal writer shares his or her journal with someone else in the group and that person writes a written response.) They also sometimes shared their journals at their meetings. In their journals and discussions, they often dealt with feelings of powerlessness and with uncertainties about their right to speak:

> I guess I feel a little more inside it, inside of the research process. Sort of like I tried to do with the problem-solving, to get inside of that concept to really understand it. That's what research is for me now. When we started this project, I was reading a lot about teacher constructs. I was trying to figure out

whose model I should use as I began my in-service work. But now I don't feel comfortable with others' models. I thought that I had to fit into some else's structure. But now I want to develop my own way of looking at these teachers and our work together. But it's still scary. I'm sure someone is going to say to me, so what? (Miller, 1990, 74–75)

But, after working together for a time, they also began to see the potential of what they were doing:

Our work in the teacher/researcher group has given me the opportunity to step back and question my motives, philosophies, desires, and responsibilities as "teacher." It has given me the strength to ask the question "who am I?," knowing that by questioning, I was actively choosing to grow and change. As a result of my question, many "tried and true" procedures and mandated techniques for classroom teaching no longer worked for me. I could no longer follow set ways for time management in my classroom but began to allow my own ways of teaching to come through. . . . It also was an honest realization on my part that I was not as comfortable with journal writing as most of the other members of our group. But their acceptance of my individuality allowed me to grow even stronger in my own personal acceptance of myself as teacher, researcher, and person. (p. 146)

As mentioned above, they also realized that it was critical not to push for conformity within the group, that their differences were OK and even valuable. This, then, was an empowering community from which they were able to draw needed support.

Activity 8.3
GETTING SUPPORT

1. Do you have support for looking honestly at your practice and making the changes you think are important? Describe the support you already have in place.

2. Now, how can you get more support? Think of other people or re-sources that are available to you. How can you tap into these?

Resource	How to connect	When to try

3. If you are thinking about joining or starting a support group, let your-self envision what it would be like, ideally:

Type of membership:

Purpose:

Meeting time and structure:

What might you get out of this?

What would make this group special?

Finding Our Voice

In the teacher research group in which I participated, we all agreed that the most powerful part of the experience was finding our own voice. Indeed, when getting ready to give a presentation on our experience, the group developed the following definition of teacher research and voice:

Teacher research is . . .

1. Learning about yourself, your students, and your classroom.
2. Finding your own voice: Recognizing the complexity of the classroom and the subjectivity of the observer and then speaking honestly about your own experience.

In the teacher research group documented by Miller (1990), voice was also a constant theme. For instance, one teacher talked about realizing that she had something important to say:

> I'm finally beginning to believe that you begin to know you're a person with possibilities of acting in charge of your own life when you don't need approval from everyone! Or if you can see ways in which to act around the stuff that's holding you down. . . . When I went to Albany a few weeks ago for another mentor meeting. . . . This time, I sat in the meeting and realized that, although no one asked about my dissertation, I knew that I had some important things to say, as a result of my research and our work here. And so, this was the first time that I spoke up at one of these large mentor meetings. I just didn't care anymore if they thought I was good, or not. I just knew that, finally, I had something to say! (p. 127)

Miller speaks of "speaking and questioning in our own voices" and "knowing that the question and our own voices will be constantly emerging" (p. 186) as one of the key elements of the experience of this research group.

Of course, finding one's voice is not as easy as it sounds, and I suspect that it is a life-long process, as is the accompanying process of empowerment. To truly feel that we have found our voice, we have to practice speaking our truth in all sorts of situations. The place to start is probably with supportive colleagues, as in the teacher research groups I have described above. Then we must also assert our right to speak authentically with our peers, with our bureaucratic "superiors," and in the community. If we write, we must continually revisit our writing for the authenticity of the voice. Is this what is expected or our honest self-expression?

To find and keep our voice, we must be involved in a continuous uncovering of layers of expectation and hegemony. We must be continually aware of our own subjectivity, our location in spheres of gender, class, race and ethnicity. We must acknowledge our own agendas as well as those of others, and we must exercise our voice in community. To do these things, we must develop a critical literacy of our own in which we read and write to make sense of and transform the world in which we live. (See chapter 6.)

Activity 8.4
PRACTICING VOICE

---

1. Write a summary of this book as it might be written for a library journal.

2. Now, write a summary of this book for a group of supportive colleagues. Use your own voice.

3. What are the differences between (1) and (2)?

Summary

This chapter has been about our relationship to community. If we are to empower ourselves to make a difference, we must acknowledge our need for a supportive, empowering community. This sort of community welcomes individual differences, honors feelings, and includes all opinions in decision-making processes. It is a community based on a ethic of care and mutual respect. We can work toward building this sort of community in the school or district in which we work, and/or we can look for networks and support groups that can sustain us. Teacher research groups are especialy useful for this because they provide a structure for looking at ourselves and our classroooms with our own eyes. Whatever type of community we find, we must learn to participate in it with an authentic voice for it is only in the honest expression of our beliefs that we can truly experience empowerment.

Partial List of School Reform Organizations

Accelerated Schools Project
Henry M. Levin, Director
National Center for the Accelerated Schools Project
Stanford University
CERAS 109
Stanford, CA 94305

American Assoc. of School Administrators
Anne Marie Rezelman or Lewis A. Rhodes
Total Quality Network
American Association of School Administrators
1801 North Moore St.
Arlington, VA 22209

American Federation of Teachers
Eugenia Kemble
Assistant to the President for Educational Issues
American Federation of Teachers
555 New Jersey Ave., N.W.
Washington, DC 20001

Association for Effective Schools Inc.
Ben A Birdsell, Director
Association for Effective Schools Inc.
8250 Sharptown Rd., R.D.
Box 143
Stuyvesant, NY 12173

Center for Educational Renewal
Roger Soder
Associate Director
Center for Educational Renewal
313 Miller Hall, DQ-12
University of Washington
Seattle, WA 98195

Center for Leadership in School Reform
Phillip C. Schlecty, President
The Center for Leadership in School Reform
950 Breckenridge Lane, Suite 200
Louisville, KY 40207

Coalition of Essential Schools
Carrie Holden
The Coalition of Essential Schools
Brown University
Box 1969
Providence, RI 02912

College Board - Equity 2000 Program
Vinetta Jones
National Director
Equity 2000, The College Board
45 Columbus Ave
New York, NY 10023

Developmental Studies Center
Christi Zmich
Development Studies Center
2000 Embarcadero, Suite 305
Oakland, CA 94502

Education Commission of the States
Judy Bray
State Systems Coordinator
Education Commission of the States
707 17th St., Suite 2700
Denver, CO 80202-3427

Effective Schools Products Ltd.
Lawrence W. Lezotte
Effective Schools Products Ltd.
2199 Jolly Road, Suite 160
Okemos, MI 48864

Efficacy Institute Inc.
Kimberly Taylor
The Efficacy Institute
128 Spring Street
Lexington, MA 02173

Foxfire Fund Inc.
Kim Cannon
Administrative Assistant
Foxfire Fund
P.O. Box 541
Mountain City, GA 30562

Galef Institute
Sue Beauregard, Vice Pres. -Programs
The Galef Institute
11150 Santa Monica Blvd., 14th floor
Los Angeles, CA 90025

Global Alliance for Transforming Ed.
Phil Gang, Director
P.O. Box 21
Frafton, VT 25146

Higher Order Thinking Skills
Stanley Pogrow
University of Arizona
College of Education
Tucson, Ariz. 85721

Impact II
Ellen Myers
Impact II
285 West Broadway
New York, NY 10013

League of Professional Schools
Lew Allen, Director of Outreach or
Carl Glickman, Chair
League of Professional Schools
University of Georgia
124 Alderhold Hall
Athens, GA 30602

National Alliance for Restructuring Ed.
Judy Codding, Director
National Alliance for Restructuring Ed.
700 11th St., N.W., Suite 750
Washington, DC 20001

National Center for Effective Schools Res. & Dev.
Florence Johnson, Director
National Center for Effective Schools
Research and Development
University of Wisconsin-Madison
Center for Education Research
1025 West Johnson St., Suite 570
Madison, WI 53606

National Coalition of Ed. Activists
P.O. Box 679
Rhinebeck, NY 12512

National Urban Alliance for Eff. Ed.
Eric J. Cooper
Teachers College, Columbia Univ.
Office of the VP for Development
New York, NY 10027

National Education Association
National Center for Innovation
National Education Association
1201 16th St., N.W.
Washington, DC 20036

New Amer. Schools Development Corp.
Fran Freeman
New Amer. Schools Development Corp.
1000 Wilson Blvd., Suite 2710
Arlington, VA

Panasonic Foundation Inc.
Sophie Sa, Executive Director
Panasonic Foundation Inc.
One Panasonic Way, 3G-7A
Secaucus, NJ 07094

Project Zero
Lisa Bromer, Staff Assistant
Project Zero
Longfellow Hall, 3rd Floor
Harvard Graduate School of Ed.
Cambridge, MA 02138

Quality Ed. For Minorities Network
Shirley McBay, President
Q.E.M. Network
1818 N St., N.W.
Suite 350 Washington, DC 20036

School Development Program
Edward T. Joyner
Acting Director
School Dev. Program
Yale Child Study Center
47 College St., Suite 212
New Haven, CT 06510

Success for All
Robert E. Slavin, Project Director
Success for All Program
Center for Research on Effective Schooling for Disadvantaged Students
Johns Hopkins University
3505 North Charles St.
Baltimore, MD 21218

For more information on these organizations see Olson (1994).

CHAPTER NINE

Teachers Speak for Themselves

Though this book is not only about empowering teachers, I do feel that it is important to look specifically at the conditions of teachers' professional lives. Teachers have traditionally been at the bottom of the hierarchy of educators, yet many have managed to manifest power-to/power-with in their work. Why is it that some teachers find their way to personal empowerment through teaching and others continue to feel powerless and overwhelmed? What early experiences are common among those teachers who seem to exemplify the empowerment concept? What beliefs and values or personality characteristics are common among these "empowered" teachers? Were they "empowered" when they began teaching or is it something they developed? What professional experiences have supported them in their growth toward self-actualization? What professional experiences have been or continue to be disempowering for them? How is their empowerment expressed in their work?

These were the questions that motivated me to begin this book and to conduct a series of brief case studies of teachers who exemplified my concept of empowerment (see chapter 1). I had worked in many in-service programs including one designed to promote teacher leadership. I had seen that some teachers were able to grow toward returning to their districts as leaders while others were not. What were the conditions that enabled these exceptional teachers to initiate and maintain high levels of professional activity expressing their own beliefs and actualizing their own visions? Why were they not discouraged by administrative blocks and bureaucratic conceptions of the teacher's role? Though I don't think these questions can ever be fully answered, the examination of the concrete conditions associated with expressions of empowerment seems critical if we are to promote empowerment as a strategy for change, and I could not possibly have written a book on this topic without grounding my theories in the lived reality of teachers.

Because they were intially the stimulus for my need to explore empowerment, I first chose to study two teachers with whom I had worked and maintained contact. Lauren and Sally had participated in my summer workshop to train teacher-leaders in the language arts. Sally had also subsequently taken courses from me at the university. Both had been active in promoting change in their districts. Because Lauren teaches second grade and Sally teaches sixth grade (fourth grade when I was planning the study), I decided that I should look for junior and senior high school teachers as well. Moreover, it seemed important to also interview teachers who had not had any previous exposure to me or my philosophy. Thus, I contacted the Connecticut Writing Project because it was also a home for teacher-leaders who were involved in change. After discussing my concept of empowerment with the director of the project, I was given the names of three teachers who, in the opinion of the director, exemplified my definition. Lee teaches seventh grade, Samantha teaches high school (9–12), and Marni teaches education courses at the college level (after fifteen years experience as a high school teacher).

I was excited about the scope of experience represented by these five teachers, but there were some limitations. First, I was unable to add a teacher who taught in an urban area or a teacher of color. Lauren and Sally taught in rural areas and Lee and Samantha taught in suburban areas. All five were white women. I didn't think of it at the time, but the age range turned out to be small: 40–58. I suspect that this was not an accident. This seems to be the age in which many people come into their own professionally (see Brown, 1983; Super and Hall, 1978; and others). I don't know if it would have been easy to find a young teacher who had achieved a very high level of autonomy, though as the profession changes and professional preparation begins to encourage reflective action, this may change. These teachers had between 15 and 28 years of teaching experience. This is, again, probably reflective of the fact that we gain confidence and reflective ability as we grow and develop as teachers (Fuller, 1969).

With each of these teachers, I conducted one two-hour semi-structured interview and followed it up with calls and letters. I also visited each of the teachers in their classrooms for one half-day each. The initial plan was for each teacher to write up a personal history by revising the tran-scribed interview. The teachers were then going to share their histories with each other so that they would actually become the researchers. We would discuss the similarities and differences in their experiences and they would decide what was most important. I thought that this sort of collabo-rative self-study would overturn the unbalanced power relationship be-tween the subject and researcher (see Lather, 1991).

This was quite a learning experience for me. Not surprisingly, the teachers were not nearly as invested in this plan as I was . . . it had been my plan. I conducted the interviews, visited each teacher for one half-day in her classroom and had the tapes of the interviews transcribed and for-warded to the teachers for revision and expansion. I held an initial meeting of the group so that they could get to know one another. Unfortunately, the teachers found that the demands of their classes were too great and only one was able to return the interview in time for any group analysis. Thus, though the data slice was rather thin for a traditional study, I changed my plans and worked with the data myself, studying each inter-view and observation for categories of information and eventually settling on those which seemed to carry the essence of each case study. I then wrote the teachers to verify and check information and I sent them all my write-ups, asking for corrections and feedback. Two of the teachers also exchanged transcribed interviews and recorded their observations.

These five case studies definitely served their purpose in stimulating my thinking as I was writing this book. I have used examples from their interviews throughout to exemplify specific concepts. However, I have decided to also assemble my observations in this chapter, so that you can get an overview of what I found and so that I can further describe how these interviews and observations ground my earlier discussions.

Scattered throughout this chapter, then, are portraits of these amaz-ing teachers as seen mostly through my eyes. The subjectivity that I brought to my examination of these teachers' lives has been clearly ar-ticulated in the previous chapters, but I want to stress that I attempted to let the categories and findings emerge from the actual words of the teachers. I tried never to impose my preconceived notions of what would be empowering onto the data. I did, perhaps, affect the topics dis-cussed by asking some of the preplanned questions. (See semi-structured interview, appendix A.) I was also guided by my genuine admiration for each of their accomplishments.

I hope that the readers of this book will not compare themselves pejoratively to any of these teachers. Each of them is in a unique situa-

P R O F I L E

Lauren

Lauren is a second-grade teacher in a small rural town in Connecticut. She has had twenty-two years of teaching experience, including teaching pre-first, teaching in a private school in Hawaii, and teaching an alternative second-grade for students who needed extra help. She has been married for twenty-five years and has two grown children.

Lauren grew up in a white middle-class rural community. Her father was a factory supervisor and her mother was a homemaker when she was young and then a librarian's assistant later. She is the older of two children. She married before finishing college and returned to college and became a teacher after her children were born.

I met Lauren when she participated in a summer institute for training teachers to be trainers of other teachers in the area of reading. When she returned to her district ready to present to other teachers, she and her colleague were told that the district could not support this. Undaunted, they became certified as in-service providers at the local teacher service center and presented anyway. They did this because they were committed to spreading the word about the possibilities of teaching literacy as a process that can actively rather than passively involve students.

Lauren has worked cooperatively with other teachers in many capacities. With the remedial teacher, she designed a literature program for poor readers when she realized how discouraging and unmotivating the basal program being used at that time was for them. She has been active in revising the district language arts curriculum in similar ways and in beginning a new early intervention program that provides in-class assessment and support for students with problems. The goals of this program are to maintain the student's self-esteem and ease the classroom teacher's burden. She has also been involved in designing a technology curriculum. (Parents and administrators were involved here, too.) She has made professional presentations at conventions and in other school districts, and she has been active on committees such as the School Improvement Team. When I asked her how she got the energy for all these things, she said that they were energizing to her, not draining. Her leadership style involves cooperative work with others. I should probably also mention that she is one of the kindest and most supportive people that I have ever met; her desire to care for others seems to be what motivates much of her professional activity.

Lauren's classroom is in what I call orderly disarray, with various learning centers in different corners and all types of materials displayed around the room. Children work mostly in small groups on projects that keep them actively involved. Lauren is patient with the children, involving them in setting their own rules and consequences and continuously reminding them to monitor their own behavior. When I visited, I saw lots of hugging and listening, and two of the learning centers involved students in thinking critically and creatively about their reading and then discussing their thoughts with each other: "It's OK to disagree as long as you do so with kindness." (When she said this, I thought how characteristic of her it was.) One group was discussing the impact of television. On the board were two questions: (1) Why do people watch television? (2) What did people do before television was invented? Lauren teaches reading with literature, uses process writing techniques and gives the students numerous opportunities to make their own choices. Indeed, she rarely gives her students an answer; rather, she guides them toward discovering the answers for themselves.

Lauren is the teacher I interviewed who seemed the most concerned about preparing kids to contribute to society. She believes in having them take action when they see injustice (see story on p. 126 about trees), and having them "look at issues beyond their community." She talked about having them get a vision of what things could be. She appreciates the diversity in her classroom and tries to help kids appreciate the differences while seeing that they also have similar needs and wants, for instance, to be acceptd, part of the group, and so on. She is aware of social issues that affect her students' performance like the changing nature of families and the lack of preparation of young

Lauren (*continued*)

Her philosophy of teaching seems to center around the beliefs that "every child can learn" and that they need to see that "the power is theirs" to make something of themselves. She works to develop self-esteem and strategies leading to independence. She is against ability grouping because of its effects on self-esteem. She believes in kids and sees them as "whole people." She is reflective about her work and likes to look for the rationale behind things. She has a clear sense of mission: "My goal for each of my students is that each will come to know what responsibility is, how to seize it, nourish and protect it, use it to govern their lives, see it as a privilege, right, and duty in their lives."

Lauren is very self-reliant and often initiates things on her own. She prefers to make her own decisions and believes that teachers should be the ones to make decisions about the students and classrooms because they, not publishers, are the ones who know their students best. She "doesn't like anyone telling her what to do," and she is quite tolerant of others: "They need to operate in their own comfort zone." She says only positive things about her colleagues and about parents (as well as students). Lauren loves challenges: "I love to do new programs because there is a challenge in it."

Lauren is now, as always, involved in new ideas. She has a vision of designing training programs for first-time parents to help them with parenting. Along the way, some could be helped to get a GED or to work with a literacy volunteer to develop reading and writing competencies. She really envisions giving the school back to the community. Also, she has been approached by a California publisher to do some curriculum designing in the area of critical thinking.

Lauren says that, for her, "empowerment is characterized by a sense of self-initiation, by commitment, faith, and an element of reflective, analytical contemplation; a global perspective of school blended with vision and action." Her advice for readers is to "Seize the moment and do what must be done."

tion as is each reader. I am not holding these people up as models who have found all the answers. Rather, I am looking at the lives of real teachers in order to uncover some of the complex factors that affect how empowerment is developed, maintained and actualized in schools.

Moreover, possibly even more informative than looking at the lives of these teachers individually was looking at their self-disclosures in terms of similarities and differences. (It is important to note that this is a phenomenological study, i.e., there is no claim that these are the facts; rather, the findings reflect how the teachers saw their experiences.) As expected, there were many similarities in the kinds of experiences they reported, but there were many interesting differences as well. It is clear to me from doing these brief case studies that each teacher's experience of empowerment is entirely unique.

Empowering Experiences: Connection, Autonomy and Self-Esteem

All of the experiences reported by these teachers as empowering seemed to fall into the categories of connection, autonomy and self-esteem, or some combination thereof. (For instance, support from family and friends gives one a sense of connection, builds self-esteem, and, if empowering, encourages autonomy.) I was amazed at how clearly these three categories, which emerged directly from the interview data, mirrored my beliefs about the importance of community (chapter 8), of personal, internalized empowerment (chapter 7), and of breaking through external barriers to authenticity (chapter 2).

Personal Background

Though I have not said much about it earlier because it is much too big a subject for this book, it is clear that one's childhood experiences and one's current family life will affect one's sense of empowerment. In terms of their family histories, these teachers look pretty much like typical teacher demographics, with a combination of rural and suburban backgrounds. Their families were a mixture of middle- and working-class, with two of the teachers being first-generation college. All of their mothers were housewives when they were little, but two of their mothers went back to work later in life. Three were oldest children, one was an only child, and one was the younger of two.

None of these teachers felt that they had received messages from their parents about limitations on women's roles, except for Lauren who felt that she had learned that "a woman's place is in the home." Though not all had perfectly secure and loving childhood experiences, most felt that they were raised to believe that they could do anything they wanted. Three specifically mentioned a high priority being put on education and achievement. None mentioned feeling pushed into marriage and family. In contrast, three mentioned their families having high expectations in terms of academics. In terms of the empowering messages identified by Cantor and Bernay (1992) (see p. 43), this could be interpreted as a form of "You are entitled to dream of greatness."

In addition, Sally spoke quite a bit about the expectation that she contribute to society:

> There was also an expectation that whatever you did or whatever you decided to do careerwise was going to be to serve others. You had to contribute to society.

Since all these teachers clearly had this value (see p. 276), one might speculate that it could also be related to the strong religious backgrounds cited by three others (though Sally said that in her case it was a family, rather than specifically a religious, value). It also indicates that these teachers were raised with a sense of a connection to a community that went beyond themselves.

In terms of family support, this group seemed to feel a lot of it, though not universally and not all the time. All felt they had some support from either parents or extended family members in their childhood, though some more than others. For instance, Lee said quite a bit about support from her mother:

> the second time my mother stepped in [the first was with a math teacher], she went to the guidance counselor at school and said, "Look, my daughter's going to college."

as well as about support from both her parents:

> [What's supported you through these changes?] The underlying support from my parents to go for it.

The three married teachers also mentioned support from their current families. For instance, when asked how she got to be a risk-taker, Lauren said:

I think it was really awakened in me by my husband. . . . My husband is a maverick of sorts.

Similarly, Samantha said:

My husband is a tremendous support. My husband would say, "Why are you putting up with that? . . . He has been one who really wants me to say what I think and feel.

Finally, three of the teachers mentioned high school teachers who strongly influenced their lives. (Interestingly, all three of these mentioned nuns, though Lee went to public school and had contact with nuns only through friends.) For instance, Lee talked about a teacher who influenced her positively:

In high school I became involved in drama and my English teacher in my sophomore year was the drama coach and he was a very important person in my life both because we had this ongoing argument in class and also because of what he was able to get me to do in plays and drama. He opened me up to the possibility that I could be more.

Samantha had a teacher who stayed after school every day to help her learn Latin:

I had a teacher in school who was very much a role model, a nun who was a remarkable teacher. She was a history teacher. She tutored me in Latin . . . for two years, giving up her own time . . . saying . . . you will go to college and find other smart people who are hardworking.

Marni had experience in the Catholic schools with nuns who provided examples of leadership and independent thought:

I think one [role model] . . . was a particular nun who was far ahead of her time. She had signed a petition saying that abortion should be allowed. . . . [N]uns provided images of women as leaders.

Thus, all five teachers had been able to find some support for their self-esteem and autonomy through connection with others in their childhood and/or personal lives.

P O R T R A I T

Sally

Sally is a sixth-grade teacher in a small rural town in Connecticut, the same one in which she was raised. She has had fifteen years of teaching experience with fourteen of them being in this district and some involving special education, resource room, and other remedial assignments. Most of the teachers in this small district have been there a long time and know each other and the people in the community very well. She has been married for thirteen years and has a child in junior high school.

When I met Sally, she was a participant in my summer institute after having taken a course from me at the university on a similar topic. (Sally repeatedly mentioned the importance, to her, of getting the knowledge she needed to back up what she instinctively felt was appropriate to her classroom.) I was struck by how firmly she grasped the philosophy behind the teaching methods and continue to be amazed at her commitment and creativity as she implements new ideas.

The following year Sally was on sabbatical with a grant to improve the content-area reading teaching in the school. When she returned to her district to work on her grant, she shared some of the ideas she had learned about teaching reading as an active process, and she modelled teaching strategies in a variety of classroom situations when she was asked to help out. As a result, she and her colleagues in the fourth and fifth grades formed an informal support group to discuss some of the issues that were arising. They met once a week after school and sometimes at one of their homes and, in the course of these meetings, decided to change from a homogeneous to a heterogeneous grouping. They worked hard to plan a new curriculum and present it to those in charge. These were all grassroots changes. . . . Sally always characterized herself as just one of the group, rather than as a leader. (Indeed, she used "we" in the interview more than anyone else did.) Now she is involved in similar changes in the sixth grade. She has also done presentations in other school districts and presentations to the board of education and to parents.

Sally's teaching style is very similar to her leadership style. She avoids being directive and works to bring out the best in others by working collaboratively. She is committed above all to helping the kids take responsiblity for their own learning. "My goal as a teacher is to have them not need me." She provides lots of opportunities for individual and collaborative activity on self-selected topics. Reading and writing are fully integrated into the content areas. She involves the kids constantly in setting goals and evaluating their own work, as well as in taking some responsibility for classroom discipline. She teaches most skills as strategies that the students can choose to use as they pursue their self-selected goals. She gives them lots of support and positive feedback.

When I visited Sally's classroom, the students were giving presentations on their individual research topics. One was on computers and one was on the pollution of the ocean. The students gave each other written feedback. Sally encouraged them to talk about why they chose their topic and how they got their information as part of their report. The students brought in a wide variety of media including posters, charts, videotapes, models, and a disassembled computer.

This teaching style seems to flow naturally from Sally's personality and personal philosophy. I would say that she is most comfortable with the "cheerleader" role of facilitating and encouraging others. "We're all here to help each other in some way." "One of our roles as humans is to care." She characterizes herself as a "supportive" person, and, clearly, this is important to her, since the word "support" came up sixteen times in her interview. She is uncomfortable with competition and is strongly in favor of decentralized authority, at least in education: "I think that it's really important to allow people to continue to have access to what they know and what they feel has worked because it may work for them and it might not work for you or me but we're not in a position to make that decision."

Sally (*continued*)

When asked about her goals at this time, she mentioned that she dreams of doing a longitudinal study of a student's growth. She said that this was important because she wanted to continue to see her work "in a larger context." When asked what advice she would give to readers of this book, she said "In a nutshell, . . . decide what you want to do first of all and base that decision on the interaction you have with your students and then get as much information as you can about it and then don't let anybody tell you anything different. . . . [I]n order for them to understand, you have to understand it first. . . . [T]he benefit of doing it that way? Because you'll develop, I think, you will develop an atmosphere in your classroom of a group of people who are empowered to learn . . . yourself and your kids"

A sign in the front of Sally's room said: Your "I will" is more important than your "I.Q."

Early Teaching Experiences

Four of the five teachers mentioned bureaucratic and technical control that they felt during their early years of teaching. They reported feeling a kind of pressure to conform or to do what was expected:

I taught the way I thought others wanted me to teach. (Sally)

We were absolutely round pegs in round holes and held there very securely. If we even tried to wiggle, we were moved to another grade level or terminated. (Lauren)

They also mentioned being worried about such things as control issues and covering the curriculum.

In contrast to this, the teachers were also very aware of their early "liberal" tendencies. Sally said that she was more traditional than now but still "unstructured." Similarly, others looked back and saw the beginnings of their current teaching style:

I had an instinct about wanting people to work independently on independent projects. (Samantha)

I was student-centered right from the beginning. (Marni)

Perhaps the one whose beginning teaching experience stood out the most was Lee. It appeared that, in some ways, that experience was more empowering for her than her experiences since. A part of this might be explained by the fact that she was teaching drama and had the opportunity to create her own program. Since that time, she has been teaching English and reading in more bureaucratically controlled programs. One might also speculate about the enthusiasm and courage of the beginner and how it might enable one to move past the conservatism of old age. Whatever the explanation, Lee looked back at this experience with longing:

The program that was really me was the shows that we did. . . . We won the state one-act competition. . . . I would work some nights until 3 o'clock in the morning building sets. It was me and the students . . . working together and there was this wonderful sense of community and being in relationship. . . . To me, it was the first real clear sense of community making a difference. I knew that I made a difference in the lives of those kids. I knew they made a tremendous difference in my life.

Clearly, it was the sense of community and connection that made this an empowering experience for her.

Ongoing Professional Life

All five of these teachers have continued to have what they see as empowering experiences throughout their professional lives. The comments they made indicated that they experienced either college or graduate school, various mentors, and collegial networking as especially empowering. Also, all had had a great diversity of experience and many collaborative experiences. Three had had administrative experience of some kind, three had done some teacher research, and all had gotten some kind of advanced training outside of their formal education. Though their experiences of these things differed, all seemed clear that these were the things that had helped them to become more self-actualized.

Samantha and Marni, for instance, both mentioned their undergraduate experiences as being especially empowering. Both attended private women's colleges and felt that there was something especially positive about the all-female environment. Samantha spoke of learning to speak up in that environment, and Marni spoke of her leadership experiences. She was student body president and a leader in various student organizations and felt that there were more opportunities for her because it was a women's college.

Lee, who attended a small private college, also mentioned the power of her undergraudate liberal arts training in helping her to see the interrelatedness of the various disciplines.

> What was fascinating was that the English class was "world" literature and the history class was world history and I was also taking an art appreciation course and music appreciation. It was the first time in my life that I had seen that it all pulled together, that the reason something was happening in music and art was because of what was going on politically and socially and economically. It was like, "My God, why don't they teach that way?"

The two teachers who attended teacher education programs at state universities did not mention these programs as being particularly empowering.

Graduate school was also mentioned as an empowering experience by four of the five teachers. This fits in with my notion of reskilling as an essential part of empowerment. Lauren mentioned that it was in graduate school that she began to ask "why" of various teaching practices (reflective teaching). Samantha similarly mentioned that her mentor in her Master of Arts in Liberal Studies program was excellent because she continually insisted on asking about the rationale behind her practice-teaching decisions. Sally pursued her graduate studies as part of her personal quest for answers and avoided going for a specific degree so that she would have the freedom to do it her way. (She seemed to feel that pursuing a degree would have been less empowering.) She used this experience to gain autonomy, and she was the one who mentioned the empowering potential of knowledge:

> I feel that I have enough knowledge now so that I'm not going to do anything that's going to hurt anybody . . . and I think that's a big thing. . . . I deliberately sought the knowledge because I saw two things happening. First, I knew that I didn't feel like what I was doing was working as effectively as it should. . . . The other thing, and this is interesting, the Connecticut Mastery Test had a lot of impact because I don't like to be told what to do. . . . If somebody was going to argue with me over how a particular student did I wanted to have my information pretty straight. . . . I wanted to be sure that if somebody was telling me what to do I was going to have some answers about why or why not it was a good idea.

Finally, Marni did not mention her graduate school experience. She was the only one currently in graduate school (a Ph.D. program).

Even more important to these teachers than their university experiences were their mentors and their other supportive professional connections. As previously stated, the theme of connection versus isolation ran through the interviews with connection as empowering and isolation as disempowering. In going over this data, I began to wonder whether the importance of these connections would have been as great for male teachers. Many have written about the fact that women in our society seem to define themselves more through relationships than through individual achievements (see Belenky et al., 1986; Gilligan, 1982; Schaef, 1983; and others), and this seemed to be true for the teachers in these interviews, though it was expressed and played itself out differently for each of them. For instance, when asked about mentors, some defined

P O R T R A I T

Lee

Lee is a middle school English teacher in a mixed suburban/rural school district. She has been teaching for twenty-three years. She has taught high school as well as middle school and drama as well as English and for twelve years she was the district reading coordinator. She went back into the classroom several years ago when her coordinator position was eliminated.

Lee grew up in a middle-class suburb of Milwaukee. She is the older of two sisters. Her parents were not college educated but respected education and always expected her to go to college. They were avid readers and have actively supported her in her school and professional choices. She began college as a music major but completed it as a drama teacher and took a job in which she created a successful drama program on her own. Later, she took a job in English teaching and returned to graduate school in the area of secondary reading.

Lee began giving workshops for teachers while she was in graduate school. She continued this as reading coordinator and as a consultant for the Connecticut Writing Project. Though she continues to share ideas informally in her own district, she feels that she has been more of a change agent in other districts due to the common prejudice that someone from outside the district really knows more.

My overall impression is that Lee has run into more administrative roadblocks in her district than have the other teachers I interviewed. Administrative shifts had forced her to choose between the classroom and remedial teaching, virtually eliminating any districtwide influence she had had as a coordinator. She also spoke continuously of a recent change in administration from one that had "heard what they [the teachers] had to say; valued what they had to say" to one that "has an attitude of us against them."

As a writing teacher, Lee believes very deeply in the concept of ownership of your own writing. She believes in letting writers choose their own topics, and she encourages writers to find their unique voices. She also talked about listening for what the students need in the moment. When I visited her classroom, the students were sharing poems that they had written. She did not analyze the poems, but, rather, encouraged the writers to share the reasons behind their choices. She also encouraged the class to experience the poem as a whole. She told me that she used to ask for more analysis but it discouraged them from sharing and experiencing the poem on nonintellectual levels, so she dropped it.

This concept of whole experience pervaded much of what Lee had to say about empowerment. It seemed to stem from her drama background. She talked often of those magical moments when "you're creating the moment together . . . when my students and I were working . . . its that community . . . that moment of creating . . . everybody makes a difference . . . everybody counts." Earlier she had spoken of that moment as

> that moment in dance when it is dance. . . . [Y]ou practice and practice and in a play you say the same lines, you do the same blocking. You do it over and over, but when you're in the middle of performing, there's a point when it's no longer that you are doing the role or doing the movement. It's the experience of being the role. It's that moment that is the expression of the meaning . . . the moment that is created by the interaction of what you're doing with the response of the audience.

This experience, which I would call synergy, was mentioned by Lee throughout the interview in various forms. It is very like the process paradigm described by Oliver and Gershman (1989) and discussed herein in chapter 4.

Lee is also strongly driven by the need to make a difference in others' lives. She talked about coming to see learning as something she does in order to share it with others. She loves to work collaboratively with others and speaks of it as energizing. She has a very strong drive to improve herself, speaking of the "drive to create, build, change and to constantly grow." She says that the changes she has made in her life have not come from a

Lee (*continued*)
plan but from the "desire for moving on to new levels of self-expression."

When asked about her goals at this time, Lee said that she wanted to seek a balance between her professional and personal life. Right now, she is totally immersed in her work. When asked what advice she would give to the reader, Lee said:

Don't try to change people who don't want to change. . . . It's a joy to work with people who are an opening for a possibility, who are an invitation; and, it is exhausting to work with people who have no interest, who don't invite you. . . . Another thing is to surround yourself with as many poeple as possible who support you and do not judge you, who will let you speak freeely and let you think aloud, who will let you talk yourself into discovering what you have to say. . . . The other thing is to try and be gentle with yourself because it is so hard . . . just accepting that I'm not going to be finished until I die . . . valuing and validating yourself . . . allowing yourself to live in the uncomfortable stage. Honor your courage for living in the chaos.

them as people who had believed in them and encouraged them (thus building their self-esteem). Others defined them as role models who had pointed the way through example (of autonomous professionalism).

Lauren only mentioned her student teaching supervisor as a mentor and a few other colleagues that she had teamed with through the years as a support network. She was clearly the most independent in this sense, though she was the one (along with Samantha) who most strongly stated the importance of the support she gets from her husband and children. When asked what "has really made the difference in your becoming as self-actualized as you are," she replied that the one main factor was her family:

> We've made it work because we knew we had each other to depend on. My children and my husband have never limited me in anything that I wanted to try. They have applauded every success, and they have rallied around me after every failure until I could turn it around. So I think that that's what it is. My husband and sons haven't put me on a pedestal, but they have allowed me the freedom to develop in any way I want and have supported me through it.

Lauren has also had lots of collaborative experiences with other teachers and seems to enjoy working that way. She talked about her sense of connection to others directly:

> You know, we can separate ourselves from one another because we're visibly different but really deep inside we're all very much the same. We need the same successes and the same nurturing. . . . I can't really say I learned tolerance from my family. It's just something that kind of developed, I guess, thinking about what is really important in the people that I meet and trying to find that important piece in connecting.

Sally mentioned only one woman administrator as a mentor who stood behind her. However, she was quite strong in her insistence on the importance for her of the supportive faculty with whom she works. Here's her description of a curriculum change process in which she was involved:

> We said "we're going to sit down and talk about this (reading instruction)." . . . We had weekly meetings. We'd meet weekly

after school and it started off by me using some of the stuff
from your book [Irwin, 1990] . . . things that I had noticed
people having trouble with. . . . It was a support group . . .
once a week after school. Not everybody did it. We arranged
with the principal for every Wednesday the 4th-grade teachers
would send . . . at three o'clock . . . their students down to the
5th-grade teachers; 4th-grade teachers would go upstairs for
. . . and then whoever was around would go up . . . and we'd
sit around the tables sometimes till 4 o'clock. The other thing
that we would do, when things got really bad, there would be
a group of us—and this is not everybody . . . we would go to
one of the other teacher's houses and sit around and . . . eat
cheese and crackers. . . . And we decided, OK, we're going to
try it [heterogeneous grouping for reading]. . . . You help each
other out. Everybody's going through the same thing usually at
different times, so you can support one another.

She also talked about her current situation:

Now, back in the classroom in a different context in a situation
that is 100% supportive . . . the situation I'm in is so positive in
terms of the people that I work with, the other 6th-grade
teachers, the group, the team, or whatever, is so positive that
I've been thinking about a project for next year, just because I
think that I have the support system to be able to pull something like that off.

Sally also talked about the positive benefit of her connections in the
teacher research group in which she participated:

The other thing it provided for me was an opportunity to talk
with people outside of the context of the school which was
really sort of getting to me [I think that whenever you're in a
situation long term it doesn't matter how positive parts of it
are, the negative parts affect you]. . . . It provided me with an
opportunity to look at things a little bit differently and I think
we all need that.

Sally aptly summarized the importance of her relationships with her colleagues near the end of the interview: "I could not possibly have been
able to make the changes that I've made if it hadn't been for the support

of the people that I've worked with." Sally had succeeded in finding empowering communities (see chapter 8), and she felt that it made all the difference for her.

Lee similarly valued the support of her colleagues. Though less formal and pervasive than Sally's support system, she spoke of good working relationships with specific teachers in the district. Her emphasis was less on the issue of support and more on the inspiration of shared inquiry and creativity:

> She'd say, "I'm having this problem with my kids . . ." and we would sit and generate ideas together and there's something that so fulfilling and so exciting to me about that. . . . That's really what I am, my inner core, . . . even in my darkest moments that was fuel for me that she and I could go out and walk and we could have a creative processing session. . . . And I also have other teachers who[m] I refer to as coaches and they're also fuel for the fire. I think they're a vital part of what empowers me. . . .
> I need people who invite me to create, who invite me to be inspired, who invite me to express myself and who make me think, who invite me to question, . . .

What a wonderful description of empowering community!

Also, in contrast to Sally and Lauren, Lee spent a lot of time giving credit to mentors who had helped her along the way. She spoke of her high school drama coach and other high school teachers who believed in her. She also spoke of the importance of her student teaching cooperating teacher and of her professor in graduate school. Finally, she included her father, mother and grandmother in the list of people who "let me know I had a brain." She said that she thought of these people as mentors because they "believed in me" and "encouraged me to take risks."

Samantha's supportive connections seemed to strike a balance among family, colleagues and mentors. She spoke of her husband and grown children as a "tremendous support" who listen to her and encourage her to "say what I think." She spoke of a wonderful teachers' room at the junior high in which she had taught which was really "a professional support network":

> Across disciplines, teachers would come into that teachers' room and talk about students and talk about teaching issues very seriously and in a very supportive way.

P O R T R A I T

Samantha

Samantha is a high school English teacher in an affluent professional suburban community. She has had twenty-eight years of teaching experience including experiences in public and private schools (one year in Hawaii), teaching English and Latin as well as writing courses, teaching junior high as well as high school, teaching all ability levels and even lecturing at a university. She is well-travelled, with her recent travels including Hong Kong and Spain. She has been married for thirty-five years to a college professor and has four grown children.

Samantha grew up in a middle-class suburb of Boston. Her father was a lawyer but died when she was a freshman in college. Her mother was a housewife with a thirst for learning (she used to quote Shakespeare) who later worked as a secretary in a library. Samantha went to private Catholic schools and to a women's college. (She attended lectures at Harvard when she was in high school.) She later got both a master's in English and a master's in liberal studies.

I had met Samantha briefly when she had taken my teacher research seminar at the university. She had taken a sabbatical to do the project and was studying kindergarten and first-grade classroooms to see how they were similar and different from her own. She left my class to go to Spain and do observations there. When she was recommended by the Connecticut Writing Project as a candidate for this study, I heartily agreed.

Samantha has been actively involved in the Connecticut Writing Project for nine years. In that capacity, she has presented workshops in other districts and at conferences. In her own school, she often makes presentations at department meetings; she has been very involved in improving the school media center; and she belongs to a "Teacher Portraiture Group" in which small groups of teachers visit each other (when invited) and then write a "portrait" of the teacher visited. She speaks of this and other activities as excellent ways to "learn from each other." She has presented workshops on "Writing Across the Curriculum" in her district and for the Connecticut Writing Project. Samantha writes regularly and has published journal articles as well as her own poetry.

When I visited Samantha in her classroom, I was especially struck by her flexibility. I observed the sophomore remedial class, a senior honors class, and a freshman "average" class. In each of these situations, she seemed to be a totally different teacher, with her style obviously attuned to the needs of the students. In the remedial class, I would have characterized her as a cheerleader or coach. The students sat in a circle sharing their writing, and she praised them extensively. The honors class was the only class in which Samantha talked to the students for any length of time without involving them. In that case, she was explaining to them a strategy for understanding Faulkner (something I have never mastered). The students were highly motivated and seemed to grasp exactly what she was saying. Finally, in the freshman class, after the students finished sharing their essays, Samantha began a unit on *Romeo and Juliet* with a survey of students' opinions on romantic love. In this class, she was, perhaps, more structured; she seemed to be leading them to an understanding of how they should behave in high school.

Samantha's style might be characterized as more "formal" than that of the other teachers. She maintains a "distance and respect" that provides a central authority which the students seem to need. She allows time for the process of writing even if that means that students don't all finish projects at the same time. She encourages them to choose their own topics whenever possible. She says that what happens in her classroom "depends on the day before."

In a later addendum, Samantha wrote me about how she sees her role as a teacher:

English teaching attempts to prepare students to be literate—as readers, writers, viewers, speakers. I believe our mission is central and serious. I also realize that teenagers are infinitely distracted and distractable. Sometimes I see myself as:

Samantha (*continued*)
- coach, cajoling students to be the best that they can be.
- model learner, reading and writing with my students—hoping to foster the lifelong joy that I continue to find in reading and writing.
- "guru," sharing the expertise I continue to seek, imparting the wisdom or shortcuts that I have spent years acquiring.
- disciplinarian, requiring a level of behavior and sensitivity to others that will preserve a civil society in our classroom.
- surrogate parent, listening to yet another story of home/school/job problems, advising or just lending a sympathetic ear
- drudge, filling out endless paperwork, making too many phone calls, keeping too many late night hours, correcting, planning, reading, writing.
- director of a play, on the magical days that students take over, in groups or individually, and I enjoy the show (so I'm audience, too).
- gardener, watering, moving, pruning, nurturing new growth.
- garage mechanic, trying to diagnose that rattle, trying to stop it, or at least keep the vehicle from breaking down.

Samantha believes that students must learn "ways of learning" in order to prepare them for the future. She tries to help them become "comfortable with ambiguity," to "read with an inquiring mind" and to "find their own voice" as writers and speakers. She encourages them to learn from each other and has concerns about tracking due to the inferior education given to kids put in the bottom track.

Samantha loves challenges. She is comfortable with risk and failure because it helps her to avoid boredom. She is constantly experimenting. When asked how she has changed over the years, she said that she is now more outspoken, sending letters or speaking up for what she believes whenever it is necessary. She deeply values individuality and says that she has a "democratic love for public education." She has a passion for her subject; she loves reading and writing and she loves literature. She spoke to me caringly about the lives of students.

Samantha's goals include explaining the value of teacher research to those in the position of making it happen, possibly conducting a longitudinal study of her own, beginning a writing lab in her high school, and working for a closer interaction between the elementary school and the high school involving both students and teachers. She also hopes to continue writing and publishing professional work and poetry. Her advice to other teachers included the importance of having supportive colleagues both inside and outside one's school district.

She also talked about her current teaching situation in which "we really have a nucleus of people who are very committed professionallly and want to talk about teaching issues." As part of her committee work, she works closely with the librarians "so they have become another support network." She also belongs to a Teacher Portraiture Group (see chapter 8) and joined an "interesting professional network of people" through her participation in teacher research. Finally, Samantha also talked of many mentors who facilitated her development, from the nun in her high school experience who stayed after school to teach her Latin and the nuns in college who provided her with models of women in leadership positions to the graduate school advisor who helped her to question teacher practice and two former administrators in her present district who encouraged her to try new things. One of them had said "Stop by my office anytime to talk about teaching":

> and I got in the habit of stopping after leaving my class . . . two or three times a week. I would go to his office and talk about issues in the classroom, or what had happened in the classroom, and he very much became a mentor. . . . How generous he was to do that.

Finally, Marni spoke of the people who had made a difference in her life and of the importance of a professional support network, though she seemed a bit more reticent about naming names and telling stories. Like Lee, she defined mentors as "people who believe in you" and who thereby help build your self-esteem. She spoke of nuns in her high school and college experience who had been independent thinkers and leaders, thereby providing her with an internalized image of the autonomous woman professional. She also spoke of the supportive relationships she enjoyed when she taught high school. Though she has found it more difficult to find these relationships at the university, she has succeeded in doing so.

Moreover, Marni also spoke of readings that had influenced her almost as if the people about whom she read were mentors. She spoke of reading the biography of Eleanor Roosevelt:

> I remember reading about her life and being struck by that and then watching her when she was appointed as ambassador to the UN and what she went though for the declaration of human rights and how she struggled at the UN for that. That re-

ally struck me; it must have been so hard to go through. She was a woman and given everything she went through and what she emerged as . . . and she never gave up . . . never gave up the fundamental rights of other people. She was always someone I wanted to know.

She also spoke of learning from the life of Marie Curie:

She believed she was going to find what she ultimately found. She believed it. She never gave that up as a possibility and it really struck me, how could she possibly all those years work in those rough conditions. . . . If you believe in yourself, it will happen.

Finally, Marni cited the quotation from Albert Schweitzer that she has kept with her since college: "You'll find success when you seek and find how to serve others."

Empowering relationships with students, another source of community connection, was mentioned by Sally, Samantha and Lee. Sally, for instance, talked quite a bit about being empowered by her caring relationships with her students:

It's been sort of a teacher empowerment through student empowerment, really. We're trying to help the kids make connections, learn more effectively, take more control over their learning and because we are doing that for them we have to do that for ourselves, too. . . . It's sort of like empowering them empowers you.

Similarly, Samantha said, "I feel empowered when they are." Lee talked about something very similar, I believe, when she described the synergistic experience of community (quoted in her portrait). She continued this by saying:

Maybe it's just about being. It's about being open, just being, being there, being present and being involved in the creation of the moment in partnership with people so that it's like you're not controlling it and then what happens is you walk away from that moment feeling inspired, feeling fulfilled, feeling like you contributed and at the same time being filled up like you were contributed to.

P O R T R A I T

Marni

Marni taught high school English in a suburban community for fifteen years and recently left there to direct a teacher/consultant network and to teach at the university level.

Marni grew up in a small working-class community in the Northeast. Her parents were not college graduates, and she was an only child. The family was Catholic and took religion very seriously. She attended Catholic schools and a private women's college where she was very involved in leadership activites, including being student government president. While in college, she worked on voter registration in the South (1960s) and volunteer social work and teaching in Appalachia. Those experiences led her to believe that "it's possible to change and I started to see that the only way we could change anything was through education and through kids."

Marni's teacher-leadership experiences began with extensive involvement in student activities. She was "involved in establishing literary magazines in the three schools in which I taught, establishing a school newspaper, working with the drama club, establishing outreach programs in the community, and running tutoring programs that were very student-centered." Several years ago, she had the opportunity to be the department chair in the large high school in which she taught. As such, she set up a K–12 writing program and began to encourage people to work collaboratively. She also promoted and was involved in numerous interdisciplinary projects. She has taught collaboratively with history, reading, and science teachers. At the university, she has similarly worked to establish a working relationship between liberal arts and education faculties.

Marni's teaching style is a curious combination: nondirective with high standards. I observed a graduate-level education class in which students worked collaboratively to investigate very difficult issues. I also observed a class discussion that was critical and dialogic; students were examining their own experience in terms of the theory in the readings as well as their own feelings and beliefs. It was hard to tell from one observation, but it certainly seemed that this was all about finding one's own voice as an educator. I know that at the university she has a reputation for working the students very hard but also being very fair. She expects a high level of performance but also provides the support needed.

Her philosophy is also focussed on the students' ability to direct their own learning: "Now I believe that you can trust the kids. They'll come up with the program and the way of evaluating it—they're better at it than we are." She also says that her role is to "provide a structure for people to be able to do what they are capable of doing on their own." In the area of writing, it is the teachers's role to "get out of the way and let it happen . . . facilitate the writers working with each other." She believes in creating community in the classroom by helping kids get beyond issues they bring in to an attitude of mutual acceptance and support. She does this by trying to get beyond the "artificial roles" that take over in the classroom so that participants can talk in a "real way."

Marni talked repeatedly of her desire to make a difference, "to give people the power to change their own lives." "There's something other than us out there and we have an obligation to it." One of her favorite quotations is from Albert Schweitzer: "You will find successs when you seek and find how to serve others." She also has a sincere belief that "if you believe in what you are doing, it will work."

Marni's goals at this time include working toward more school/university collaboration. She would also like to see teacher training programs taking more advantage of all the excellent teachers in the public schools. Her advice to readers was to take it one step at a time: "You don't have to do everything all at once. You can take small steps." She also said that "you have to do the thing you think you can't."

This seems to me to be a wonderful description of a teaching moment that is empowering for both teacher and student alike. It is also reminiscent of the discussion in chapter 1 that we cannot be empowered ourselves if we are involved in power-over relationships. It is power-to/power-with relationships that empower us.

Finally, all of these teachers had had many experiences working collaboratively with other teachers and one wonders whether this is where they began to see the value of teacher networking. Lauren has collaborated on a remedial literature program, an early intervention program, a language arts curriculum and a technology curriculum. Sally worked collaboratively on completely changing the reading curriculum (see above). Lee is a middle school team leader. Marni has team taught with reading, history and science teachers.

All of these teachers have also had many opportunities to build their self-confidence related to teaching, and this seemed to be another significant theme for them. For instance, Samantha talked about the Connecticut Writing Project "and learning to become a better writer has really helped . . . has given me confidence." She also reported that she has become more of a risk-taker as she has gotten older and that she has gained professional confidence from publishing her own work. Marni characterized the classroom as an apprenticeship for leadership, one presumably that gave her the confidence to go outside the classroom. Sally described how having knowledge gave her confidence in what she was doing.

Three of these teachers have had significant administrative experience that they seemed to feel was empowering, possibly because of the self-confidence it developed in them. Sally had spent a year as "lead teacher." In that role, she refused to evaluate and carved out a role for herself as a "coach" for the other teachers. Later, she got a sabbatical to work on teaching reading in the content areas, using the year to model teaching strategies in various classrooms. Lee worked for twelve years as the coordinator for reading in her district, thus having the opportunity to visit and coordinate programs across the grades and schools. Marni was interim department head for one year. As such, she had the opportunity to observe the classroooms of fourteen other teachers. She said that this experience helped her to see the "bigger picture" of issues across kids and classes and curricula.

Indeed, several of these teachers mentioned that seeing the "bigger picture" was important to them. Sally talked about the opportunity she had to work with the same kids in fourth, fifth and sixth grades:

So the opportunity for that kind of longitudinal look at kids and how they develop between the ages of 9 and 12 or whatever was very, very valuable, very valuable. My dream is to start with a kid, a child in kindergarten and take him all the way through, whether it be 6th grade or 8th grade. That's something that I think would give me so much more perspective about the whole learning process.

For her teacher-research project, Samantha had gone into first-grade classrooms to see how they were the same and different from her own experience. She also dreams of doing a longitudinal study, and of facilitating collaboration between the elementary and secondary schools. Lauren dreams of connecting the school with the community by offering parenting classes for new parents, clearly seeing the connection between early parenting and student success. She also wants to help these parents with their job skills in order to increase family stability in the area, again showing her awareness of the "big picture" and her willingness to address it.

All of these teachers, as evidenced in their portraits, have had a great diversity of experience, which may have increased their confidence in going into new situations. Also, it was clear that these experiences were the most empowering when they involved the freedom to create new programs and make teaching decisions on their own. (Indeed, self-esteem can develop only when we are able to make our own decisions to actualize our true beliefs. See chapter 7.) When Lauren moved to a private school in Hawaii, she had to design the curriculum "from the ground up." She has also had to design programs for pre–first grade and for an alternative second-grade class of children at risk. Sally began her career teaching special education, then teaching in a resource room, then as a Title I tutor and most recently as a 4th-, 5th- and 6th-grade teacher. Lee designed the whole drama program she ran in her first years of teaching and has taught both high school and middle school English with her graduate work being in reading. Samantha has taught in private and public schools, middle schools and high schools and has taught and assisted in college courses. She taught in Hawaii for one year, and she has taught Latin. She spoke of these experiences giving her "a distance from her situation." Marni is now teaching teacher preparation courses in a college after many years of teaching high school English. Moreover, her in-service work includes offering workshops to teachers teaching grades K–12.

Finally, all of these teachers have had extensive advanced training. (See reskilling in chapter 7.) Lauren spoke of the summer institute funded by the state that she attended in 1989 (at which I met her) in terms of the confidence she gained:

As I reflect on the changes in my professional life in the past five years, I realize that few of them would have occurred if I had not attended that institute. I would not have been able to make the contributions to our language arts curriculum. I could not offer the workshops about reading comprehension strategies. I would not have the confidence in the quality of the literature units. I no longer use a teachers' guide in language arts. . . . I have the utmost confidence in my ability to deliver instruction meaningfully and effectively.

As mentioned earlier, Sally put top priority on gaining knowledge to increase her self confidence, and she pursued this knowledge in graduate courses and the summer institute. Lee and Samantha similarly mentioned the confidence they gained from their training in the summer institute of the Connecticut Writing Project. Several also mentioned specific educational writers who had made a difference for them, like Donald Graves and Donald Murray.

All five of these teachers still regularly attend professional conferences, and several present at them periodically. Samantha wrote me later about these experiences, "The renewal one gets from seeing the profession in global ways is so energizing." I also suspect that the connection to the larger community of educators who are making changes is a vital part of this experience.

So what have we learned from these teachers in terms of empowering ourselves and others? First, if their perceptions about the influences in their life are accurate, it may be possible for messages about achievement and community service given to children to help them achieve power-to/power-with values later in life. Secondly, it may be possible for teachers to influence the empowerment of their students by encouraging them to feel self-confident and by providing positive role models.

Our ongoing professional experiences should probably connect us to others in supportive communities, build our self-confidence and expertise, and give us practice with autonomous decision-making. Pursuing advanced training is helpful especially if it is the kind that encourages us to reflect critically on our practice and if it builds self-confidence and comfort with autonomous decision-making. Supportive professional connections seem essential and can take many forms. Mentors can encourage us or provide us with positive role models. Colleagues can stimulate us and encourage our creativity. Supportive communities can connect us to something larger than ourselves. A variety of experiences and independent projects can help us to build our self-esteem and ability to work independently.

Thus, the perceptions of these teachers echo much that I have said earlier in this book. Though early teaching experiences involve adjusting to bureaucratic and technical control, these can be overcome by empowering oneself and surrounding oneself with a supportive community. Empowering ourselves involves becoming reflective about our practice, reskilling ourselves and building expertise, gaining self-confidence by taking risks, and pursuing our own visions. Empowering communities are ones in which our opinions are valued, in which we feel respected and in which members gain power rather than lose it by belonging. They can be within the school, or they may consist of persons from a variety of places. Though each of these teachers' stories was unique, these general characteristics seemed universal.

Disempowering Experiences: Discrimination, Domination and Isolation

When I began to look at the experiences that the teachers cited as particularly disempowering, I saw the same themes emerging as when I looked at their empowering experiences. However, instead of connection, I saw experiences of isolation. Instead of independent decision-making, I saw pressure to conform. Instead of opportunities to build self-esteem, I saw social interactions that implied that they were in some way lesser or less able than someone else. As you read through these experiences, you will see that they are not at all unusual. It may be that these teachers have had fewer of these than others. Or, it may be that their empowering experiences were sufficient to override them. Or it may be that their beliefs or personalities enabled them to rise above these disempowering experiences. Whatever the reason, these teachers have succeeded in becoming "empowered" in spite of fairly typical disempowering experiences.

For instance, I asked the teachers if they had experienced any limitations because they were women. Lee told a story of a high school teacher who refused to help her because he believed that females couldn't do math. She said that "he didn't believe much in educating women" and that it was then that she began to think that she was "just a girl." This reminded me of Gilligan's (1991) findings that self-esteem plummets for white girls during the adolescent years. Samantha told about how she was socialized to be "quiet and reticent" and how the difficulties of speaking up still plague her: "There is still some voice deep inside of me that says not in quite these words, but says in a sense "you're being a pushy broad.' " Other childhood messages about gender roles included Lee's feeling that she had to choose between career and family and Lauren's family message that "a woman's place was in the home."

Messages about gender continue in the lives of these teachers, though they do not seem to consciously affect them. Lee talked about seeing the same kind of discrimination toward girl students in math classes today. She speculated on the possiblity that she would have been on the administrative team when reading coordinator had she not been a woman. She also suspected that some of the lack of administrative support for teachers in her district might have a sexist motivation. Moreover, she could remember administrators who had treated her in a condescending, paternalistic way. Lauren also could cite instances of being treated paternalistically, and she told a story of being put on a committee for planning a technology curriculum, presumably because of her expertise on technology, and then finding out that they really wanted her to be the secretary because she took such good notes. "So, needless to say, I've never lifted a pencil or brought a piece of paper to those committee meetings." (She was also the only elementary teacher on this committee.) These are excellent examples of messages female teachers often get that they are lesser or more limited in their abilities.

Numerous examples of other kinds of prejudicial discounting of their abilities based on a hierarchical ordering of persons were also freely cited by these teachers. Both Lee and Samantha mentioned the prejudice against middle school teachers that says that they are less capable, intelligent or educated than the high school teachers. For instance, Lee said that she lost her power base in the district when she became a teacher in the middle school. When I asked if this was because she was moving back to teaching from administration, she said, "Well, no; I think that the distinction is secondary versus the rest of us." She said that she had lost power and prestige in the district specifically because she moved from the secondary to the middle school:

The high school people view themselves as the intellectuals and as the people knowledgeable in their fields and the people who are in the middle schools and the elementary schools [are not]. . . . [T]hat middle school instruction is all about the students feeling good and the parents just want to know if the students are happy. It's not about teaching the kids anything, and so I think that elementary teachers view themselves as teachers of students and high school people as teachers of content, that there really is this undermining demoralization of elementary school teachers and middle school teachers because there is that feeling of embarrassment or "I'm not as good." Because I am not a trained English teacher or a trained science teacher or a trained math teacher, somehow I am less of an intellectual.

Lauren similarly said that she experienced prejudice against elementary teachers:

Part of it is . . . it may not be so much being a woman but being in an elementary school—that we may not understand issues the way others do because we're so nurturing; we're so busy nurturing that the great world out there doesn't impact us like it does other people. The ideas we have can't possibly have the content or the importance of our colleagues up at the high scool or up at the middle school. Even when we talk, we speak about going *up* to the high school. When you're at the high school you talk about going back *down* to the elementary school. So there's even that perception, although we don't really state it, that one is less than another, less important or less equal in terms of what we are doing.

Lauren and Lee also experienced the prejudice that says that outsiders inherently know more than the teachers in our own district. When Lauren and her colleague returned from the summer institute ready to present what they had learned, they were told by their superintendent that he would not support their offering a workshop for continuing education credits (CEUs) required of all teachers by the state. (They went to the local teacher service center and got certified as CEU providers and presented there.) I asked Lauren if she thought this was gender discrimination. She said:

I don't think so much that it was because we were women. . . .
There were issues that the superintendent really felt were more
important than having two of his teachers present. Also, you
know there's a lot more credibility given to somebody who's
had to travel 50 miles to present. They live further away so
their IQ is elevated by about 30 points. . . . So I think that too
may have had something to do with it.

Lee has had a similar rejection of her writing expertise:

The irony is that every time my district over the last four years
has called the Writing Project for people to come out and
present workshops, the head of the Writing Project says to
them, "You have one of the best presenters for the Writing
Project right in your own district," and they know that. They
know that I've done the writing project but the impression is
that somebody from outside will better be able to tell us, or get
us to change.

Because of this, Lee believes that she has been a much more effective
change agent in other districts than in her own.

Marni has also experienced these kinds of discriminations but
mostly at the university where she says there is a "caste system" that
orders people according to status and worth. When asked why what she
called internal class and gender impediments did not stop her from
moving to the university to teach, she said:

I didn't know what the university was like. Perhaps if I had
known, those impediments would have stopped me. . . . My
experience is that (I don't know if this is true for everybody,
for every university) but it's definitely a caste system that is
predicated on very clear class distinctions on some intellectual
level. I understand why some of the things are there, but who's
published and how and in what journal makes one person an A
and one person a B; and being in one school makes one person
better than a person in another school; and that respect for a
different kind of knowledge, very often it strikes me, is not
there and that was the most appalling shock to me. . . . It
seems that people who are very very bright, and I'm not dis-
missing them, they're doing wonderful things in their own
classrooms and have excellent publications, but some are also

very judgemental of others' work. The categorizing by publication levels seems to ignore an important part of a university: the quality of teaching. I also have trouble with levelling comments such as the School of Education educators are the lowest of the university hierarchy because "they can't do anything else" . . . talk about stereotypes.

She then talked about being able to deal with this by realizing within herself that "it did not make me a lesser person in terms of being able to contribute to a discussion if I did not fit into the hierarchical system." Marni also talked about finding a support group of university colleagues who did not hold such rigid assumptions.

Of course, all of this levelling of persons is about the myth of the variability of human worth (see p. 65). For these teachers, it was experienced as demoralizing and, in at least two cases, it limited options. Their descriptions provide us with concrete instances of how this mentality plays itself out in schools. Women are sometimes seen as less likely administrators and more likely secretaries, as are elementary teachers when compared to high school teachers. Outsiders are seen as knowing more than teachers within the district. The standards by which educators are arranged according to status are complex and pervasive.

Marni's reference to her internalized working-class consciousness was also interesting in terms of internalized messages about being lesser.

I can think of externals too [obstacles] but the internal ones are more clear and some of those are issues related to gender and class. Class has a lot of significance. Sometimes we talk about gender and don't look at class issues as a part of it. I see many of my colleagues in the writing project who I look at as very committed people who could be doing X, Y or Z in many other capacities but they don't see themselves that way. I started about 4 or 5 years ago trying to look at that and in my own little mini research study I've noticed that there is a correlation to one's socioeconomic background. The background they came from, a . . . or lower middle class background that didn't see education beyond a certain point as something that was in their bailiwick, whereas if I look at many of my colleagues in my department that I'm in [university], I don't think there was a doubt ever in their mind about going on for their Ph.D.

Because these things are so unconscious for many, it is impossible to assess how much class and gender consciousness promotes the tendency of some teachers to give their power away.

Moving away from such overtly prejudicial assaults on their self-esteem, these teachers have also experienced such assaults in the form of external controls and the resultant lack of autonomy. Lauren spoke of being restricted early in her career by a rigid curriculum, having to go to in-services that were really "cattle calls," and being evaluated on the basis of how neat her room was (thus devaluing all the real teaching that was going on). Sally talked about technical control in terms of the pressures of accountability and testing (as did Lee) and how that prompted her to educate herself so that she would have answers when she was told what to do.

In terms of overt bureaucratic control, Samantha described the time when she literally had to punch a time clock (early in her career) and the time when she got a negative evaluation just because she sat on her desk. Lee felt the most pressure from the central office in terms of implementing curriculum whether she agreed with it or not. Moreover, her administration seems to be the least supportive of those experienced by these teachers:

[The bureaucracy] totally disempowers teachers. The other major shift that's occurred in our district with the two administrations (I see it as two administrations), the early administration that I worked with . . . had nothing but positive good things to say about the teachers. This district has an outstanding teacher staff. They empowered the teachers; people who were the team leaders were trusted as team leaders and they were given the time to do the job that they needed to do. If they made a request then the request was granted. The principals heard what they had to say, valued what they had to say. The current administration has an attitude of us against them. What they put out in the paper is appalling. . . . It's like the administrators are the only people who care about the students. . . . What kind of garbage is that? I know these teachers . . . they are committed people who work hard and are constantly trying to stay up on it, trying things in their classrooms, supportive of kids and now there's this, this snide, undermining, demoralizing attitude, that is, this "us against them" attitude, and it's damaging.

Related to this was the issue of time. As stated in chapter 2, technical control is often accompanied by intensification of the workload. Though only two teachers mentioned this, Samantha wrote me later to make sure that I was aware of it as an issue for her:

> Do you address, anywhere, the idea of *time* as empowering, or the lack of time as disempowering? This year, as I rush from lunch duty, to two classes, then to our new writing conference center, without even time to go to the bathroom, I wonder a lot about time. As I read drafts late into the night, or get up early to plan what to do that day, I wonder about time. Then there are all the commitments that I haven't done yet—a full month into the school year: seeing the librarian about collaborating later this month; meeting with my teacher portraiture group; seeing the preschool teacher who said last year that she is willing to do a project with me; filling out the paperwork for an Emily Dickinson conference that I want to go to with a colleague; gathering materials to Xerox for an I-Search project I want to start this month in two classes. As our local superintendent and board of education plan a campaign to require English teachers at the high school to teach five classes instead of four, I think of how teachers need *time.*

It was Marni who most overtly raised the issue of isolation as disempowering, though it runs as a theme through all of the interviews.

> You have to have a support system. I was very, very fortunate in my teaching career to have a wonderful network of colleagues who would work together with me. . . . [T]hat was the greatest stress in coming to the university, where things are much much more isolated than in the public school. Even though teachers in the public school are isolated, it's nothing like it is at the university.

When asked about external obstacles to her development as a change agent, Marni also said:

> The educational structure. It's predicated on isolation and individualism which can be plusses but it's not collaborative or empowering.

Samantha echoed this theme when she was talking about needing more professional support. She said that she was "perceived as somewhat of a zealot . . . as far as being willing to work maybe too hard." She also talked about how the departments in her high school are isolated from one another and how the teacher portraiture group and her work with librarians has really been about breaking down that isolation. (Also, her dream of creating collaborative projects between the elementary schools and the high school is really about breaking down the isolation between those communities.)

Another disempowering experience having to do with separation and isolation was the teachers' experience of teachers who resist participation and collaboration. Both Lauren and Sally specifically mentioned these colleagues as worrisome to them. Lauren spoke about colleagues that were afraid to take risks. Sally spoke about a colleague who was an "obstructionist":

> The other reason that it was difficult was because of a member of the faculty who[m] I saw as very obstructionist to any kinds of changes that might occur. This person was very happy to maintain the status quo and he wanted to be able to do things the way that he did them and he didn't really want anybody's input. I think that he felt very threatened by any kind of change and as a result through passive resistance probably did just about anything that he could to prevent that from happening. You can only work with that kind of a negative influence so long before it really starts to affect you. So I was seriously thinking about whether or not I was going to be able to do what I believed should be going on in my classroom. I decided to take a sabbatical rather than quit my job.

I suppose that for Sally, who was, more than the others, characterized by a commitment to connection and community both personally and philosophically, this is the downside of connection . . . not being able to work effectively with others is disturbing. Another downside for her was the stress she felt about others' stress during the period of change:

> I would almost say it's meeting the needs of other people in a weird kind of a way . . . that was [stressful]. There were a whole lot of people who were anxious about change. There were a whole lot of people who were having difficulties and there were a lot of people having a lot of personal difficulties

that I was very close to during that period. That creates a lot of stress. You know there's a part of me that has always wanted everybody to be happy . . . everybody to be OK. That gets you into trouble and that was going on then.

Finally, Sally's deep sense of connection to her students also caused problems when she took the year off from teaching her own class:

Terrible, terrible, because I discovered that I get my energy from working with a group of students and I had no way of monitoring long-term progress on any of these kids. I had no way of just developing any kind of in-depth knowledge about any of these kids. I had no way of knowing if anything that I'd done had much impact and I couldn't survive with that. It was really difficult for me because I realized that my feedback comes from the students, not from the adults I'm with.

This reminded me of Nel Noddings' (1984) point that the one caring needs to see a response, in terms of growth, in the one cared for in order to sustain the caring. (See chapter 4.) Lee also talked about the disempowerment that came from being away from students and teaching when she was in graduate school:

I did that for two years and then at the end of that time I was beginning to feel like a "go-for" and I was losing my sense of who I was and I needed to get back to teaching, and that was the first indication to me that most of my life is about my teaching and I was having some physical problems as well as some emotional problems at the end of the two-year period because I just needed to get back in touch with who I regarded myself to be and that was a teacher.

This suggests that teachers who are thinking about taking on leadership responsibilities should think carefully about how far out of the classroom they are willing to go. (Cohen [1991] in a study of outstanding teachers also found that they had a lack of interest in upward mobility in the traditional sense.)

Beliefs, Values and Personalities

So these teachers have experienced a broad range of disempowering experiences involving technical and bureaucratic control, hierarchy, domination, and isolation. But these teachers were able to overcome the negative effects of these experiences in fairly direct ways. They overcame isolation by finding support networks. They overcame assaults on their self-esteem by asserting their worth (as when Marni decided that she did have something to offer), and by taking risks. They overcame external controls by looking for ways around them (as when Lauren presented her in-service at a local teacher service center) or by educating themselves sufficiently to be able to answer their detractors (as when Sally took graduate courses to be able to defend her opinions).

Why were these teachers able to overcome these obstacles to their development while others are not? It is impossible to say if they experienced fewer disempowering experiences than other teachers who are less self-actualized. All but Lee did seem to have fairly supportive administrations, for instance. Another possibility is that they had more empowering experiences to draw on; positive messages about their abilities given in childhood, support from family and friends, opportunities to exercise their autonomy and so on. A third possibility is that they were able to draw on a set, of beliefs or values that sustained them. Or, perhaps, they had personalities that were more resilient than others'. Hence, I began to look for commonalities in these areas based on what they had told me and what I had observed.

One of the most outstanding similarities among these teachers in terms of values was their commitment to "making a difference" (hence the subtitle of this book). Cantor and Bernay (1992) have coined the term WomanPower to express the view of power held by the politically successful women they interviewed. Though most of the women in government that they interviewed defined power as the ability to get things done, they also talked about using power to help others. "Power in itself means nothing. . . . I think power is the opportunity to really have an impact on your community." "To me power means being able to do something for others. I use the power of my office to help other people" (p. 40). They go on to say that "WomanPower also emcompasses the notion of empowering others" (p. 57).

Though I did not ask these teachers how they defined power, this concept of WomanPower seemed to emerge in their value and goal statements. (Note: Though I did not interview any men, I suspect that empowered men would have the same concept of "caring power," so I prefer to call it that.) Lauren talked about her mission in terms of preparing kids to "contribute to society." Sally said that "We are all here to help each other in some way" and that "One of our roles as humans is to care about everybody and to do what we can." Lee got into theater when she saw that it could be "a catalyst for social and political change." She talked about learning so that she would be "able to give it away" and the importance to her when she "knew that I made a difference." Later she said more strongly, "My life has to be about making a difference." Samantha talked about having a "democratic love for public education" and about her "belief that I can make a difference in students' lives." Finally, when speaking of the social work she had done in the Appalachians, Marni said "It made me believe that we could change or it's possible to change and I started to see that the only way we could change anything was through education. . . . [I]ndividually we can make a difference . . . to give people the power to change their own lives and I believed that when I went into teaching." Later, in a more obvious value statement, she said "There's something out there and we have an obligation to it."

There was something quite striking to me about this universal dedication to improving the lives of others. These sorts of statements ran through all the interviews, and I suspected that this moral or ethical commitment was what sustained these teachers in their difficult moments. Indeed, if one looks at the phrasing they used, it was not only a moral commitment to others but a belief that things could change, that they could get better, at least for individuals. It reminded me of part of my description of empowered educators, as stated in chapter 1: "They are strong, practical and compassionate as they work individually and with others to support the self-realization of all persons in their classrooms, schools, and communities." The only difference I saw among the teachers was whether they saw this commitment in a larger social sense or as a commitment to individuals.

If we go back to Nel Noddings' definition of caring, we can see numerous instances of caring in many of the statements made by these teachers. If caring involves understanding the goals of the other and displacing one's motivation in the service of those goals, we see this again and again in these teachers' lives. Lauren described herself as "dedicated to the kids," who are "whole people" who have the "power to make their own choices." She also talked about other teachers who change as "courageous," thus understanding their stresses. Sally spoke about helping the kids to select their own goals and then supporting their efforts. She talked often about herself as a "supportive" person and stressed that teachers should be allowed to do "what works for them." Also the stress she felt from others' problems (see above) shows her level of care. Lee also referred to such mutuality when she said, "You are contributing and being contributed to." Samantha talked with me a lot about specific kids and their needs and problems in a very caring way. Marni even pointed out that her students know she cares.

These teachers also evidenced a commitment to the value of diversity. This commitment, which I see as part of caring, came out in different ways. Lauren talked about understanding minority status from her experiences in Hawaii. She also pointed out that underneath our differences we all "all really the same." Sally spoke about how her students showed a tremendous variety in terms of their strengths and difficulties and that this was OK—even good. Lee worried about her students' lack of exposure to kids from other cultures. Samantha brought in multicultural materials and built in individual projects to capitalize on the diversity of student interests.

Similarly, the views on power in education expressed by these teachers reflected an emphasis on caring, on power-to/power-with rather than power-over. All believed in involving kids in making their own choices and in teachers making administrative decisions. Lauren talked about the "power to learn and make choices is theirs [the students'], not mine, to control." She also stated clearly that she believed that it is the teachers rather than textbook publishers or curriculum coordinators who should make the decisions about teaching:

> We are indeed the practitioners. We are the closest to what's going on in our classrooms. We're the ones who do most of the journal reading, etc.

Similarly, Sally said she was "extremely uncomfortable with external decision-making" and that we should let teachers "do what works for them." She said that she doesn't "believe in telling people what to do," and, as said earlier, she encourages her students to make their own choices and to take responsibility for their own learning. Also, Marni said straight out that the teachers and students should make most of the decisions.

Indeed, all these teachers seemed uncomfortable with domination especially when it was aimed at them. Thus, I would characterize them as having empowering values (see above) and autonomous personalities. Lauren and Sally both said that they "hated" being "told what to do." Lauren said that she wanted the "freedom to make her own decisions."

The other three teachers evidenced their autonomy more through their actions than their words. All were viewed as mavericks in their schools and districts; I would suspect that this was partially because of the sheer number of their professional activities and even more so because of the innovative nature of these activities. Moreover, what is probably most informative is that these teachers maintained a high level of autonomy while also remaining deeply connected to others, or possibly because their connection with others supported it. This goes against the patriarchal assumption that autonomy requires separation.

In addition, all these teachers were able to reflect critically on their own practice. They talked about their own teaching decisions, what they are still working on, why they do what they do, and so on. Both Lauren and Samantha mentioned that a big turning point in their career was when they began to ask "why" regarding teaching practices. For both, this was in graduate school. Similarly, Sally went back to graduate school to get the answers she needed about what worked and why. Lee was really struggling with a conflict between the feeling that instruction should be student-centered and the feeling that direct instruction is sometimes more efficient. Samantha said that observing other teachers in her teacher portraiture group "is a great way to reflect on one's own teaching."

Similarly, all five of these teachers seemed to be risk-takers, to be drawn to challenges and to enjoy the opportunity to be creative. Lauren said that she "love[d] to do new programs because there is a challenge in it." Similarly, she said that she loved designing curriculum because "you're creating something that never existed." Sally spoke about being always willing to try something new because she "always feel[s] that something good will come out of it." Lee said that though she was aware of her limitations, still, underneath, "I really believe this: Any human being can do anything." When asked if she was a risk-taker she said:

> Yeah, I do, because in each stage of my life, in each change of direction, I've had to let go the security of feeling competent and feeling accomplished at whatever I had been doing. I've had to take on being a learner again, a beginner. I think that is courageous. . . . I think that the desire to be better, to take that challenge . . . is honorable.

In a letter to me she said that she had "the desire to create, build, change and to constantly grow." Similarly, when asked how she took on so many projects that would frighten others, Samantha said "I was scared before I did it but I think . . . I liked the challenge." She also said that she has "become a risk-taker and become comfortable with risk-taking because it's satisfying." Finally, Marni said that she felt that "if you believe in what you are doing, it's going to work." She talked about getting around obstacles and taking a risk in leaving the public schools.

There were other personality characteristics that came up in various interviews that were not necessarily universal. (I had no way of knowing.) Sally spoke about being "confident" in her ability to learn. Lauren spoke about being a "positive thinker." (They all seemed to be positive thinkers to me.) Samantha spoke about her love for her subject. Lee talked about her drive to improve herself. Marni talked about her tenacity. These different self-characterizations reflect that fact that these five teachers had distinctly different personalities in spite of the commonalities I have discussed.

Leadership and Teaching Styles

Clearly, the leadership activities of these teachers alone qualify them as "empowered." (See portraits.) Further evidence of this, however, can be seen in both their leadership and teaching styles which seem to reflect their desire to empower others. The key words that came up when discussing how they worked to affect change were *collaboration, voice* and *acceptance*. Words that came up in their descriptions of their role as change agent included *collaborator, cheerleader* and *coach*. This was the model of teaching and leading that I discussed in chapter 4, and all of them seemed quite comfortable with it.

For instance, in talking about working collaboratively with others, Lauren showed her accepting style:

> But basically, they have to operate in their own comfort zone too. So you have to be really careful not to make someone feel that they are less worthy. Their opinion/style might be different, but they're not less worthy. There's room for change in all of us. So we must learn to appreciate that and to remember that we are all developing human beings. We're never finished.

Marni talked about the need to be flexible, letting her agenda change according to the needs of the group . . . that is, accepting them where they were. Lee talked about finding out what teachers needed in the moment and beginning to "coach" them from there.

Both Lauren and Samantha talked about being better able to state their opinions than they used to be. I would reframe this as finding their professional voice. (Lee and Samantha also talked about finding their voice as writers.) This ability to speak out, either at meetings or in writing, seemed to be very useful for all these teachers in influencing the changes in their district. For instance, Samantha said:

> I have certainly become more outspoken. When I disagree with something, I do not sit silently. I will articulate my disagreement. I'll do it verbally or in writing. I'm much better at . . . protesting in writing than I am verbally.

Finally, Sally provided an excellent example of the power-to/ power-with rather than power-over style of these teachers. She talked extensively about herself as part of a group, rather than as a leader. Indeed, she tried very hard to avoid taking any credit for affecting change, though I finally got her to say that she had had an influence. She first said that she thought of herself as a "cheerleader." When asked if she saw herself as a change agent, she said:

> I think that I don't. It's not something that I deliberately try to be. I don't work with my colleagues with the perception that things that I do are going to change what someone else is doing because I see the impact that we all have on one another and I think we all change one another. . . . I think of myself as a supportive person.

Later, however, when talking about the change to heterogeneous grouping, she said "I think part of the reason for that decision was that I had gone into people's reading classes and done things." Sally's sense of connection to her colleagues precludes her from seeing herself in a way that she would see as separating her from them. Instead, for all of the changes she discussed in her interview, she said "we."

The teaching styles that I observed also reflected empowering beliefs and values. I visited each of the teacher's classrooms to see if I would see the kind of teaching practice they described in their interviews, and I found that they had been very accurate. Though I occasionally saw some activities that I would classify as somewhat less than

Table 9.1. Empowering Behaviors

	Lauren	Sally	Lee	Samantha	Marni
Lots of student talk	✗	✗	✗	✗	✗
Independent projects	✗	✗	✗	✗	✗
Collaborative activities	✗	✗	n/a	n/a	✗
Opportunities to be creative	✗	✗	✗	✗	✗
Metacognitive discussions	✗	✗	✗	✗	✗
Merging of disciplines	✗	✗	n/a	✗	n/a
Content connected to students' lives	✗	✗	✗	✗	✗
Multicultural or social justice issues discussed	✗	n/a	n/a	n/a	✗
Critical thinking opportunities	✗	✗	✗	✗	✗
Feelings, images valued	✗	✗	✗	✗	✗
Heterogenous grouping in class	✗	✗	✗	✗	✗
Seats arranged nonhierarchically	✗	n/a	✗	✗	✗
Expressions of caring valued	✗	✗	✗	✗	n/a
Use of dialogue & student voice	✗	✗	✗	✗	✗

✗ = observed; n/a = not applicable during observation.

empowering, these were rare, basically limited to the use of a work-sheet and workbook and the use of rows for the students' desks. By far the majority of methods I observed reflected the philosophy of this book. Table 9.1 lists the empowering behaviors that I observed in these classrooms. When they were not observed, it was easy to see how the specific context of the lesson did not really provide the appropriate setting (n/a). Because I only observed for one half-day, it is impossible for me to say if I would have seem all of these behaviors in all the classrooms, but I suspect that this is so.

As you can see, there were rather remarkable similarities among these teachers in terms of categories of teacher behaviors observed. Certainly, none of them used a power-over model of teaching. All created space for a considerable amount of student talk, independent projects, creative, critical and metacognitive thinking, active involvement with relevant activities, responses that went beyond the intellectual, and the creation of community in the classroom, even in the short time that I was observing.

There was, however, a difference in the degree of emphasis on any one thing. For instance, given some sort of continuum, I could say that the middle and high school teachers were more focussed on product than the elementary school teachers, more willing to be the one making the decisions, and more content- as opposed to strategy-oriented. These are only differences in degree, however. The middle and high school teachers (Lee and Samantha) were still focussed on process, student choice and reading/writing strategies more than many of their colleagues.

Summary

When we revisit the definition of empowered educators given in chapter 1, we can clearly see that, as a group, these five teachers provide us with excellent examples:

> Empowered educators are ones who believe in themselves and their capacity to act. They understand systems of domination and work to transform oppressive practices in society. They respect the dignity and humanness of others and manifest their power as the power to actualize their own unique humanity. They are strong, practical and compassionate as they work individually and with others to support the self-realization of all persons in their classrooms, schools and communities.

Each of the teachers I interviewed believed in her own ability to make decisions and to carry them out. They were sensitive to issues of diversity and segregation by ability and did what they could to overcome these social problems. They were also aware that total domination by the teacher would not empower their students. They showed almost no need to dominate over either their students or their colleagues; in contrast, they built empowering relationships based on mutuality and respect whenever possible. My observations indicated to me that they manifested their philosophy of teaching in their daily classroom life as well as in their other leadership activities. They were able to get things done, practical in their methods and goals, and caring (compassionate) in their relationships. They sometimes worked alone but they also drew strength from the support of others with similar values. They were committed to making a difference in the lives of others.

Moreover, I also saw definite differences among these teachers. Lee was still struggling a little with self-confidence in the face of disempowering administrative policies. Marni saw oppression in a larger social context, whereas others saw it mostly in terms of the lives of individuals. Lauren was the only one who spoke of trying to have an impact on the entire community by educating young parents. I think these differences were as important as the similarities that I found. They indicated that empowerment doesn't mean that we are all the same or that we have it all worked out. These teachers all agreed with me when I said that empowerment is a lifelong process that is never fully completed.

Moreover, these five teachers also differed in their emphases on the common factors. When thinking about how to explain the differences among the teachers, I discovered that I could find one or two words or themes that were prominent for each of them, though these were characteristics that they all shared. For Lauren, for instance, these were "choice" and "caring." She wanted to make her own choices and she wanted to support others in doing the same thing. She wanted to provide help to other teachers, to young parents and to kids in a way that expressed a deep level of caring and her commitment to their self-actualization. Belonging to a group and changing society were concerns that grew out of her respect for choice and caring.

For Sally, the words were "connection" and "support." Sally was the one teacher who most deeply thought of herself as a member of a group. For her, decisions were made by the group. Though she sometimes exerted her "power-to" she was much more comfortable with "power-with." Moreover, she expressed her caring, to use her words, by showing support for others when they had realized what they wanted to do. Thus, caring and choice were also important themes for her, but they grew out of her clear sense of embeddedness.

For Lee, the words that stood out for me were "dance" and "experience," even though she only used the word "dance" once in her interview. Nevertheless, her explanation of the significance of this term was by far the longest and most moving section of our time talking together. I could see how it guided much of what she did in other areas. For her, the dance metaphor captured the moment of group's synergy in which everyone is involved and the process has taken on a meaning of its own. This, then, is a moment of power-to/power-with in which choices are being made organically within a group experience. Thus, connection was deeply involved in this experience, too. Moreover, she also made it clear that it was her caring, her desire to make a difference, that motivated her commitment to creating such synergistic experiences. For her, it was clear that these moments involved creativity and wholeness.

For Samantha, the word that stood out the most for me was "voice." Within her commitment to helping her students to find their unique voices, she evidenced her sense of caring and her commitment to choice. As a reading and writing teacher, she supports her students in thinking critically and creatively about their own lives. Even in her own experience of empowerment, finding her own voice seemed to be a model that worked for her. She mentioned that speaking up and writing in her own voice were abilities that she had developed over the years.

Finally, for Marni the phrase that seems most appropriate is "social action." Beginning with her experiences in Appalachia and her voter registration work in the 1960s, it was clear that she had a vision of social change. She was the only one who analyzed her sense of gender oppression in terms of how it intersected with her internalized class oppression. She was the one who most strongly protested against the levelling of people and the separation of theory from practice and K–12 teachers from university faculty. All of this, of course, expressed her deep level of caring for others as well as her sense of connection and her commitment to individual choice.

When I looked at these themes and the ones that emerged in regard to experiences that the teachers found to be empowering or disempowering, one umbrella theme seemed to emerge. That is the idea of the empowering nature of experiencing autonomy *within* community. In contrast to theories of power-over which dichotomize autonomy and community (the more embedded you are in a community, the more you lose your autonomy), these data indicate that autonomy with isolation is still disempowering and community with domination is also disempowering. Only the experience of autonomy within a caring community that accepts and supports difference is going to empower us.

This implies that those interested in empowering teachers (so that they can empower students) must create *both* opportunities for individual decision making *and* a supportive community. My investigation of these five teachers' lives leads me to believe that an atmosphere of acceptance and encouragement is far more important than control and criticism; that opportunitites for advanced training are critical but must make space for an individual's creativity and value system; that opportunities for teachers to build programs and take on administrative responsibilities build self-esteem but should not take them totally away from their students. School districts would be well advised to respect the expertise of their own teachers rather than always bringing in outsiders, and high school teachers need more opportunitites to observe the impressive expertise of their elementary-level counterparts. These and other opportunities to connect within an atmosphere of respect for difference may help teachers to overcome the effects of earlier disempowering experiences which they, I believe, have all had, either through gender, class, race, ethnic or status discrimination and domination, through self-imposed isolation in the search for autonomy, or in their own experience of a disempowering education. The changes we are talking about are not small, but, as these teachers show us, they are possible.

CHAPTER TEN

Empowerment and Education: Past, Present and Future

So what have I learned in the process of writing this book? What have you learned in the process of reading it? This answer will probably be different for each person. The path to personal and professional empowerment winds in many directions. In the past nine chapters, I have discussed the relationship between empowerment and education in a variety of areas, but every chapter has been based on the central premise that empowerment stands opposed to domination, that it involves power-to/power-with rather than power-over. In this last chapter, I would like to summarize and synthesize my ideas and to encourage you to do the same. Then we will be ready to reflect on the future of empowerment and education.

Why "Empowerment"?

So why did I write a book on empowerment anyway? Certainly, this is an overused and misused term these days. The fact is that I couldn't find another term that so aptly described my understanding that the organization and conceptualization of power is central to understanding what is needed in the schools. Also, it is an all-inclusive concept that allows us to speak in terms that don't demand that we separate the personal and the professional, the mental and the emotional, the real and the ideal. Empowerment includes all of these. Seeing this all-inclusiveness can help us to see that empowerment in one area of our lives will probably lead to empowerment in other areas of our lives.

Moreover, empowerment is an internal as well as an external state. This is also an important characteristic of this term: we need to pay attention to both our internalized attitudes and the actual situations in which we live and work. It is difficult to empower ourselves fully if we live or work in situations of domination, and we cannot empower ourselves fully if we are given all the external autonomy we need but internally we do not feel powerful.

Thus, in chapter 1 I provided a description of empowered educators that stressed their expression of power-to/power-with rather than power-over. I also included the internal experience of empowerment as well as the natural external expression of this in the empowerment of others through action. Rather than repeat that description here, I think it might be better for you to define what empowerment is to you.

Activity 10.1
DEFINING YOUR OWN EMPOWERMENT

Close your eyes and picture yourself three years from now, after you have become as empowered as you can imagine. I am assuming that you have also found an empowering community that can support you. Describe yourself. What are you doing? What are you feeling? What do you look like?

What does this tell you about what empowerment is to you?

Empowerment in the Lives of Teachers

There are many internal and external factors that can interfere with our empowerment. We often lose control of our work life in the face of the bureaucratic and technical demands of the job. These factors are less obvious than direct control but just as insidious. For instance, if we can't do something because it isn't in our job description or because someone else outside the situation decides that we can't, then we are dealing with a bureaucracy. If we have to teach a certain way because "the book says so," then we are dealing with technical control. Of course, technical control is supported by a scientific rationality that obscures the bias of the program designers.

The first thing we have to do to deal with these kinds of external controls is to recognize them. Then we can refuse to be limited by them. We can speak with the administrator that has doubts about our idea, or address the school board directly. We can question the scientific basis of the prepackaged program. We can do our own research to show that our programs have merit, too.

In order to do these things, we will have to develop excellent communication skills. We need to listen for feelings as well as ideas and to frame our suggestions in ways that show that we respect the other person's point of view. We need to involve our colleagues and be willing to compromise. We need to take the time to educate and collaborate with others interested in improving our educational system.

Of course, we may also be limited in these actions by internalized oppression. The assumption that things should stay the same, or cultural hegemony, is pervasive. It is difficult constantly to question our assumptions and common practices. There are many not-so-liberating practices that we take for granted, just because we never thought about them in this way. Moreover, most of us have internalized a certain amount of domination in the form of not feeling confident about questioning authority. A little voice inside of us says something like "Who are you to make these decisions? What do *you* know?" Along the same lines, most of us learned at an early age to feel less powerful than we really are. We tend to blame ourselves for our own unhappiness and dissatisfaction rather than looking outward for things that can be changed. This is reinforced by the isolation of individualism: "Everyone else seems OK, so there must be something wrong with me."

Sexism, classism, and other forms of discrimination also affect us more than we realize. Most fundamentally, sexism breeds a split between power and love. In a sexist society, men are encouraged to be powerful and to suppress their natural caring, whereas women are encouraged to be loving but from a powerless position. Neither of these works. If we are to really help our children, then we must demand that we have the power to implement caring policies. Those of us who are women must connect with our suppressed personal power, recognizing and then rejecting any beliefs that we have internalized about the inferiority or limited role of women. Those of us who are men must release our natural caring and feeling side.

Similarly, we must examine our own internalized classism, racism or homophobia before we can truly accept ourselves. All these prejudices are based on the myth of the variability of human worth, so we must examine this as well. Do we believe that some people have more worth than others? If so, then we live constantly with the threat of losing our worth, and we are controlled by a frightened inner critic who wants to keep us in line so that this won't happen. If these feelings of vulnerability are serious, then you may wish to consider getting professional support. If you seek help from a counselor, make sure it is one who is growth-oriented and respects you as a person in control of your own life. Or, you may wish to use such things as journaling and forming a support group to provide yourself with a safe space to examine your own internalized oppression.

Getting Support

The first thing you will want to do to support your own empowerment is to determine what it is you really believe. What is it you want to be empowered to do? Or, in a more general sense, who are you as an educator? This forming of personal and professional identity is not something that ends after our teenage years. We may need to revisit questions of identity and values throughout our life. Along with this, we need to go through a process of rejecting the school practices that do not feel empowering and revisioning an empowering education.

We also need to be very conscious about when we feel empowered and disempowered and what is making us feel that way. We can sensitize ourselves to identify these situations on the spot so that we can take action to change them if necessary. We also need to become conscious about the true nature of these experiences. Rather than blaming ourselves or our students or our administrators, we need to understand these problems in terms of the larger social system of which they are a part. We need to reflect on our practice in terms of this awareness of the larger society.

All of this will require that we do a certain amount of reskilling as well. We need to learn about options and theories that provide us with the tools we need to design an empowering education in the first place. It is impossible for us to feel really confident about what we are doing if we have not investigated all that is out there to help us.

To support ourselves psychologically, we may need to do some mental clearing of our self-limiting beliefs. We need to make sure that we are taking responsibility for our actions without blaming ourselves or others when things do not go as expected. We need to build our self-esteem and self-confidence by taking risks and giving ourselves positive messages. We need to develop a sense of trust in ourselves and others, a positive attitude about events, and an ability to flow with change. All of these were definitely characteristics of the five teachers I studied.

Those five teachers also had a profound sense of connection to others and a deep commitment to the well-being of others. I believe that these are natural feelings that we all have unless we have suppressed them because of old wounds or because of fear. If you are having trouble caring or feeling connected to others, then you may wish to get some help with clearing your internalized disconnection or your criticism of yourself. Usually, we feel about others the way we feel about ourselves. Whatever you do, don't "beat yourself up" for your feelings of anger or isolation or jealousy or lack of caring. Have compassion for yourself and the injuries that have gotten you to this place, just as you would have compassion for a colleague who is struggling with the disempowering experiences of power-over.

All of these personal empowerment strategies are most possible when we are a part of a supportive community that lets us know that we are accepted as we are. Ideally, your school and district will be such a "conscious community." In a conscious community, members relate to each other in an attitude of mutual respect and acceptance. Feelings are accepted and the expression of them is welcomed even when they involve anger or fear or sadness. Each member realizes that the self and the whole are inseparable and *neither* should be sacrificed. Individuals need autonomy within community and communities need individuals who are autonomous. This will lead to a feeling of synergy, of the whole being greater than the sum of its parts.

To build a conscious community, we have to get rid of competition and the idea that some people are worth more than others. Each person deserves praise and support for his/her own growth process. Diversity must be valued. Communication must be authentic. Constructive problem solving can be substituted for complaining (which is usually a technique for avoiding action and responsibility). A caring atmosphere can encourage risk-taking which can lead to empowerment. Talk to your colleagues about these concepts and work out a way to make your community processes conscious. Make time to discuss how people are feeling and whether the change to conscious community is happening in an authentic way.

While having a conscious community in our school or district is ideal, these communities will not be free from difficulties and conflicts. It may take many years to get to a place in which you feel supported in your school building. Thus, you may wish to form or join a smaller support group of your own. The teachers I interviewed all felt that they gained valuable perspectives when they talked to teachers from other districts and situations. Journaling and writing, peer coaching, collaborative planning, reading, and empowerment itself all provide excellent foci for such groups. Indeed, one purpose of this book is to provide a structure for empowerment groups that would like to work through these issues collectively. (I would love to hear from these groups!) Teacher research also provides an excellent focus for a support group. Doing teacher research helps us to validate our own perceptions and to think reflectively about our classroom experiences.

Being in these groups and communities can help us find the authentic voice that many of us have lost. It has been my experience that, as we find our own voice, we are more and more able to help our students find theirs.

Activity 10.2
PUTTING IT TOGETHER FOR OURSELVES

First, think about the internal factors that are limiting you. Describe them in your own words.

What are some things that you can do to overcome these internal inhibitors?

What are the external factors in your life as an educator that keep you from the full expression of your best self?

What are some specific things you can do to change external inhibitors?

What are some community-based things you can do to support you personal development as well as help you to overcome the external limitations?

Good Luck!

Empowerment in the School Experiences of Students

As we have seen, it is impossible to feel empowered ourselves if we are involved in the domination of others. This keeps us locked in a tyrant/rebel duality in which everyone is dependent on the reactions of the other. Thus, a large part of empowering ourselves involves changing our relationships with students. This was verified for me by the statements of the teachers I interviewed. For instance, you may remember that Sally said "It's like empowering them empowers you."

Of course, there are many current practices that disempower students. Ability grouping and tracking separate kids into the "have's" and "have-not's" at an early age. A disproportionate number of "have-not's" are from the nondominant cultures, probably because the knowledge bases and learning styles they bring to school are not the ones that are valued there. Research indicates that girls are sometimes treated differently than boys, with boys being encouraged more. Similarly, grading and evaluation promote a sense of competition and hierarchy that leaves no one unscathed. The students' own cultures are usually left out of the classroom, and many students feel that their authentic voices are not valued.

Moreover, schools are typically run according to a patriarchal paradigm that suppresses feelings, views knowing as a purely cognitive experience and makes little space for process or process time. Communication usually involves one-upmanship; the individual is expected to fend for him/herself; morality is seen as a set of rules that, in many cases, takes the place of love and caring. In such a system, differences are feared, and rule-following and acquiescence are praised. Students are viewed as objects that can be measured, treated and produced through a kind of factory-line procedure.

In an empowering education, students are subjects with important voices and needs of their own. Students participate in the decisons that affect their lives. They are involved in setting goals and evaluating their own progress. Learning involves thinking, feeling, intuiting, sensing and wanting. The classroom is a community based on relationships of cooperation, mutuality and respect. Caring is central, with space made both for autonomous and collective action. Attention is paid to the process of learning. Differences are seen as beneficial. The worth of each individual is seen as inviolate. Dialogue is authentic. The teacher is a coach, facilitator, instructor, mentor, collaborator and listener both in the classroom and in the larger school community.

Moreover, in an empowering curriculum, the relationship between knowledge and power is made clear. Empowering knowledge is alive, honest and culturally relevant. It is seen as embedded in a social context which legitimates it. It includes technical, practical and emancipatory knowledge and begins with the actual lives and needs of the students and their community. Empowering classrooms take a stand for social justice. As caring communities, they are antiracist and antidiscriminatory. Spirituality and creativity are promoted in their nonreligious aspects. The barriers between the disciplines are broken down. Literacy is seen as the ability and practice of using language skills to understand and transform one's life. This would include using reading and writing for adaptation to the larger society when freely chosen, for self-improvement and growth, and for political and social critique and action.

Activity 10.3
PUTTING IT TOGETHER FOR OUR STUDENTS

Perhaps it would be useful to develop an action plan for our classrooms. Begin with thinking about things you do that don't really feel right . . . things that make the students dependent on the teacher. Then, think about alternatives. Finally, set a target date for taking action.

Student Empowerment Action Plan

What Is Done Now	What Could Be More Empowering	Target Date
Good Luck!		

A Personal Statement

Of course, it is not an accident that I have chosen to take a year of my life to write about power-to/power-with. I have struggled with my own relationship to power for most of my professional life. As I have become more authentic and actualized in my work, I have realized the enormous sense of fulfillment this can bring. I have also realized how difficult it is to achieve. Moreover, my professional and personal empowerment have not been totally separate. Though I chose to focus this book on professional aspects of empowerment, it should be obvious that as we change toward more self-confidence and self-knowledge, our personal lives will change, too.

Much that I have written about in this book has been validated by my own experience. I began teaching seventh-grade English underprepared and insecure (deskilling?). I was treated like a child who could not make her own decisions (sexism?). I was evaluated on the basis of my bulletin boards (bureaucracy?). I was told that I had to use the textbook even when I had evidence showing that my students could not read it (technical control?). My colleagues resented me because I had just studied at a prestigious university, and because I worked very hard (competition?). They also interpreted my shyness as snobbery (surplus powerlessness?). We were all caught up in doubting our self-worth and this made authentic communication almost impossible (self-esteem?). None of us thought that it was possible to change things for the better. (Variability of worth, hierarchy, self-blaming, surplus powerlessness, hegemony!)

Graduate school, for me, was not particularly empowering either. Statistics indicate that the further women go in school, the lower our self-esteem (Project on the Education and Status of Women, 1982). Many graduate programs consist of a series of hurdles one jumps over in order to prove oneself worthy of respect (meritocracy). Hierarchy and competition are rampant among faculty and students. Though I was successful, I was haunted by the sense that I could fail at any moment. All my full-time professors were male. All the "leaders" at the conventions were male (sexism). Moreover, I studied primarily cognitive psychology and statistics . . . using my mind to study the mind! (Separating forms of knowing; excessive rationalism.) I felt quite alienated from myself.

During my first college teaching job, I got a lot of support from colleagues. Unfortunately, the word around campus was that nine out of ten assistant professors never got tenure. So I continued jumping through hoops, turning out research that could be published in prestigious journals and feeling alienated from my work (scientific rationality). I was teaching "how to" reading courses in ways that felt controlled by state certification requirements (bureaucracy and technical control).

Luckily I found a feminist support group during this time that exposed me to political theory and philosophy that gave me names for the kinds of discomfort I was feeling (reskilling). I was caught in the split between love and power . . . trying to be strong and powerful at work without supporting myself by letting my natural caring for others direct my energies (caring power). I began to understand that I had been objectified, even in my own mind, as a woman, and I began to develop my theory that students could be treated as subjects rather than objects. I discovered critical educational theorists like Giroux (1983) and Freire (1973) and began to keep notes on both feminist and critical educational theory. I just couldn't quite see yet how this could become part of my work on reading education. I also first read about the difference between power-over and power-from-within (Starhawk, 1982) during that time. Finally, the support of this feminist group provided me with a glimpse of the potentially empowering nature of community.

I changed jobs to one in Chicago, where I hoped to make some significant contributions to inner-city education. I was especially excited about working in a multicultural environment. Looking back, I can see that this was the first, though small, step toward integrating my commitment to social justice more openly into my work with literacy, and, thus, it was another step toward my own professional empowerment. I also see now that it was then that my teaching became less about "how to" teach reading and more about critically examining these practices.

At that time, I began to feel confident enough to take risks. While in Chicago, I wrote a book about reading education that was to be my last magnum opus on the subject (*Teaching Reading Comprehension Processes*, 1986, 1991). A supportive colleague included me in a grant that allowed me to "teach" this book to a large group of inner-city teachers, many of whom were teaching in quite adverse circumstances. Thus, I now got involved in issues related to school change.

The feedback I got from this program was both exhilarating and confusing. I was getting feedback like, "I enjoy teaching for the first time." What I realized was that there was something about my book that went beyond methods of teaching reading. Something about it was empowering. What was it? I have been searching for the answer to that question ever since, as you can see from this book. It has been a process of clarifying my own beliefs and searching for ways to put them into practice.

Writing this book has been the most empowering experience of all, for I am doing it because it is important to me, not to please others or to secure my job. It has also been empowering for me because it has allowed me to synthesize all the parts of myself by seeing how they all provide pieces to a much larger puzzle. In this context, I have seen the limits of the scientific rationality that had guided my earlier work. I have allowed my intellectual side to merge with my feeling side and my intuitive side to "construct" knowledge (see Belenky et al., 1986). Finally, this work has been empowering to me because it is inherently empowering to empower others.

While I have been on this professional quest for full self-expression, I have also gone through many personal changes involving more self-esteem, more autonomy and more trust that things will work out for the better. All of the mental clearing that I discussed in chapter 7 has been important for me. Indeed, many of the books I have cited are books that I read in the quest for my own personal empowerment. I have worked on positive thinking (Burns, 1980), befriending my inner critic (Stone and Stone, 1993), and overcoming the internalization of inferiority (Bartky, 1980). For me, feminist, Buddhist, psychological and Native American teachings have also been helpful in learning nonjudgemental, nonhierarchical ways of thinking.

In my teaching, I have gone though a gradual shift from setting all the goals, delivering lectures, and giving tests to allowing students to pursue individual projects, involving students in teaching the class, and using journals and portfolios of students' work for evaluation. I have also moved from presenting one right way to teach reading to relating each method to the philosophical and political beliefs that support it. I try to run my classes as seminars in critical inquiry and encourage my students to examine and actualize their own beliefs. We pay attention to our classroom processes and try to insure that no one's voice is silenced. Like the teachers I interviewed, I feel more empowered when my students do also.

Moreover, I have been privileged to have some of the community support I discussed in chapter 8. Though I have sometimes experienced fairly typical bureaucratic undermining, I have also had some moments of support in smaller groups. Professionally, the most meaningful of these was the teacher research group in which I participated. Though I never completed a study because of personal reasons, I loved going to this group. Each member had air time, and we supported each person in her own unique agenda. I felt very accepted and cared for in this group.

I have also been able to experience autonomy within community in the psychosynthesis counselor training program in which I have been participating for the past three years. Psychosynthesis is a holistic, growth-oriented transpersonal psychology founded by Roberto Assagioli, a contemporary of Jung. Though there are Synthesis Centers throughout the world, it is, unfortunately, not very well known in the United States. To me, its essence involves getting to know and accept all the parts of the Self, including the Higher Self (see Assagioli, 1976), the end result being the progressive synthesis of those parts. As my colleagues and I went thorough this process together, we came to know and accept all the parts of each other as well. Such a community in which all of our feelings are accepted can be incredibly healing. (For more information on psychosynthesis, see Brown, 1983; Ferrucci, 1986; Parfitt, 1990; Sliker, 1992; and others.)

Of course, I can still see ways in which I need to grow toward greater personal empowerment (as I always will). While writing chapter 9, I realized that though I have achieved a great deal of professional autonomy, I have also accepted a great deal of isolation. When I return to the university in the fall, I hope to be even more outspoken about my beliefs and feelings, with the assumption that others might feel the same and that this will help us to create more genuine community. I also want to find the time to offer more support to my colleagues, many of whom are untenured. I hope to take better care of myself by saying "no" when I need to and by identifying disempowering situations overtly, even if it means that I must ask colleagues to look at their own feelings and processes.

I should also mention that for the past few years I have had to struggle with potentially debilitating health issues. I mention this because even this has helped me to become more empowered by requiring me to say no to experiences of domination and by requiring me to spend long periods away from "normal life," thus providing me with long periods of time for reflection. I also mention this to suggest that almost every adversity can be an opportunity in the process of personal empowerment.

The Future of Empowerment in Education

I truly believe that now is the time to empower ourselves to empower our students. While I would agree that it may have been difficult before, there is much in our current society and educational system that opens the door to these changes.

First, these are hard times, so it seems relevant to note that I have not suggested anything that needs to cost any more money than we are spending now. Indeed, I can think of ways that some money could be cut from prepackaged programs and standardized testing and refunneled into libraries, computers and other resources. Moreover, the money saved by the larger society from the education of children who are currently failed by the schools would be enormous. There are simply no jobs in our current economy for people who cannot read and write and reason independently, so, even for economic reasons, we must stop disempowering such large groups of kids.

Secondly, the trend "from power to partnership" is a global one. Montouri and Conti (1993) document the change toward developing work groups in which everyone has input, and Shaffer and Anundsen (1992) describe new styles of leadership and community in the workplace. Senge (1990) describes a new type of corporation, one in which personal visions are valued. As a society, we seem to be learning that rigid hierarchical control is not the most effective way to conduct business. Workers are more productive when they have input. People are more happy when they are a respected part of a community. Multinational corporations are spreading these ideas around the globe.

This global change is related to what many are calling a paradigm shift from hierarchy and separation to cooperation and connection. Psychologist Mikhail Csikszentmihalyi (1993) suggests that individuals develop from an emphasis on safety to one on cultural conformity to one on individualism to one on connection and altruism. He speculates that the society seems to be going through these phases of development as well.

When we look at education specifically, we can see that curriculum changes that emphasize cooperation and empowerment are already underway. Whole language and process writing are examples of these sorts of changes. In these programs, children have input into the books they read and the projects they complete; there is an opportunity for sharing and getting input from others; writing is about self-selected topics for self-selected goals, though children help each other through peer coaching and group feedback. In many of these programs, children are involved in self-assessment through portfolios that are shared with teachers, parents and others, and the development of voice and critical thought is a central objective. Moreover, ability grouping is being challenged in many communities as inherently biased, and multicultural education and cooperative learning are more and more common. School reform networks are multiplying (see chapter 8).

In addition, many programs preparing teachers are now emphasizing reflective thinking, decision-making and leadership skills. At the University of Connecticut, for instance, we require that students complete a master's degree as part of their teacher preparation. As part of this master's program, the students complete an internship that involves leadership experiences beyond student teaching, like coordinating a tutoring program or implementing a curriculum change, and they complete a research study on their experience. During the entire three years that they are in the School of Education, the students participate in seminars focussing on reflection and critique.

Similarly, the move to "empower teachers" is also currently in vogue. Site-based management, career ladders, and semi-administrative positions like "lead teacher" are all giving teachers more responsibility and control than ever before. Though such initiatives have the potential to simply integrate teachers into a different place in the hierarchy, many changes are being designed in ways that question hierarchy altogether. What we need now is a realization that all educators are in this together and that they cannot be empowered by someone above them in the hierarchy. The commitment to power-to/power-with involves everyone in the district equally. Teachers need not be singled out as the only group that needs to be empowered.

My hope is that we will be able to avoid the typical pendulum swing that many of us have seen over and over again. To do this, we must not implement any of these changes in a shallow way. What worries me most is that many of the people involved in these change processes do not fully understand their democratic rationale. Programs to involve teachers in curriculum planning often add to their workload without truly adding to their control over their situation. Similarly, such programs often involve teachers and parents in decision-making without simultaneously offering to reskill them so that they can make the best decisions possible. Teacher research is often expected to be an imitation of the generalizable, quantitative, positivistic "objective" research it is supposed to be replacing. Whole language programs are often implemented as add-ons to rigid curriculums. Heterogeneous grouping is used as an excuse to teach everyone as if they were the same. Multicultural education is more like cultural anthropology than the mutual accommodation of cultures in a proactively antidiscriminatory way. Implementing these changes in such a superficial and bandwagon manner will lead the pendulum to swing in the other direction, because nothing will have really changed.

It seems to me that the only way that these changes can be implemented effectively is to do so with a clear understanding of the big picture, the total context in which they are taking place. They must be grounded in an understanding of their moral implications, the relationship of these decisions to other paradigmatic shifts going on in our society, and the interconnected nature of all of these changes. Whole language is about sharing authority and reconnecting knowledge to its meaningful use. Heterogeneous grouping is about celebrating difference rather than ignoring it. Multicultural education is pervasive and overtly antiracist and antidiscriminatory. Teacher empowerment is about truly redistributing power and questioning hierarchy and requires the reskilling and building of self-esteem of individuals within the context of supportive, conscious communities based on the experience of power-to *and* power-with (synergy).

These profound changes cannot occur without the commitment and energy of thousands of educators and communities working together. We know how to improve teaching but we need a new system for making change happen. "The current bag of tricks won't work. There isn't enough foundation money to transform 80,000 public schools. There is no way to re-educate 2.4 million teachers relying on the existing system of professional development. There aren't enough charismatic reformers to reach every school" (Olson, 1994, 30). Michael Fullan, dean of education at the University of Toronto, responds to this when he says "It is people who change systems through the development of new critical masses" (Olson, 1994, 31). The purpose of this book is to inspire people like yourself to take the responsiblity to work for the changes we know will improve our schools. To do this, we will all need to empower ourselves to empower our students.

For the amazing, empowering, frightening and inspiring fact is that it is up to us. The potential result is the fuller self-actualization of all persons. The potential result of failing is increased alienation, frustration and separation. Teachers, parents, administrators, lawmakers and concerned citizens can each do his or her part to transform an authoritarian educational system that has outlived it usefulness into a truly democratic one capable of preparing students for their roles in a changing world.

Interview Questions
and Sample Interview Protocol

Note: You will be able to add or delete later so just relax and say what comes to mind. Don't force yourself to answer any question that seems irrelevant. I have more questions than we can possibly cover in two hours. I just want to make sure that we cover everything that is important to *your* story. Feel free to digress if you think of something else that you think is important.

General History

1. Where did you grow up? What kind of community? Where did you go to college?
    (*a*) Occupation of parents?
    (*b*) Type of family? (roles)
    (*c*) Messages about "femininity"?
    (*d*) Tell me about your mother.
    (*e*) Tell me about your father.
    (*f*) Any other mentors who were particularly important?

2. Why did you go into teaching?

3. What was your view of yourself and teaching when you entered the profession. What was your classroom like?

Development

4. What is (or would be) your classroom like now? (In your opinion, what led to these changes?)

5. How has your concept of yourself changed since you went into teaching? (In your opinion, what led to these changes?)

   (Do you think of yourself as a *courageous* person? Why or why not?)

6. How else have you changed personally? (What led to these changes)

   (Do you believe you can do anything you want? If not, what can't you do and how does that interfere?)

7. Can you summarize how your philosophy of teaching has changed over the years? (What caused it to change?)

8. Self-reflection (Teaching)
   (a) Was there any *group* or *person* that was particularly helpful to your development as a teacher?
   (b) Was there any *information*—books, training sessions, etc.—that was particularly helpful?
   (c) *Personal experience* that was particularly helpful?
   (d) *Community experience* that was particularly helpful?
   (e) Anything about your *childhood* or *upbringing* that was helpful?
   (f) Any *personal belief* or *religious belief* that has been helpful?

9. Obstacles
   (a) Was there any *group* or *person* that presented an obstacle to your development as a teacher?
   (b) Was there any *information*—books, training sessions, etc.—that presented an obstacle?
   (c) *Personal experience* that was an obstacle?
   (d) *Community experience* that was an obstacle?
   (e) Anything about your *childhood* or *upbringing* that was an obstacle?
   (f) Any *personal belief* or *religious belief* that was an obstacle?

Experience as a Change Agent

10. Do you see yourself as a change agent in your school or community? Why or why not?

    (Do you see yourself as a *risk-taker*? Why or why not?)

11. How did you get involved in changing things? What kinds of things did you do?

12. How do you feel about what has happened?

13. What are you working on now?

14. At this point, what plans, or long-term goals or hopes do you have?

15. At this point, what does the concept of teacher as leader mean to you?

Self-Reflection (Leadership)

16. Do you feel that it has been more difficult for you to contribute because you are a woman? Why or why not?

17. Looking back, what aspects of your *childhood* or upbringing may have contributed to your active involvement in school change today?

18. Looking back, what *personal experiences* have contributed to your active involvement in changing things? What *personal beliefs* are most important to you as you do this work?

19. What *professional experiences* may have contributed to your commitment to change?

20. What *external characteristics* in your situation most facilitated your involvement in school change?

21. What *internal characteristics* drive you to try to change things? What internal characteristics sustain you when things get difficult?

22. Finally, what have been the major obstacles to your involvement as a change agent? How have you overcome them?

Closing Statement

23. Is there anything you would like to say to teachers who might be reading this book by way of inspiration or advice?

Pebbles Along the Path: On the Process of Becoming a Teacher-Researcher

CHERYL S. TIMION

GROWTH

WISDOM
KNOWLEDGE

It is spring, the point on the Native American Medicine Wheel when inspiration and intuition come to light. It is also time for me to begin the culmination, the write-up, of my case study. I pray for inspiration. I try to unravel the layers of confinement, give vent to my intuition. However, paying heed to my intuitions does not come easily, for I am a person well schooled in the traditional attitudes of research.

As the year draws to a close I find my confidence in my research project is waning. For my case study is not based on statistics gathered from test scores and sterile statistics that do not take the human element into account. My data consists of field notes, classroom observations, journal entries, interviews with my students and their parents, visits with librarians, excerpts from my students' reading logs, photographs of students and diagrams of our classroom floorplan.

I have been convinced that as classroom teachers we must allow our voices to break the barriers of isolation that are formed by the walls of our individual classrooms. In my heart I also know that research that considers how educational practices affect our students is worthy of scrutiny. But I find myself wondering who will consider this subjective data valid? What can I tell about my classroom that will be of interest to anyone beyond the walls of Room 2? Who will be interested in my story?

These feelings of insignificance and inadequacy are the same powerful mufflers that have silenced many teachers' voices. They have kept us from sharing our stories, from putting the *learners* back into our search to discover how individuals learn. So I look back over the field notes and the data I have collected in the course of the school year. Back to the beginning. On the Native American Medicine Wheel it would be *summer*, the point for growth . . .

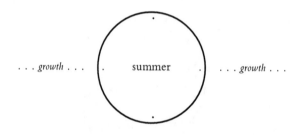

. . . *growth* . . .   summer   . . . *growth* . . .

I had just returned from my course work at Northeastern University's Summer Institute on Writing and Teaching. With the serene backdrop of Martha's Vineyard, I had studied case-study design with Glenda Bissex. Under her tutelage, I had thought back to the events of the past school year in my classroom. I'd written about my students and the ways that they learned, as well as the ways that I evaluated their learning. Eventually, I had developed questions about the learning process and things that had surprised or puzzled me as I worked with the students.

By the end of my course with Glenda, I had decided on a question that focused on some aspect of the educational process; something that I wanted to learn more about in the coming school year. My students the previous year had told me that the most difficult aspect of learning to read had been finding a book that they wanted to read. I had anticipated that sounding out unfamiliar words would have been the most difficult part of learning to read, so my students had totally surprised me with their response that *choosing the book* was the hardest part of learning to read.

As I prepared to leave the Vineyard, I could feel the momentum for my research project building; I couldn't wait to get started. My classmates and I had arrived as a group of classroom teachers. We left the island as ethnographers and returned to our classrooms throughout the country anxious to embark on our fieldwork. *Growth* had taken place as we had made plans to expand our role in our classrooms.

I bought notebooks and set up a schedule for transcribing my field notes. I set aside one night per week for journal writing and for reviewing the data I had collected for the week. I had the proper mindset as I launched into this new project. I would look at the events in my classroom as open mindedly as possible . . . and then the students arrived.

As I read over my field notes from September, I could feel the energy leap from the page. At times in my classroom journal I had referred to what I was doing as classroom inquiry; at other times I called it ethnographic research or qualitative research. Toward the end of September, I was able to enroll in a graduate seminar, Teacher As Researcher, at the University of Connecticut. Judith Irwin would lead the seminar. Still the momentum was building; discussions with the other seminar participants were invigorating. We read descriptions of many ethnographic studies and found these narratives had the effect of taking us into other teachers' classrooms. It was refreshing to focus on the *students* and not the test scores. We discovered that this type of research did not make generalizations; the studies often looked at learning as a process. This alone had value for me as a classroom teacher; the momentum continued to build.

Next our seminar group read about how to conduct qualitative research. Contrary to our previous schooling in the principles of educational research, we were now reading that a teacher's description of what takes place in a classroom is acceptable, even encouraged! Our group discussions became even more lively. After years of having to preface any personal comment with the phrase "it appears," or "it seems as though," this was mind-boggling. However, at the same time I realized that I was a trained teacher who had practiced my profession for over fifteen years. Why did I not feel qualified to share what was taking place in our classroom? Why did I not trust my ability to report the findings about my students' learning process?

This new information that I was digesting was having a profound affect on me as a classroom teacher. I was experiencing the sensation of a caged bird being set free. Perhaps it was my intuition, which I had been trained to keep at bay, now being allowed out into the fresh air. Ever so gradually, my role as a teacher began to change as I entered our classroom each day as a researcher. I was looking at my students from a new perspective. I was no longer the sole disseminator of knowledge in the classroom.

I watched the students and wrote down what I saw and what the students did. My field notes were filled with questions and *my* perception of what was taking place. I began to notice that my note-taking was having an affect on the students as well. The fact that they could see that I cared about *how* each student was learning seemed, in itself, to create a different atmosphere.

The other participants in the seminar group were reporting each session on the status of their research as well. They were observing in other teachers' classrooms, so their perspective on the whole process was somewhat different than mine. They were in the role of an outsider trying to establish rapport with the teacher and the students, trying to become an insider. While I was trying to distance myself from the front-and-center position, I was attempting to become an outsider looking in. Neither role is an easy one to play. Through our seminar discussions we discovered firsthand that what we had read from other researchers rang true, that the most valuable thing that we could do was to *write*. All of us were finding that we needed to write about what we saw, what we heard and overheard, what we were thinking and feeling in our research settings.

My enthusiasm remained in high gear. One journal entry in October ended, "I'm excited about the year ahead, the uncharted waters." But those *uncharted* waters almost engulfed me as the school year progressed. Qualitative research is open-ended; its premise is a question which leads to more questions which lead to more questions. The more I looked at my class with wondering eyes, the more questions I had. In both of my graduate classes that were involved with teacher as researcher, we had discussed the idea that it was OK to change your question. Another October journal entry dealt with this. "I'm now not totally sure what I want to research, what my *big* question should be. I see many possibilities in my classroom each day. I'm like a ship lost at sea."

My original purpose was to investigate how my six-and seven-year-old students select the books from which they learned to read. My students last year had told me that selecting the books was the hardest part of learning to read, but this year's class was a much different group. Perhaps my question was not as appropriate for the class. Was the Medicine Wheel pulling me in the wrong direction? Autumn *introspection* was having the effect of driving me off course.

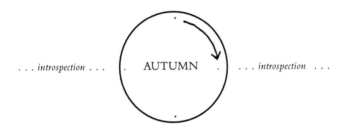

About this time I received a letter from a classmate in my case-study class. Reading over her letter brought me up short. I realized that I had strayed from my pre-plotted schedule for conducting my case study, and a very uneasy feeling began to rise from the pit of my being. Glenda wrote to me to addressing this concern, and my seminar group reassured me as well that this problem would resolve itself as my study progressed. So I continued to write and collect data, but now that I was aware of how my path had changed. I lacked a sense of direction or purpose in my project.

I was acquiring the spirit of being a teacher-researcher. I was looking at my students from a different perspective. But I knew that I needed to do more journal writing; I needed a more systematic way to document conversations that were taking place; I needed to record student behaviors.

I was now nearing the point on the Medicine Wheel when knowledge and wisdom are said to predominate. Discovering the value of writing on a regular schedule was leading me toward this point in the cycle. Both my seminar group and my case study class had discussed the fact that we should be writing in our research journals daily; in fact many times during the day was preferable. We were then to look for patterns or new questions that appeared as we reread our journal entries.

Now as I poured over my notes, I realized that the focus of my study had changed. I had strayed from my original question. I had begun to zero in on one of the students in my classroom who had a diagnosed learning disability, attention deficit disorder (ADD). However, a conversation with my administrator just before Christmas made me realize that there was a possibility that this student could be removed from our classroom and placed in a different educational environment. In the middle of the night I awoke with a start. I lay there with my eyes wide open. The implications of the conversation with my principal hit me full force. If there was a possibility that the student would be removed from our classroom, I would be up a creek without the proverbial paddle as far as my case study was concerned. I got up and wrote.

In the wee hours of the morning, I tried to rethink the options for my case study. As I wrote, I came to the realization that it would be safest for me to drop the idea of focussing on one student. I wrote about my class as a whole and I wrote about the excitement that I felt about the literature-based reading program that was evolving in our classroom. There were many issues that were intriguing to me. But as I wrote, my original question—how my students select the books they read—surfaced again. I was back to square one and I was five months into my case study.

After the holidays I approached my research project with new resolve. I still did not have the feeling that my study had a clear focus. But once again I was advised that this too was all right and that I should just keep collecting data, taking field notes and writing in my research journal. I also continued to read independently, chapters here, paragraphs there, about how to be a teacher and a researcher at the same time. Very gradually, without my realizing when it began, a tension began to develop between these two roles, one as a teacher and the other as researcher. The two roles kept vying for the position of prominence in my daily interactions with the students.

I would spend an evening transcribing data or reading over my field notes, reflecting on my class as a researcher. I'd arrive in the classroom the next morning anxious to continue in my role as a researcher. Some mornings I would be posted at the book shelves, with clipboard in hand, ready to record what I observed as my students selected their reading materials for that day. But all too often, the researcher was called to be the teacher when a child could not find a particular book she wanted, when the lunch count and attendance slips had to be filled out or when there was an altercation in the coatroom.

I realized that I had to find an uninterrupted block of time when I could write. I wanted to write at the scene, at school where the sights, sounds and smells of my case study existed. So I found a table in the teachers' room where I could write during the first few minutes of my lunch period each day. This plan allowed me the break away from my teaching room which I needed but I was still at school. It also gave me a routine which allowed me to relax a bit as things happened in the classroom that needed to be recorded because I know I could write it down at lunchtime. Also, jotting a phrase down on a scrap of paper that I could slip into my pocket was enough to jog my memory when I got to the teachers' room and was able to write about the experience . . . Then a student teacher was assigned to me. She and I needed to talk about what had happened in the morning and what we needed to do in the afternoon. My lunchtime plan was short-lived. Consequently, in January every aspect of my case study was in a state of flux.

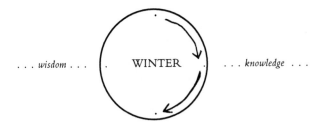

. . . wisdom . . .   WINTER   . . . knowledge . . .

Had I pulled away from the path of the Medicine Wheel? I should be at the point where wisdom and knowledge are predominant. However, I had shifted my focus from my original question; I wasn't sure where this whole experience was leading me; and my plan for writing my classroom observations had to be changed constantly.

I continued to drag myself through the one-hour commute to my teacher-researcher seminar meetings twice a month. However, once I got there, my energy level rose, for the isolation that I was experiencing as a teacher-researcher could melt away during our discussions. I did not have to worry about bruised professional egos or eyeballs rolling if I dared to share some of the things that were happening in our classroom.

Our group discussions truly were helpful, but I felt as though I was trying to play a game with no rules. One journal entry stated, "There are books and articles on the subject of teacher as researcher. I've been to see many leaders in the field give talks *about* it. But no one tells me exactly *how* to do it! I guess that the answer is that no two teachers are the same, thus no two case studies can be the same. You have to feel your own way." Later in January I wrote, "I feel so scattered. My focus is constantly changing. If I were to draw it, at this point my case study would look like a modernistic painting created with a brush full of paint that has been splattered onto the canvas by a flick of the wrist."

I had heard that some teacher-researchers refer to this phase of a case study, when your focus is scattered, as being in a state of muddlement. By whatever name you call it, it is terribly unsettling. I floundered in this tempest for quite awhile.

In my seminar group, as I listened to the other participants discuss the status of their research projects, I realized that each one of them was experiencing this same feeling of drifting, being carried along by the current. We encouraged one another while we were together. We said all the right words, but alone in my car on the drive home prickles of panic returned. Where was this all leading? How could I ever bring closure to this whole mess?

Then a letter came from Glenda. She addressed this uneasy feeling when she said, "What you are feeling now—if it's not clarity and certainty about your study—may not indicate failure at all but that you're in the midst of a messy research process." It was somewhat reassuring to know these feelings of fragmentation indicated that I was "on schedule" with my case study, but it did not dispel my lack of a sense of accomplishment with my project. At the same time, however, my journal entries reflected the sense of excitement that I was feeling toward the process approach to reading that I was implementing in our classroom. The momentum from that aspect of my work was carrying me through this period.

In retrospect, I realize that even during this period of "muddlement," I had gained *wisdom*. For I had become more adept as a questioner, often rephrasing my question or asking additional questions of the same student. I began to get more varied responses from my students to my question of how they had selected the book they were reading. One question often led to yet another one. If they responded that they were reading the book because they liked it, I might then ask how they had found out about the book in the first place. If they replied that they had picked the book because they could read it, I might then ask them how they knew they could read it.

I also realized that I needed to include parent input in my study so I developed and sent home a survey. I interviewed librarians in the school libraries and in our town library as well. Only in retrospect did I come to realize that this period that had seemed to be so stagnant at the time was in fact a pivotal point in my case study. For during the winter I had gained *wisdom* as a questioner, though at times this simply led me to have still more questions. I had also gone digging for more information from other teachers who had conducted research on topics related to the subject of my research. My winter season had been a time of *wisdom* and *knowledge* after all.

Reading back over my field notes, journal entries and other data, I saw that as the season brightened, so did my feelings about my case study. One day toward the end of February I wrote, "For the first time since September I have begun to feel the momentum building in my case study. I find that almost every day I have a new question. It's like peeling away the outer layers of an onion. I feel as though I am now getting to the real meat of what I am after . . . whatever that may be." I was so fortunate to have my teacher-researcher seminar group. Being able to connect with others who were going through this research process was affirming.

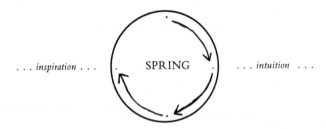

. . . *inspiration* . . . SPRING . . . *intuition* . . .

I was rounding out the circle of the Medicine Wheel as spring came to New England . . . and my case study. Spring, the season of intuition and inspiration. In fact, in a letter to Glenda in March I wrote, "It is liberating to at last have an outlet for my intuition. After almost half a century of trying to beat it into submission, it has taken me time to learn to listen to and follow my hunches, to bring them to the fore and pursue their dictate."

I began to feel real pressure to start organizing the data I had amassed. I sensed that this would be a first step in the process of writing up my case study. Members of my teacher-researcher seminar group also began voicing their concerns about how to work through this stage of the research process. The thought of organizing and interpreting all the data I had collected seemed to be an overwhelming task. As a first step to writing up our studies, we all focussed again on our original questions. Once again the *messy* process of qualitative research reminded us how distinctly different it is from quantitative study. For only one seminar member opted to write about her original question; others had changed their questions. I decided to expand on my original topic.

Then came another letter from Glenda. She reminded me that I was not trying to *prove* anything. She cautioned that in this type of research we are not charged with making generalizations. She advised, "Move away from what you think your research *should* be and to see what it actually is."

I had planned to do some major writing on my case study over my April vacation from teaching. But once again my plan fell victim to the process. As I addressed my word processor, fingers poised to tap out my case study, I came to the realization that this was one paper I could not just sit down and pound out. I had to *look* at what I had collected . . . from as many different angles as possible. I also needed to give it time, time to turn it over in my mind. I needed *time* to think about what I had found. I began to graph and chart my students' responses to my questions about how they were choosing the books that they read. I reread all the information I had gathered. I organized it chronologically, then I rearranged it into folders by categories. As I read, I wrote in the margins with different colors of ink the thoughts and questions that occurred to me. I wrote on the covers of folders a synopsis of what I had discovered or uncovered each month. I penciled in new approaches that might lead me to what it was I was trying to discover.

While all this made sense to my intuitive side, I constantly had to be conscious of the fact that I had to shed the baggage of a conditioned attitude schooled by traditional educational research, that inner voice that said, "so what, educational leaders will dismiss this project as subjective gobbledygook." Another inclination I had to quell was the temptation to jump to conclusions.

Thank goodness I was committed to completing this research project and finally I began to write my case study. It was not until I came to this point that I truly began to discover that I had been learning all year. I began to realize the larger scope, the impact of what I was looking at. By taking time to step back and reflect on my data, I could see my students' book selection process as a pre-reading activity. I could see how I, as a teacher, had affected this aspect of the reading process by setting the stage, making books accessible, reading to my students at least twice a day and sharing my genuine love for books.

Through my data, I saw my students developing into very diverse independent readers. I began to see evidence of ways that the traditional basal reading systems had worked against the very premise of our democratic society. Instead of encouraging individuality, the basal system of "teaching" reading had fostered sameness. It had assumed that all students learn the same way at the same pace. There was little room for creative thinking and individuality. I began to wonder if by pre-selecting and packing the doses of reading material, we were not so subtly telling the students that choosing their own reading materials was too difficult. Rather than helping the students to make good choices, we were taking the freedom to choose away from them and then wondering why they were not choosing to read.

Individuality and ownership of the reading process are very basic to beginning readers just as they are to adult readers. It was not until I began to write that I truly could see the power that I had given to my students as I allowed *them* to choose the books that they were using to learn to read.

As a teacher-researcher I have set the atmosphere in our classroom as a place where learning is valued. By writing down the students' responses to my questions during our interviews, they could see that I valued their thoughts and opinions. The experience of being a teacher-researcher led me to watch my students, to record their ways of knowing. It has had the affect of giving me permission to look at teaching methods and practices and ask, *why?*

In the process of conducting qualitative research, I have taken my teaching cues from my students. For example, from my anecdotal record of my individual reading conferences with the students, I noted that some of the students learn best from a phonetic approach, while others seem to function best when they can develop a sight vocabulary. I planned my lessons so that I could teach to each student's individual strengths. I was learning to be quiet and to listen and to watch for the clues that can show me each student's best way of knowing, each student's learning style.

Looking back, I have found this teacher-researcher experience to be rather like the walk in the woods that I once took with a friend who was a Ph.D. candidate in entomology. As we walked along I was enjoying the out of doors and the fresh clean air. I occasionally swatted at a pesky insect. My friend, on the other hand, was in total rapture of the beauty that was before us. He would exclaim, "Oh look, there's a ———, aren't its markings beautiful! See the velvety emerald stripes? Those are quite rare, we're fortunate to see one of those." By the end of our walk, I too was in awe of the new-found beauty that surrounded us. It was as though a whole new world had opened up before my eyes. I feel as though I have had a similar experience this year as a teacher-researcher. And likewise, it is an awe-inspiring experience. I'm sure that there had been teaching clues there all along. I was just not aware of them.

I believe that I had the best of both worlds, so to speak, during the course of my case study. I had the opportunity for the exchange of ideas with fellow researchers during the discussions with my seminar group. But I also had deadlines in my case study class that forced me to collect my thoughts about the process of classroom research and to *write* about it, to bring closure to my project.

Though at times it was frustrating to me that I could not concentrate on my case study without the interruption of teaching, this research experience has affected my approach to the classroom. It has changed me as a teacher, for I'm sure that I will never again teach the way that I used to. The last few years we have had many visitors in our classroom. But this year I found myself reluctant to have visitors because I could sense that my teaching was in a state of flux. However, in retrospect, I have come to realize that as long as I approach the classroom as a learner, as a researcher, I will always be in a state of flux. In the future, I will have cause for alarm if I feel as though I have all the kinks worked out, when I have all the answers.

Reading over the data that I have collected and reflecting on all that has transpired in our classroom this year, I realize that I do have a story to tell. It may not change the world, but is has changed *me* and therein lies its value. For among the pebbles along the path I have unearthed new insights that have broadened my inner circle of knowledge.

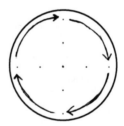

Bibliography

American Association of University Women (1992a). *Short-changing Girls, Short-changing America.* AAUW, 1111 16th Street NW, Washington, DC 20036.

———— (1992b). *How Schools Shortchange Girls: A Study of Major Findings on Girls and Education.* AAUW, 1111 16th Street NW, Washington, DC 20036.

Allington, R. L. (1978). Are good and poor readers taught differently? Is that why poor readers are poor readers? Paper presented at the annual meeting of the American Education Research Association, Toronto, March.

———— (1977). If they don't read much, how they ever gonna get good? *Journal of Reading, 21,* 57–61.

———— (1980). Teacher interruption behaviors during primary grade oral reading. *Journal of Educational Psychology, 72,* 371–377.

———— (1994). Reducing the risk: Integrated language arts in restructured elementary schools. In L. Moerden, L. Cherry-Wilkensen & J. Smith (Eds.), *Integrated Language Arts: From Controversy to Consensus.* Boston: Allyn and Bacon.

Aloise, C. (1992). Conversations and co-authorship: Listening to the undersounds. In *Teacher Research: Guess Who's Learning,* Connecticut Writing Project, Storrs, CT.

Anderson, R. C., Mason, J. & Shirey, L. (1983). The reading group: An experimental investigation of a labyrinth (Technical Report No. 271). Urbana-Champaign: Center for the Study of Reading, University of Illinois.

Anyon, J. (1981). Social class and school knowledge. *Curriculm Inquiry*, *11*, 4–42.

Apple, M. (1979). *Ideology and curriculum*. Boston: Routledge & Kegan Paul.

——— (1982). *Education and Power*. Boston: Routledge & Kegan Paul.

——— (1988). *Teachers and Texts*. New York: Routledge.

Arnold, K. (1987). Values and vocations: The career aspirations of academically gifted females in the first five years after high school. College of Education, University of Illinois, Champaign-Urbana, IL.

Arnold, K. & Denny, T. (1988). The lives of academic achievers. College of Education, University of Illinois, Champaign-Urbana, IL.

Ashcroft, L. (1987). Defusing "empowerment": The what and the why. *Language Arts*, *64*, 142–156.

Assagioli, R. (1973). *The Act of Will*. New York: Penguin Books.

——— (1976). *Psychosynthesis: A Manual of Principles and Techniques*. New York: Penguin Books.

Atwell, N. (1987). *In the Middle: Teaching Reading and Writing to Adolescents*. Portsmouth, NH: Heinemann.

Balbus, I. (1982). *Marxism and Domination: A Neo-Hegelian, Feminist, Psychoanalytic Theory of Sexual, Political, and Technological Liberation*. Princeton, NJ: Princeton University Press.

Ball, S. (1987). *The Micro-Politics of the School: Towards a Theory of School Organization*. New York: Methuen.

——— (1991). *Foucault and Education*. London: Routledge.

Banks, J. A. (1991). A curriculum for empowerment, action and change. In C. Sleeter, (Ed.), *Empowerment through Multicultural Education*. Albany, NY: SUNY Press.

Barth, R. S. (1990). *Improving Schools from Within: Teachers, Parents, and Principals Can Make a Difference*. San Francisco, CA: Jossey-Bass.

Bartky, S. L. (1990). *Femininity and Domination: Studies in the Phenomenology of Oppression*. New York: Routledge.

Belenky, M. F., Clinchy, B. M., Goldberger, N. R., Tarule, J. M. (1986). *Women's Ways of Knowing*. New York: Basic Books.

Bell, L. A. (1991). Changing our ideas about ourselves: Group consciousness raising with elementary school girls as a means to empowerment. In C. Sleeter, (Ed.), *Empowerment through Multicultural Education*. Albany, NY: SUNY Press.

Bernstein, B. (1971). *Class, Codes, and Control*, Vol. 1: *Theoretical Studies Toward a Sociology of Language*. London: Routledge & Kegan Paul.

Bissex, G. L. (1987). What is a teacher researcher? In G. L. Bissex, & R. H. Bullock, (Eds.), *Seeing for Ourselves: Case-Study Research by Teachers of Writing*. Portsmouth, NH: Heinemann.

Bissex, G. L. & Bullock, R. H. (1987). *Seeing for Ourselves: Case-Study Research by Teachers of Writing*. Portsmouth, NH: Heinemann.

Blachowicz, C. (1983). Commentary. In L. Gentile, M. Kamil and J. Blanchard (Eds.), *Reading Research Revisited*. Columbus, OH: Merrill.

Bogden R., & Bilkin, S. (1982). *Qualitative Research in Education*. Boston: Allyn & Bacon.

Bohm, D. (1991). *Consciousness*. New York: Harper and Row.

———— (1994). *Thought as a system*. London: Routledge.

Bookman, A., & Morgan, S. (Eds.) (1988). *Women and the Politics of Empowerment*. Philadelphia: Temple University Press.

Bourdieu, P. & Passeron, J. (1977). *Reproduction in Education, Society, and Culture*. Translated from the French by Richard Nice. London: Sage Publications.

Bowles, S. & Gintis, H. (1976). *Schooling in Capitalist America*. New York: Basic Books, Inc.

Bozza, M. A. (1994). One school's random acts of kindness. *Instructor*, November/December, 57–59.

Bradshaw, J. (1988). *Healing the Shame that Binds You*. Deerfield Beach, FL: Health Communications.

Brake, M. (1980). *The Sociology of Youth Culture and Youth Subcultures*. London: Routledge & Kegan Paul.

Branden, N. (1992). *The Power of Self-Esteem*. Deerfield Beach, FL: Health Communications.

———— (1987). *How to Raise Your Self-Esteem*. New York: Bantam Books.

———— (1971). *The Psychology of Self-Esteem*. New York: Bantam Books.

Bromley, K. D. (1991). *Webbing with Literature: Creating Story Maps with Children's Books*. Boston: Allyn & Bacon.

Brophy, J. (1984). The teacher as thinker: Implementing instruction. In G. Duffy, L. Roehler, & J. Mason. *Comprehension Instruction*. White Plains, NY: Longman.

Brown, M. Y. (1983). *The Unfolding Self: Psychosynthesis and Counseling*. Los Angeles: Pscyhosynthesis Press.

Bruckerhoff, C. (1990). Conversation as centerpiece for reflective practice. *Curriculum and Teaching, 5*, 14–24.

Burns, D. D. (1980). *Feeling Good: The New Mood Therapy*. New York: NAL Penguin.

Camp, R. (1990). Thinking together about portfolios, *The Quarterly, 12*, 8–14, 27.

Cantor, D. W. & Bernay, T. (1992). *Women in Power: The Secrets of Leadership*. Boston: Houghton Mifflin.

Carter, M. & Tierney, R. (1988). Reading and writing growth: Using portfolios in assessment. Paper presented and the annual meeting of the National Reading Conference, Tucson, AZ.

Christensen, L. (1992). Tales from an untracked class. *Rethinking Schools, 2*, 1, 14–16.

———— (1994). Building community from chaos. *Rethinking Schools, 9*, 1, 14–17.

Clark, C. (1984). Teacher planning and reading comprehension development. In G. Duffy, L. Roehler, & J. Mason, *Comprehension Instruction*. New York: Longman.

Cochran-Smith, M. & Lytle, S. (1993). *Inside/Outside: Teacher Research and Knowledge*. New York: Teachers College Press.

Code, L. (1991). *What She Can Know: Feminist Theory and the Construction of Knowledge*. Ithaca, NY: Cornell University Press.

Cohen, R. M. (1991). *A Lifetime of Teaching*. New York: Teachers College Press.

Collins, P. (1990). *Black Feminist Thought: Knowledge, Consciousness, and the Politics of Empowerment*. London: Harper/Collins Academic.

Combs, M. & Yellin, D. (1986). Beliefs about education and reading: Looking at beginning and preservice teachers. Paper presented at the annual meeting of the National Reading Conference, Austin, TX, December.

Cook, J. M. (1970). Paper delivered at the Philosophy and the Black Liberation Struggle Conference, University of Illinois at Chicago Circle, November.

Cooper, J. D. (1993). *Literacy: Helping Children Construct Meaning*. Boston: Houghton Mifflin.

Corwin, R. G. (1973). Models of educational organizations. *Review of Research in Education, 2*, 247–295.

Csikszentmihalyi, M. (1991). *The Evolving Self: A Psychology for the New Millennium*. New York: HarperPerennial.

———— (1990). *Flow: The Psychology of Optimal Experience*. New York: HarperPerennial.

Cullinan, B. E. (Ed.) (1987). *Children's Literature in the Reading Program.* Newark, DE: International Reading Association.

Cummins, J. (1986). Empowering minority students: A framework for intervention. *Harvard Educational Review, 56,* 18–36.

Darder, A. (1991). *Culture and Power in the Classroom: A Critical Foundation for Bicultural Education.* New York: Bergin & Garvey.

Davis, F. B. (1944). Fundamental factors of comprehension in reading. *Psychometrika, 9,* 185–197.

Depree, M. (1989). *Leadership as an Art.* New York: Dell Paperbacks.

Deschl, R. A. & Wright, E. (1989). A case study of high school teachers' decision making models for planning and teaching science. *Journal of Research in Science Teaching, 26,* 467–501.

Dewey, J. (1963 [1938]). *Experience and Education.* New York: Collier.

Diamond, I. (1994). *On Fertile Ground.* Boston: Beacon Press.

Diamond, I. & Orenstein, G. F. (1990). *Reweaving the Web: The Emergence of Eco-Feminism.* San Francisco: Sierra Club Books.

Duffy, G. & Roehler, L. (1993). *Improving Classroom Reading Instruction: A Decision-Making Approach.* New York: McGraw-Hill.

Duffy, G. Roehler, L. & Putnam, J. (1987). Putting the teacher in control: Basal readers, textbooks and instructional decision making. *The Elementary School Journal, 87,* 357–366.

Durkin, D. (1978). What classroom observation reveals about reading comprehension instruction. *Reading Research Quarterly, 14,* 481–533.

Edelsky, C. Atwerger, B. & Flores, B. (1991). *Whole Language: What's the Difference?* Portsmouth, NH: Heinemann.

Edwards, R. (1979). *Contested Terrain: The Transformation of the Workplace in the Twentieth Century.* New York: Basic Books.

Eisler, R. (1987). *The Chalice and the Blade.* San Francisco: Harper & Row.

Eisner, E. (1991). *The Enlightened Eye: Qualitative Inquiry and the Enhancement of Educational Practice.* New York: Macmillan.

Elasser, N. & John-Steiner, V. (1977). An interactionist approach to advancing literacy. *Harvard Educational Review, 47,* 355–369.

Ellsworth, E. (1989). Why doesn't this feel empowering? Working through the repressive myths of critical pedagogy. *Harvard Education Review, 59,* 297–324.

Evans, C. L., Stubbs, M. L., Freechette, P., Neely, C., and Warner, J. (1991). *Educational Practitioners' Absent Voices in the Building of Educational Theory.* Working Paper No. 170, Center for Research on Women, Wellesley, MA.

Everhart, R. B. (1983). *Reading, Writing, and Resistance.* Boston: Routledge & Kegan Paul.

Faidley, R. & Musser, S. (1991). National Education Standards: The Complex Challenge for Educational Leaders. *NASSP Bulletin, 75,* 23–27.

Farr, R. & Tone, B. (1994). *Portfolio and Performance Assessment: Helping Students Evaluate their Progress as Readers and Writers.* Fort Worth, TX: Harcourt Brace College Publishers.

Fay, C. (1990). Teaching and leading: In the teacher's voice. Paper presented at the annual meeting of the American Educational Research Association, Boston, April.

Ferrucci, P. (1982). *What We May Be: Techniques for Psychological and Spiritual Growth through Psychosynthesis.* Los Angeles: Jeremy Tarcher.

——— (1990). *Inevitable Grace.* Los Angeles: Jeremy Tarcher.

Fine, M. (1991). *Framing Dropouts: Notes on the Politics of an Urban Public High School.* Albany, NY: SUNY Press.

Firestone, W. A. & Bader, B. D. (1991). Restructuring teaching: An assessment of frequently considered options. *Educational Policy, 5,* 119–136.

Follett, M. P. (1924). *Creative Experience.* New York: Longman, Green.

Fordley, R. & Musser, S. (1991). National Education Standards: The complex challenge for educational leaders. *NASSP Bulletin, 75* (537), 23–27.

Foucault, M. (1977). *Discipline and Punish: The Birth of the Prison.* New York: Pantheon.

——— (1980). C. Gordon (Ed.), *Power/Knowledge: Selected Interviews and Other Writings.* New York: Pantheon.

Freidman, S. Jackson, J. & Boles, K. (1984). The other end of the corridor: The effect of teaching on teachers. *Radical Teacher, 7,* 2–23.

Freire, P. (1973). *Pedagogy of the Oppressed.* New York: Seabury Press.

——— (1978). *Pedagogy in Process: Letters to Guinea-Bissau.* New York: Seabury Press.

——— (1987) with D. Macedo. *Literacy: Reading the Word and the World.* S. Hadley, MA: Bergin & Garvey.

Fullan, M. (1982). *The Meaning of Educational Change.* New York: Teachers College Press.

Fuller, F. (1969). Concerns of teachers: A developmental characterization. *American Educational Research Journal, 6,* 207–266.

Fuller, M. (1983). Black girls in a London comprehensive school. In Rosemary Deem (Ed.), *Schooling for Women's Work.* London: Routledge & Kegan Paul.

Galda, L., Cullinan, B. E. & Strickland, D. S. (1993). *Language, Literacy, and the Child*. Fort Worth, TX: Harcourt Brace Javonovich.

Gallegos, S. (1992). *Animals of the Four Windows: Integrating Thinking, Sensing, Feeling and Imagery*. Santa Fe, NM: Moon Bear Press.

Gambrell, L. (1987). Children's oral language during teacher directed reading instruction. In J. E. Readance and R. S. Baldwin (Eds.), *Research in Literacy: Merging Perspectives*. 36th Yearbook of the National Reading Conference.

Gang, P., Lynn, N. M., Maver, D. J. (1992). *Conscious Education: The Bridge to Freedom*. Grafton, VT: Dagaz Press.

Gatto, J. (1995). A different kind of teacher. *Conference Papers of the First International Conference on Holistic Teacher Education*. Available at PO Box 21, Grafton, VT.

Gawain, S. (1986). *Living in the Light: A Guide to Personal and Planetary Transformation*. Mill Valley, CA: Whatever Publishing Co.

———— (1993). *The Path of Transformation: How Healing Ourselves Can Change the World*. Mill Valley, CA: Nataraj Publishing Co.

Gee, H. (1990). *Social Linguistics and Literacies*. London: Falmer Press.

Gershon, D. & Straub, G. (1989). *Empowerment: The Art of Creating Your Life as You Want It*. New York: Dell.

Gilligan, C. (1982). *In a Different Voice: Psychological Theory and Women's Development*. Cambridge, MA: Harvard University Press.

Gilligan, C., Lyons, N., and Hanmer, T. (1990). *Making Connections: The Relational Worlds of Adolescent Girls at Emma Willard School*. Cambridge, MA: Harvard University Press.

Giroux, H. A. (1983). *Theory and Resistance in Education: A Pedagogy for the Opposition*. Boston: Bergin & Garvey.

Goodlad, J. (1984). *A Place Called School: Prospects for the Future*. New York: McGraw-Hill.

Goodman, J. (1988). The political tactics and teaching strategies of reflective, active preservice teachers. *Elementary School Journal, 89*, 23–41.

Goodman, K. (1987). *What's Whole in Whole Language?* Portsmouth, NH: Heinemann.

Goodson, I. & Dowbiggin, I. (1991). Docile bodies: Commonalities in the history of psychiatry and schooling. In S. Ball, (Ed.), *Foucault and Education*. London: Routledge.

Gordon, T. (1970). *P. E. T.: Parent Effectiveness Training*. New York: Peter H. Wyden.

Goswami, D. & Stillman, P. (1987). *Reclaiming the Classroom: Teacher Research as an Agency for Change*. Portsmouth, NH: Boynton/Cook.

Grace, G. (1978). *Teachers, Ideology and Control: A Study in Urban Education*. Boston: Routledge & Kegan Paul.

Gramsci, A. (1972). *Selections from the Prison Notebooks*. Ed. and trans. by Q. Hoare and G. Smith. New York: Irvington Press.

Graves, D. (1995). *A Fresh Look at Writing*. Portsmouth, NH: Heinemann.

——— (1983). *Writing: Teachers and Children at Work*. Portsmouth, NH: Heinemann.

Griffin, S. (1978). *Women and Nature: The Roaring Inside Her*. New York: Harper & Row.

——— (1981). *Pornography and Silence: Culture's Revenge against Nature*. New York: Harper & Row.

Grumet, M. (1988). *Bitter Milk: Women and Teaching*. Amherst, MA: University of Massachusetts Press.

Habermas, J. (1972). *Knowledge and Human Interests*. Trans. J. J. Shapiro. London: Heinemann.

Hansen, J. (1987). *When Writers Read*. Portsmouth, NH: Heinemann.

Havel, V. (1995). A time for transcendence. Acceptance of the 1994 Philadelphia Liberty Medal, reprinted in the *Utne Reader, 67*, 53, 112–113.

Heath, S. B. (1978). *Teacher Talk: Language in the Classroom*. Center for Applied Linguistics, Washington, DC.

——— (1983). *Ways with Words: Language, Life and Work in Communities and Classrooms*. New York: Cambridge University Press.

——— (1989). The sense of being literate: Historical and cross-cultural features. In *Handbook of Reading Research*, 2nd ed., New York: Longman.

Heider, J. (1986). *The Tao of Leadership*. New York: Bantam Books.

Henderson, J. G. (1992). *Reflective Teaching: Becoming an Inquiring Educator*. New York: Macmillan.

Heubner, D. (1987). The vocation of teaching. In F. Bolin and J. M. Falk (Eds.), *Teacher Renewal: Professional Issues, Personal Choices*. New York: Teachers College Press.

Hirsch, E. D. (1987). *Cultural Literacy: What Every American Nees to Know*. Boston: Houghton Mifflin.

Hoffman, J. O'Neal, S., Kastler, L., Clements, R., Segal, K. & Nash, M. (1984). Guided oral reading and miscue focussed verbal feedback in second grade classrooms. *Reading Research Quarterly, 16*, 14–20.

Holly, M. L. (1989). *Writing to Grow: Keeping a Personal-Professional Journal.* Portsmouth, NH: Heinemann.

Houston, S. (1973). Black English. *Psychology Today,* March, 45–48.

Howard, K. (1990). Making the writing portfolio real. *The Quarterly, 12,* 4–7, 27.

Hubbard, R. & Power, B. (1993). *The Art of Classroom Inquiry: A Handbook for Teacher-Researchers.* Portsmouth, NH: Heinemann.

Hunt, D. & Hait, P. (1990). *The Tao of Time.* New York: Henry Holt & Co.

Irwin, J. (1991). *Teaching Reading Comprehension Processes,* 2nd ed.. Englewood Cliffs, NJ: Prentice Hall.

Irwin, J. & Baker, I. (1989). *Promoting Active Comprehension Strategies.* Englewood Cliffs, NJ: Prentice Hall.

Irwin, J. & Doyle, M. (1992). *Reading and Writing Connections: Learning from Research.* Newark, DE: International Reading Association.

Irwin, J. W. & Schiller, D. (1987) From product to process in comprehension instruction. Unpublished paper, Loyola University of Chicago.

Johnson, D. D., Toms-Bronowski, S. & Buss, D. (1983). Critique of Davis's Study. In L. Gentile, M. Kamil and J. Blanchard (Eds.), *Reading Research Revisited.* Columbus, OH: Merrill.

Johnston, P. (1992). *Constructive Evaluation of Literate Activity.* New York: Longman.

Johnston, P. & Pearson, P. D. (1982). Prior knowledge, connectivity, and the assessment of reading comprehension (Techinical report no. 245). Urbana-Champaign, IL: Center for the Student of Reading, University of Illinois.

Johnston, P. & Winograd, P. (1985). Passive failure in reading. *Journal of Reading Behavior, 17,* 279–299.

Karp, S. (1993). Montclair finds many pieces to "detracking" puzzle. *Rethinking Schools,* 8, 16–17.

Katz, R. (1983/1984). Empowerment and synergy: Expanding the community's healing resources. *Prevention in Human Services, 3,* 201–225.

Kaufman, B. (1994). *Son-rise: The Miracle Continues.* Tiberon, CA: H. J. Kramer, Inc.

Kemmis, S. & McTaggart, R. (1982). *The Action Research Planner.* Victoria, Australia: Deacon University Press.

Kestenbaum, C. J. (1986). The professional woman's dilemma: Love and/ or power. *American Journal of Psychoanalysis, 46,* 15.

Kleinfield, J. & Yerian, S. (1995). *Gender Tales: Tensions in the Schools.* New York: St. Martin's Press.

Knoblach, C. H. & Brannon, L. (1993). *Critical Teaching and the Idea of Literacy*. Portsmouth NH: Boynton-Cook.

Kochman, T. (1981). *Black and White Styles in Conflict*. Chicago, IL: University of Chicago Press.

Kohl, H. (1994). *I Won't Learn from You*. New York: Norton.

———— (1995). *Should We Burn Babar?* New York: Norton.

Kohlberg, L. (1981). *The Philosophy of Moral Development*. New York: Harper & Row.

———— (1983). *The Psychology of Moral Deveopment*. New York: Harper & Row.

Kohn, A. (1986). *No Contest: The Case Against Competition*. Boston: Houghton Mifflin.

Kozol, J. (1975). Great men and women (tailored for school use). *Learning Magazine*, December, 16–20.

Kotlowitz, A. (1991). *There Are No Children Here: The Story of Two Boys Growing Up in the Other America*. New York: Doubleday.

Kreidler, W. J. (1994). Nurture the instincts for caring. *Instructor*, November/December, 25.

Kreisberg, S. (1992). *Transforming Power: Domination, Empowerment and Education*. Albany, NY: SUNY Press.

Lankshear, C. with M. Lawler (1987). *Literacy, Schooling and Revolution*. London: Falmer Press.

Lappe, F. M. & DuBois, P. M. (1994). *The Quickening of America: Rebuilding Our Nation, Remembering Our Lives*. San Francisco: Jossey-Bass.

Larson, M. (1980). Proletarianization and educated labor. *Theory and Society*, *9*, 166.

Lather, P. (1984). Critical theory, curricular transformation and feminist mainstreaming. *Journal of Education*, *166*, 5–23.

———— (1991). *Getting Smart: Feminist Research and Pedagogy within the Postmodern*. New York: Routledge.

Lerner, M. (1986). *Surplus Powerlessness*. Oakland, CA: The Institute for Labor & Mental Health.

Levi, R. (1990). Assessment of educational visions: Engaging learners and parents. *Language Arts*, *67*, 269–273.

Lieberman, A., Saxl, E. R. & Miles, M. B. (1988). Teacher leadership: Ideology and practice. In A. Lieberman (Ed.), *Building a Professional Culture in Schools*. New York: Teachers College Press.

Linn, M. C., DeBendicts, T., Delucci, K., Harris, A. & Stage, E. (1987). Gender differences in national assessment of educational progress science items. What does "I don't know" really mean? *Journal of Research in Science Teaching, 24*, 267–278.

Loevinger, J. (1976). *Ego Development*. San Francisco: Jossey-Bass.

Loewen, J. (1995). *Lies My Teacher Told Me*. New York: Norton.

Luke, A. (1988). *Literacy, Textbooks, and Ideology: Postwar Literacy Instruction and the Mythology of Dick and Jane*. London: Falmer Press.

Maeroff, G. (1988). *The Empowerment of Teachers: Overcoming the Crisis of Confidence*. New York: Teachers' College Press.

Maher, F. A. (1987). Toward a richer theory of feminist pedagogy: A comparison of "liberation" and "gender" models for teaching and learning. *Journal of Education, 169*, 91–100.

Manly-Casimir, M. & Wasserman, S. (1989). The teacher as decision-maker: Connecting self with the practice for teaching. *Childhood Education, 65*, 288–293.

Maslow, A. (1968). *Toward a Psychology of Being*. New York: Van Norstrand Reinhold.

Maxcy, S. J. & Caldas, S. J. (1991). Moral imagination and the philosophy of school leadership. *Journal of Eduational Administration, 29*, 38–53.

Mayeroff, M. (1971). *On Caring*. New York: Harper & Row.

McCaleb, S. B. (1994). *Building Communities of Learners: A Collaboration Among Teachers, Students, Families and Community*. New York: St. Martin's Press.

McDermott, R. P. (1977). The cultural context of learning to read. In S. F. Wanat (Ed.), *Papers in Applied Linguistics: Linguistics and Reading*. Series I. Arlington, VA: Center for Applied Linguistics.

McDonald, J. P. (1986). Raising the teacher's voice and the ironic role of theory. *Harvard Educational Review, 56*, 356.

McGill-Franzen, A. & Allington, R. (1991). The gridlock of low reading achievement: Perspectives on practice and policy. *Remedial and Special Education, 12*, 20–30.

McLaren, P. (1989). *Life in Schools: An Introduction to Critical Pedagogy in the Foundations of Education*. New York: Longman Press.

Meier, D. (1995). *The Power of their Ideas*. Boston: Beacon Press.

Merchant, C. (1980). *The Death of Nature: Women, Ecology, and the Scientific Revolution*. San Francisco: Harper & Row.

Michelsen, S. (1991). The university collaborator: Empowering teachers' thinking. Paper presented at the annual meeting of the National Reading Conference, Palm Springs, CA.

Miller, J. (1992). *Creating Spaces and Finding Voices: Teachers Collaborating for Empowerment.* Albany, NY: SUNY Press.

Miller, J. B. (1987). Women and power. *Journal: Women and Therapy, 6,* 1–11.

Mills, C. W. (1959). *The Sociological Imagination.* New York: Oxford University Press.

Mohr, M. & Maclean, M. (1987). *Working Together: A Guide for Teacher-Researchers.* Urbana, IL: National Council of Teachers of English.

Montouri, A. & Conti, I. (1993). *From Power to Partnership: Creating the Future of Love, Work, and Community.* San Francisco: Harper San Francisco.

Newman, J. M. (1988). Sharing journals: Conversational mirrors for seeing ourselves as learners, writers, and teachers. *English Education, 20,* 134–156.

Nieto, S. (1992). *Affirming Diversity: The Sociopolitical Context of Multicultural Education.* White Plains, NY: Longman.

Nieva, V. F. & Gutek, B. A. (1980). Sex effects on evaluation. *The Academy of Management Review, 5,* 267–275.

Noddings, N. (1984). *Caring: A Feminine Approach to Ethics and Moral Education.* Berkeley, CA: University of California Press.

Noddings, N. & Shore, P. J. (1984). *Awakening the Inner Eye: Intuition in Education.* New York: Teachers College Press.

Norton, D. E. (1992). *The Impact of Literature Based Reading.* New York: Merrill.

Oakes, J. (1985). *Keeping Track: How Schools Structure Inequality.* New Haven, CT: Yale University Press.

Oliver, D. & Gershman, K. (1989). *Education, Modernity and Fractured Meaning: Toward a Process Theory of Teaching and Learning.* Albany, NY: SUNY Press.

Olson, L. (1994). Growing Pains. *Education Week,* 2 November, 29–48.

Olson, M. W. (1990). *Opening the Door to Classroom Research.* Newark, DE: International Reading Association.

O'Neil, W. (1970). Properly literate. *Harvard Educational Review, 40,* 124–138.

Orenstein, P. (1994). *Schoolgirls: Young Women, Self-Esteem and the Gender Gap.* New York: Doubleday.

Ornish, D. (1990). *Dr. Dean Ornish's Program for Reversing Heart Disease.* New York: Random House.

Pang, V. O. (1991). Teaching children about social issues: Kidpower. In C. Sleeter, (Ed.), *Empowerment through Multicultural Education*, Albany, NY: SUNY Press.

Parfitt, W. (1990). *The elements of psychosynthesis.* Longmead, England: Element Books.

Patterson, C. H. (1986). *Theories of Counseling and Psychotherapy*, 4th ed. New York: Harper & Row.

Patterson, L., Santa, C., Short, K. & Smith, K. (Eds.) (1993). *Teachers are Researchers: Reflection and Action.* Newark, DE: International Reading Association.

Patterson, L., Stansell, J. & Lee, S. (1990). *Teacher Research: From Promise to Power.* Katonah, NY: Richard C. Owen.

Peck, M. S. (1993). Stages of community building. In C. Whitmeyer (Ed.), *In the Company of Others: Making Community in the Modern World.* New York: Jeremy Tarcher Press.

Perry, W. G. (1970). *Forms of Intellectual and Ethical Development in the College Years.* New York: Holt, Rinehart, & Winston.

Peshlein, A. & Glesne, C. (1992). *Becoming Qualitative Researchers: An Introduction.* White Plains, NY: Longman.

Peterson, M. F. & Cooke, R. A. (1983). Attitudinal and contextual variables explaining teachers' leadership behavior. *Journal of Educational Psychology, 75*, 50–62.

Pflaum, S., Pascarella, E., Bostwick, M. & Auer, C. (1980). The influence of pupil behaviors and pupil status factors on teacher behaviors during oral reading lessons. *Journal of Educational Research, 74*, 99–105.

Piaget, J. (1965). *The Moral Judgement of the Child.* New York: Free Press.

Pinnell, G. S. & Matlin, M. L. (1989). *Teachers and Research: Language Learning in the Classroom.* Newark, DE: International Reading Association.

Pipher, M. (1994). *Reviving Ophelia: Saving the Selves of Adolescent Girls.* New York: Ballantine Books.

Powell, M. & Solety, J. (1990). *Teachers in Control: Cracking the Code.* New York: Routledge.

Project on the Status and Education of Women, Association of American Colleges (1982). *The Classroom Climate: A Chilly One for Women.* Washington, DC: Association of American Colleges.

Putnam, J. (1984). One Exceptional Teacher's Decision-Making Model. Institute for Research on Teaching, Michigan State University, East Lansing, MI.

Rayman, P. (1990). Envisioning good work: Thoughts on women, work and health in the 90's. Working paper no. 205, Wellesley College Center for Research on Women.

Robbins, M E. & Brown, G. (1991). Transforming teaching and learning through collaboration. Paper presented at the annual meeting of the National Reading Conference, Anaheim, CA.

Rosenshine, B. (1980). Skill hierarchies in reading comprehension. In R. S. Spiro, B. C. Bruce & W. F. Brewer (Eds.), *Theoretical Issues in Reading Comprehension*. Hillsdale, NJ: Lawrence Erlbaum.

Ross, D. D., Bondy, E. & Kyle, D. W. (1993). *Reflective Teaching for Student Empowerment: Elementary Curriculum and Methods*. New York: Macmillan.

Roszak, T., Gomez, M. & Kanner, A. (1995). *Ecopsychology: Restoring the Earth, Healing the Mind*. San Francisco: Sierra Club Books.

Routman, R. (1991). *Invitations: Changing as Teachers and Learners K–12*. Portsmouth, NH: Heinemann.

Rowe, N. M. (1994a). Creativity as a natural component to language arts education. In the proceedings from the annual conference of the Global Alliance for Transforming Education, Rhinebeck, NY.

——— (1994b). Lifestyles and activities that nourish creative process and spirit: Nine artists. Unpublished Masters Thesis, Institute of Transpersonal Psychology, Palo Alto, CA.

Sadker, M. & Sadker, D. (1994). *Failing at Fairness: How Our School Cheat Girls*. New York: Macmillan.

Safilios-Rothschild, C. (1979). Sex role socialization and sex discrimination: A synthesis and overview of the literature. National Institute of Education, Washington, DC.

Sapon-Shavin, M. & Schniederwind, N. (1991). Cooperative learning as empowering pedagogy. In C. Sleeter, (Ed.), *Empowerment through Multicultural Education*. Albany, NY: SUNY Press.

Schaef, A. (1981; 1992, third printing). *Women's Reality: An Emerging Female System in a White Male Society*. Minneapolis, MN: Winston Press.

Schon, D. (1983). *The Reflective Practitioner: How Professionals Think in Action*. New York: Basic Books.

Scribner, S. (1984). Literacy in three metaphors. *American Journal of Education, 93*, 6–21.

Selye, H. (1978). *The Stress of Life*. New York, McGraw-Hill.

Senge, P. M. (1990). *The Fifth Discipline: The Art and Practice of the Learning Organization*. New York: Doubleday.

Shaffer, C. R. & Anundsen, K. (1993). *Creating Community Anywhere: Finding Support and Connection in a Fragmented World*. New York: Jeremy Tarcher.

Shannon, P. (1983). The use of commercial reading materials in American elementary schools. *Reading Research Quarterly*, *19*, 68–85.

———— (1987). Commercial reading materials, a technological ideology, and the deskilling of teachers. *The Elementary School Journal*, *87*, 307–329.

———— (1989). *Broken Promises: Reading Instruction in Twentieth-Century America*. E. Granby, MA: Bergin & Garvey.

Sher, B. & Gottlieb, A. (1989). *Teamworks!* New York: Warner Books.

Shor, I. (1987) *Critical Teaching and Everyday Life*. Chicago: University of Chicago Press.

———— (1992). *Empowering Education: Critical Teaching for Social Change*. Chicago: University of Chicago Press.

Sleeter, C. (Ed.) (1991a). *Empowerment through Multicultural Education*. Albany, NY: SUNY Press.

———— (1991b). Multicultural education and empowerment. In C. Sleeter (Ed.), *Empowerment through Multicultural Education*. Albany, NY: SUNY Press.

Sleeter, C. & Grant, C. A. (1991). Mapping terrains of power: Student cultural knowledge versus classroom knowledge. In C. Sleeter (Ed.), *Empowerment through Multicultural Education*. Albany, NY: SUNY Press.

Sliker, G. (1992). *Multiple Mind: Healing the Split in the Psyche and World*. Boston: Shambala.

Smith, C. B. (1989). Teachers as decision makers. *Reading Teacher*, *42*, 632.

Sorensen, M. (1993). Teach each other: Connecting talking and writing. *English Journal*, *82*, 42–47.

Spaulding, C. (1992a). *Motivation in the Classroom*. New York: McGraw-Hill.

———— (1992b). The motivation to read and write. In J. Irwin & M. Doyle (Eds.), *Reading and Writing Connections: Learning from Research*. Newark, DE: International Reading Association.

Sprague, J. (1992). Critical perspectives on teacher empowerment. *Communication Education*, *41*, 181–203.

Stanley, W. B. (1992). *Curriculum for Utopia: Social Reconstructionism and Critical Pedagogy in the Postmodern Era.* Albany, NY: SUNY Press.

Staton, J. (1980). Writing and counseling: Using a dialogue journal. *Language Arts, 57,* 514–518.

———— (1987). The power of responding in dialogue journals. In T. Fulwiler (Ed.), *The Journal Book.* Portsmouth, NH: Boynton/Cook.

Starhawk, R. (1982). *Dreaming the Dark: Magic, Sex and Politics.* Boston: Beacon Press.

Stein, A. (1993). Camelot reborn in 2nd grade Northfield classroom. *Chicago Tribune,* 4 February, sect. 2, p. 4.

Steinem, G. (1992). *Revolution from Within: A Book of Self-esteem.* Boston: Little, Brown, & Co.

Stevenson, C. (1988). *Teachers as Inquirers.* Columbus, OH: National Middle School Association.

Stone, H. & Stone, S. (1993). *Embracing your Inner Critic: Turning Self-criticism into a Creative Asset.* San Francisco: HarperSanFrancisco.

Strober, M. & Tyack, D. (1980). Why do women teach and men manage? A report on research on schools. *Signs, 5,* 499–503.

Super, D. & Hall, D. (1978). Career development, exploration and planning. *Annual Review of Psychology, 29,* 333–372.

Thomas, C. (1980). Girls and counter-school culture. Melbourne Working Papers, Melbourne.

Thompson, J. (1987). Language and ideology. *The Sociological Review, 35,* 516–536.

Tierney, R., Carter, M. A. & Desai, L. E. (1991). *Portfolio Assessment in the Reading-Writing Classroom.* Norwood, MA: Christopher Gordon.

Timion, C. (1992). Children's Book-Selection Strategies. In J. Irwin & M. Doyle (Eds.), *Reading and Writing Connections: Learning from Research.* Newark, DE: International Reading Association.

Tompkins, G. E. (1990). *Teaching Writing: Balancing Process and Product.* Columbus, OH: Merrill.

Vacca, R. & Rosinski, T. (1992). *Case Studies in Whole Language.* Fort Worth, TX: Harcourt Brace Javonovich.

Vacca R. & Vacca, J. (1989). *Teaching Reading in the Content Areas.* Glenview, IL: Scott Foresman.

Wagner, L. (1986). A state perspective on teacher leadership roles: The potential of the California mentor teacher. Paper presented at the annual meeting of the American Educational Research Association, San Francisco, April.

Wallis, C. (1994). A class of their own. *Time, 144,* 52–61.

Weaver, C. (1990). *Understanding Whole Language: From Principles to Practice.* Portsmouth, NH: Heinemann.

Weick, K. (1976). Educational organizations as loosely-coupled systems. *Administrative Science Quarterly, 21,* 1–19.

Weikel, B. (1995). "Girlspeak" and "Boyspeak": Gender Differences in Classroom Discussion. In J. Kleinfield & S. Yerian (Eds.), *Gender Tales: Tensions in the Schools.* New York: St. Martin's Press.

Weiler, K. (1988). *Women Teaching for Change: Gender, Class and Power.* S. Hadley, MA: Bergin & Garvey.

Weis, L. (1991). Disempowering white working-class females: The role of the high school. In C. Sleeter (Ed.), *Empowerment through Multicultural Education.* Albany, NY: SUNY Press.

Wheelock, A. (1994). *Alternatives to Tracking and Ability Grouping.* Arlington, VA: American Association of School Administrators.

Whitmeyer, C. (Ed.) (1993). *In the Company of Others: Making Community in the Modern World.* New York: Jeremy Tarcher Press.

Whitmore, D. (1986). *Psychosynthesis in Education.* Rochester, VT: Destiny Books.

Williams, R. (1973). Base and superstructure in Marxist cultural theory. *New Left Review, 82.*

Willinsky, J. (1990). *The New Literacy: Redefining Reading and Writing in the Schools.* New York: Routledge.

Willis, P. (1977). *Learning to Labour.* Farnborough, England.

Winograd, P. & Smith, L. (1986). Improving the climate for reading comprehension instruction. Paper presented at the annual meeting of the National Reading Conference, Austin, TX, December.

Wise, A. E. (1979). *Legislated Learning: The Bureaucratization of the American Classroom.* Berkeley, CA: University of California Press.

Wood C. (1991). Maternal teaching: Revolution of kindness. *Holistic Education Review,* Summer, 3–10.

Woog, D. (1995). *School's Out: The Impact of Gay and Lesbian Issues on American's Schools.* Boston: Alyson Press.

Zeichner, K. M. & Liston, D. P. (1987). Teaching student teachers to reflect. *Harvard Educational Review, 57,* 23–48.

Index

Accountability, 20

Action, 124; autonomous, 294; collective, 38, 294; counter-hegemonic, 62–63; reflective, 168–173; research, 195; responsibility for, 25, 173; and self-confidence, 4; social, 285; social consequences of, 194; transformative, 205

Activities: ability grouping, 56–57; assessing control, 208–209; bureaucracy, 26; caring, 44–45, 103–104, 127–128; change, 192–193; collaborative, 94, 282*tab*; control, 9–10; defining empowerment, 288; emancipatory, 126; empowering experiences, 165; empowerment defining, 6–7; empowerment process, 167–168; "flow," 68; gender bias, 58; getting support, 224–225; grading, 52–53; on hegemony, 31; internalized domination, 33–35; literacy, 149–150, 152–153, 159; metaphoric thinking, 99–100; multiculturalism, 134–135, 136–137; paradigm change, 81–82; political, 126; positive thinking, 190–191; power, 9–10; practicing voice, 227–228; programmed, 93; reflective action, 173; reflective implementation, 195–200; responsibility, 182–183; school/community, 117–119, 213–215; on scientific legitimacy, 19–20; self-esteem, 187–188; service, 102; sharing authority, 92; student resistance, 61–62; subjects/objects, 89–90; on surplus powerlessness, 38–39; teacher roles, 110–112; for technical control, 23–24; visualization, 177–180; ways of knowing, 95–96; whole, 157

Affirmation, 129, 182

Alienation, 17, 49, 50, 72, 83

Altruism, 300

Anorexia, 57

Assertiveness training, 186

Authoritarianism, 32

Authority, shared, 14, 91, 119, 148

Autonomy, 17, 29, 243, 279, 285, 288; in communication, 75; individual, 75; lack of, 272; limitations of, 32; parent, 116; teacher, 116; value of, xvi

DATE DUE

JAN 1 7 1998			
SEP 1 0 1998			
JUL 1 3 2000			